BIOGRAPHY

BIO
LUCARELLI

Lucarelli, Leonardo

Mincemeat

JAN 0 5 2017

Mincemeat

Mincemeat

THE EDUCATION OF AN ITALIAN CHEF

Leonardo Lucarelli

Translated from the Italian by
Lorena Rossi Gori & Danielle Rossi

 Other Press
New York

Production editor: Yvonne E. Cárdenas
Text designer: Julie Fry
This book was set in Scala Pro and Trade Gothic by
Alpha Design & Composition of Pittsfield, NH

10 9 8 7 6 5 4 3 2 1

LIBRARY OF CONGRESS CATALOGING-IN-PUBLICATION
DATA

Names: Lucarelli, Leonardo, 1977– author.
Title: Mincemeat : the education of an Italian chef / Leonardo
    Lucarelli ; translated from the Italian by Lorena Rossi Gori
    and Danielle Rossi.
Other titles: Carne trita. English
Description: New York : Other Press, [2016] | Description based
    on print version record and CIP data provided by publisher;
    resource not viewed.
Identifiers: LCCN 2016017889 (print) | LCCN 2016017657 (ebook)
    | ISBN 9781590517925 (ebook) | ISBN 9781590517918
    (hardcover)
Subjects: LCSH: Lucarelli, Leonardo, 1977– | Cooks—Italy—
    Biography. | Restaurateurs—Italy—Biography.
Classification: LCC TX649.L84 (print) | LCC TX649.L84 A3 2016
    (ebook) | DDC 641.5092 [B]—dc23
LC record available at https://lccn.loc.gov/2016017889

Publisher's Note: Although the events described in this memoir
are true, the names and identifying characteristics of some people
and places have been changed.

for Giuli

If you put aside those prodigious, singular moments that destiny gives us, love of one's work (a privilege enjoyed, unfortunately, only by a few) is the best, most concrete approximation of happiness on earth—but most people don't realize this.

Primo Levi, *The Monkey's Wrench*

You start working in a kitchen because you stumble into it. Because when you were growing up, you would get home after school and you were alone or, at most, it was you and your kid brother. Because at some point you thought you knew how to cook. And when you saw someone working in a kitchen you thought that he was some modern-day hero, a daredevil, a sultan, or an impostor, and if an impostor can cook, then so can you.

You start working in a kitchen because when you're a cash-strapped student, nothing could be easier than slaving away in a restaurant, and since kowtowing to spoiled customers isn't your thing, it's way better being a cook than a waiter. Because you want to grow your hair and a beard, and cooks are junkies and alcoholics and womanizers and artists. Because Orwell worked in a kitchen, and even if you can't imagine yourself as the next Gordon Ramsay, you can still dream of being the next George Orwell. Because there comes a time when it seems all too easy, before it becomes insurmountably difficult, but then it slips back into easy again. Because at twenty you crave a job to call your own, and it's not too hard to get one in a kitchen.

You start working in a kitchen because you couldn't get it across to your mother that you really wanted to do something else, but more than that, you couldn't explain it to yourself. Because you came across some cooks with a heart, and at first, cash in hand is easier to deal with than a regular job—but then again, who in their right mind would ever give you a regular job? And you like being able to quit at the drop of a hat knowing that there's another job just across the piazza. Because deep down you like to keep saying you'll quit this shitty job for good, but then you never do, because you can't, and opportunity doesn't come knocking at your door all that often. Because food nourishes you, but it also makes you happy.

You start working in a kitchen because every restaurant is a world unto itself and the chef is always at the top of the heap and if a cute girl is out to fuck someone, she'll start at the top.

Because for you cooking is an act of love, but you don't give a shit about love. And if someone like Joe Bastianich can make money, then so can you. Because you know there are lots of jobs behind the kitchen door. And you are genuinely convinced that every man, woman, and kid should know how to cook.

Because you like to lean out over the edge and survey the scene below.

You start working in a kitchen because you're good at it. Because you get a kick out of pulling rank. And kitchens still let you start from the bottom and sweat your way up the pecking order. Because creative jobs usually call for expensive schools and expensive equipment. And everyone knows that the greatest chefs are the ones who have washed mountains of dirty dishes and that MasterChef is a scam. Because you like being an artisan of your craft.

Because once you discover the power of food, you just can't give it up, not even when the shattered shards of your life are being hurled all over the place.

Because being a chef is an alibi. And cooking is like telling a story or writing a book and you think you have tons of things to say.

Because deep down you feel like a loser, but you're the prince of losers. And maybe, just maybe, everyone feels like that, at first.

You start working in a kitchen because you can tell tall tales about what you do. Because while others might work in a kitchen to pass time, you'd do anything else to pass the time away from the kitchen. Because making a living by cooking makes you feel important. And there's something irresistible about working at night. Because you like having the keys to the restaurant and suppliers on speed dial.

You start working in a kitchen because a chef's wages are still pretty decent, all things considered.

You start working in a kitchen because you've never minded teetering on the edge of legality; otherwise you'd be an architect or a doctor. But you've never had the doggedness and dedication to be an architect, or a doctor, or anything else, for that matter. Because food never lies but everything else connected to it does. Because you like being a bullshit artist, yet in all that heat and sweat and shouting you learn to understand people, and kitchens breed friendships with people you'd never talk to otherwise and probably won't, if you come across them anywhere other than a kitchen.

Because professional chefs are the only ones left who are passing on traditions. And you enjoy handling tons of meat, you love the smell of cold rooms and porcini mushrooms and fresh fish arriving at the crack of dawn and the moist panties of waitresses at the end of the day.

Because outside the kitchen you are a misfit and you know you'd be torn to shreds. And you can be called a chef without knowing how to cook all that well, and you can earn the respect of your coworkers even if you are a son of a bitch. And your grandma used to say that undertakers and cooks will never be out of work, and even though you think she's just a little old lady thinking little old lady thoughts, at the end of the day she's telling it exactly how it is.

Because if you didn't cook, you wouldn't know where to put that stomach-churningly dangerous desire to settle a score with the world. Because in reality you have always, always gotten a kick out of discovering new flavors. And when you're filling people's bellies, they adore you.

Because it's tough feeling lonely on your own; it's easier when everyone else is lonely too. And it never occurs to you to work as an undertaker and no one's ever asked you to dig a grave. And the flabbergasted looks you get when you julienne something in a matter of seconds make you cocky. And you've always loved knives anyway, and what else is there for jerks and rejects like you? Because you are scared of just drifting and never amounting to anything. But if you're cooking, nothing else matters. Because before you went to work in a kitchen you thought you weren't worth much, and maybe you still aren't, but nobody seems to have noticed. And it's soothing to be surrounded by order when there's no order inside you. Because there are plenty of people you should have told to fuck off and now you can.

The truth is that sometimes there is no alternative but to run, because food is both a divine precept and a mortal sin. And when they told you that entering a restaurant kitchen was like feeding yourself into a meat mincer, you replied that mincers transform scraps into great food.

You start working in a kitchen because it's just another job.

You start working in a kitchen because you think it will make all your dreams come true.

You start working in a kitchen because one day the orders, the diners, the waitstaff, the raging chef—they come down on you like a ton of bricks, leaving you gasping, overwhelmed. But you get back up dazed and exhausted, and something in your head asks: Do you really want to be a chef? You never thought this was a question you'd ask yourself, and when you answer "Yes," you don't even realize you've said it.

You start working in a kitchen because you have to start somewhere.

You start working in a kitchen because you're not thinking straight.

1.

The walls are all far away except for the one right in front of me. I'm wearing whites at least two sizes too big, instead of the usual blacks with my name embroidered in dark red over the left pocket: Leonardo Lucarelli. There's nothing written on this uniform, I'm only a cook in a vast, anonymous commercial kitchen, puffing and panting, yelling and getting frazzled. All around me people are dashing about, blabbering in some thick dialect. I don't understand a word. I know I'm in a kitchen in Thiene, up north in the Veneto region of Italy. The restaurant is packed. Orders are shooting out from the printer in front of me at such a rate that I can barely tear off and pin up the tickets. They're getting all scrunched up, falling to the ground like streamers, and in the end there's just a long strip of dishes I should already have prepped and loaded on the pass, bellowing "Go!" Instead, I don't even know where to begin. It's unbearably hot. The kitchen is too big. The uniform is too loose. The tickets are coming in too fast. Everything is wrong. I'm in the wrong place. I don't like these people and they don't like me, but the thing is that I can't move my hands, get into the groove, utter a word. The chef arrives (I'm trying to remember—what's his name?) and tells me what to do but I don't understand him. I should know what to do. But I don't and I can't understand what he's saying. So I move out of his way. I see hands opening and closing the oven, drizzling reductions and sauces over dishes. I see a perfect assembly line, timers going off, crockery clinking, a full pass, servers sprinting. I see the Nigerian dishwasher, Sofia, swamped under a heap of filthy pots and dishes. Hers is the only face I recognize. Her slop sink is tiny and I ask myself how she can possibly get everything washed in that woefully cramped space. She doesn't look at me, she's too busy. I return to my station, determined to pull myself together. I'm back in the game now, I understand what I have to do. Can I still save the evening? By now, we're up to our necks in shit. And when you're struggling to keep your head above the shit, there's nothing you can do about it, the night is ruined. You work your knuckles to the bone and your only reward is frustration. You hope it will all end soon and that the machine on the counter will stop spitting out tickets and the waiters will stop yelling: Get a move on with table 36! Rush table 15 to the front of the line but without the lobster, the lady doesn't want it now! Five walkins, no reservation. Fire the appetizers! I turn around and take a step back. If I'm no use at my station, the least I can do is give Sofia a hand.

I move toward the sink and start emptying and refilling the dishwasher, but there are too many plates, I can't cope. Sofia sighs and rinses, and says, "Be careful!" while I grab another stack of plates. Maybe I can do something useful, put the dishes away and make space for others. Make space, leave space, take space: A kitchen is a bit like a video game, and I'm wondering if I'll ever advance to the next level. The stack of plates sways perilously and crashes to the floor, smashed to pieces. It literally explodes. Everything stops. Time is a bubble and Earth is galaxies away from here. For a fraction of a second there is absolute stillness and silence. The dishwasher is the only thing that doesn't react to the crash and continues sloshing away. Sofia covers her gaping mouth with both wet hands, scared they'll take it out on her. I raise my arm and immediately shout out, "It's my fault, I picked up too many plates at once, it's all my fault."

That's what happens in a commercial kitchen: If you screw up, if you forget something, and above all, if someone is about to get the rap over something you did, you've got to own up immediately. But if you are blamed for someone else's screwup and that person doesn't speak up, you must not rat them out. In a kitchen, rot, like denatured protein in a good piece of boiled meat, rises to the surface immediately. There's no faking it. You can sweet-talk other people, fool people outside the kitchen (with them you have to, it's the other unwritten law), but not your kitchen buddies.

In a flash, I feel the adrenaline surging to my temples, my heartbeat quickens, my mouth dries up, and I shriek like a wounded animal in a forest of glass shards. Flushed, the veins in my neck bulging, I have no idea what I am screaming. I hear the words only after they have left my mouth. I scream at the chef and at all those freaking frustrated hypocritical brownnosers. I scream at Sofia too, who should know how to stand up for herself but doesn't. I keep screaming and start waving my arms about, angrily, incoherently. I scream and flail as if in the throes of some bizarre exorcism. But inside, my thoughts are calm, deliberate, tuned to the soft sloshing of the dishwasher. This is no way to behave, what the hell am I doing? This is so wrong. In the meantime I hurl a plate at the wall. Open and slam the oven door a few times. You have to buckle down, I tell myself, show them the stuff you're made of. I throw a punch at the fridge. Then I open it and start flinging its contents onto the floor. Thoughts course through my brain: I will not let them screw with me, I will show them I can rise above everything and deal with whatever comes my way. I stomp on milk cartons, showering the kitchen in white rain. I have come out on top, I win, I am the best, I have nerves of steel. A slab of beef slams against the door separating us from the dining room. Because if it weren't for me in here, everything would just hit the fan. I throw pans on the floor and thump the exhaust hood. Because, I'm thinking, you're the only one who can keep his cool after slaving over a hot flattop for ten hours, the only one who can find a solution—a quick one—to unforeseen calamities. Now I start taking my clothes off. I'm screaming, tossing everything to the floor, slapping the air around me. I peel off the white jacket that is way too big for me, popping the buttons. But my thoughts are calm. I am the Incredible Hulk on weed. I'm thinking, if you can't be convincing, at least bamboozle them. So now I'm grabbing the chef's head and pushing it in the sink, thinking, this is the only way people will recognize who's the boss, the alpha male in the kitchen, whether or not you really are. Now I'm kicking the fat pastry chef's ass. It's not enough to be hired as the chef; you have to be acknowledged as one by your peers. Otherwise, there's absolutely no point. My mind is calm. Now I go to the sink and turn the hose on everyone in sight, soaking them. I'm screaming, throwing punches, nearly naked. But inside I'm completely serene. I'm thinking, a crew that doesn't look up to you and respect you when things fall apart will turn against you, and you will sink to the bottom of the heap because a leader alone is nothing but a man alone. Now I start sobbing, screaming that they all make me sick, that this is no way to work, that I don't give a shit about the restaurant, about Rotzo potatoes or Borso del Grappa peas, that they can all go to hell. I am the Incredible Hulk when he was a little boy and lost his way home. I'm weeping. Exhausted. Enough already.

I open my eyes suddenly, and it's dark. It takes me a few seconds to collect my thoughts and realize I'm in bed. I swallow hard. My throat is parched. I hear the central heating pumping hot water through the radiator. Someone is snoring. I'm covered in sweat but I'm shivering. My pillow is on the floor. I start by whispering my name: Leonardo Lucarelli. I say it again. And yes, I am a chef. Height five foot seven, weight 160 pounds, and I've never bitten my nails.

2.

I'm in a hotel, room 204. It's winter, January 4, 2013, about
six o'clock in the morning, up in the mountains. Yesterday it
snowed heavily, and a few miles from here, on the Asiago plateau, there's the little house my girlfriend and I have rented.
The house is empty, she's pregnant and living down south in
L'Aquila. "Chef" is a French word that simply means "leader,
chief." Asleep in the other bed is Federico, my second in command. What a relief. If Federico is there, then I must be me,
no ifs, no ands, no buts. It's always the same nightmare, and
once again I am safe, my head bursting with crap and a powerful need to share the highlights of my dream. Sometimes
the dream is less violent, there's no one shrieking or shatter-
ing things, and I am simply a minor cast member. There's a
feeling of total emptiness, of having crossed an unwritten line
beyond which you can be as great as you like, but you are an out-
cast, unwanted and useless. These are not just recurring work-
related nightmares, they're intolerably frightening, given the
state I wake up in, distraught and alone.

What could be simpler than a kitchen? There are certain
fundamentals that need to be learned and respected, no fifty
shades of anything, it's all either black or white and nothing in
between. Years ago, Orlando, my chef in San Piero a Sieve, used
to say, "There are only two ways to do things in the kitchen:
the right way and the wrong way." He was talking about food
and recipes, but the same rule applies to social and professional
relationships. There are some things that you have to do and
others that you must never do. If I have been able to get myself
back on track, it is because I reset my dreams, my plans, my

vision of the future to this kitchen-based belief in absolute right and absolute wrong. Is your mise en place never ready at the beginning of service? Wrong. Does someone always have to keep an eye on you, fix your mistakes, settle your skirmishes with colleagues? Wrong. Are you anything less than absolutely self-assured as you bark orders to your staff or manage your walk-ins? Very wrong. Did you call in sick on a Saturday night? Oh, so wrong. Did you flip off the chef in front of the whole kitchen brigade? Totally wrong.

In the kitchen I keep dreaming about, the one who's always wrong is me. Same name, same height, same weight, same well-groomed nails.

A quick glance at the phone: 6:34. There're a couple of hours before I have to get up. Federico is still snoring, louder than before. I hold my cell phone over his mouth and record him. Tomorrow, I'll turn down the radio and play it back at full volume in the kitchen.

I get up in silence, stepping over the sheets that are in a damp, crumpled heap on the carpet. I go into the bathroom that stinks of smoke, and drink straight from the faucet. I swallow an aspirin, my first of the day. The dream starts to fade away into a niggle in the center of my chest that won't let me go back to sleep. It's not the nightmare that's worrying me, it's the party of 150 people who are arriving in a very short while. They only told me about it yesterday afternoon. The bastards. They think that everything will somehow work itself out, that the pantry is stocked and that the chef is on top of things, plus he makes a heap of money. In the distance, I can hear the noise of the snow plows. I have to prepare the menu du jour, check the inventory sheets, find someone to replace Xiong, the Chinese dishwasher who has to take his wife to the airport, make sure that the freezer isn't acting up again and, while I'm at it, go down to the kitchen and remove the strudels we made yesterday from the blast chillers: They should all be frozen by now.

Outside, in the distance, mountain peaks are etched against the morning sky, ski trails are turning pale pink. I put on my black uniform. It fits perfectly. The corridor lights are on, the hotel is silent, the carpet's dusty and so are the walls. Feeble light filters through the windows, and the world is bewitchingly frozen. I breathe in the '80s-style atmosphere of this hotel. As it is, empty and eerily silent, it reminds me of *The Shining*, and there's something about it that I like. It's my kingdom, I can wander down to the bar, go into the kitchen, turn on the computer at Reception. Nothing out of the ordinary. I don't eat or drink, but I take pleasure in not having to worry about anything. Because even if this is the asshole of creation, it's mine and I'm in charge here.

I'm thirty-six years old. I started working in kitchens alongside nutcases and geniuses, people with troubled pasts and present lives wasted by drugs and alcohol. Characters with irresistible charm, especially when handling a knife or a pan like master jugglers. I have lost my temper dozens of times. I've had to swallow many a bitter pill. I've washed hundreds of pans hurled violently into sinks, and the same thought would go through my mind, over and over again, my scorched hands stinging inside sodden, worn-out gloves: Sooner or later I will be a chef and my kitchen hand will have it better than this. Screw it. That's what I would say to myself, with a precise plan of revenge all mapped out in my mind.

These days, the food service industry has cleaned up its act. Growing up right smack in the middle of these profound professional and social changes, has, in some ways, allowed me to get ahead fast.

I relished watching my profession gradually turn into entertainment for the masses. Nouvelle cuisine came on the scene in 1972, signature dishes began appearing, and over the last fifteen years or so, everything has snowballed to the point that you now see naked women clinging to Carlo Cracco on the cover of *GQ* and Matias Perdomo starring in Benetton ads, not to mention the hordes of cheftestants on ready, set, cook shows and nightmare kitchens and recipes packed into every damned glossy magazine on the shelf.

These days, chefs are hip, they're top guns. Those big glass windows and open kitchens are there to give naïve and gullible diners the impression they are seeing what actually goes on inside. But what's cool about this profession, even now that it's in the spotlight, is the blend of cockiness and complicity that lies behind the swinging doors.

Even in outdoor cooking events, some very heavy shit goes on behind the scenes.

There is always a commander at the helm who, besides knowing how to create delicious food, knows how to manage a crew of shady characters with vastly diverse and seldom entirely transparent backgrounds: illegal immigrants, runaway kids, fifty-somethings looking for a sea change (or being forced by unemployment into one), inexperienced and arrogant (but occasionally, also enlightened) restaurant owners, and scheming suppliers. The chefs are the ones who have to think on their feet and solve emergencies, pronto; the ones who, amid the crashing of plates, the swearing, and the beeps of the oven timers, must always have a ready answer, because every single question is addressed to them. Chefs need to stay unruffled and clearheaded during service, but at the end of the night, they can drink like a fish, heat up cocaine in the microwave on porcelain dessert plates, cultivate a colossal ego, clown around or withdraw into depression, and maybe enjoy the favors of a waitress or barman.

But well before being overwhelmed by the allure of the chef's almightiness, when those stacks of greasy pans were well and truly pissing me off, above all—and I mean absolutely all—I was driven by the emotional power of good food. I was captivated by the thought that behind those kitchen doors was this sweaty chaos from which dishes would emerge with the perfect crunch, the perfect color, the perfect aroma, the sprig of marjoram set at just the right angle, and that all of this made perfect sense. I discovered the tenderness, the joy, and the attention to detail of cooking well for our own satisfaction, even before that of our customers.

Food deserves respect. Food is both a friend and a catalyst, food tells no lies. If you know how to cook well, all is good with the world. One night as a cook is more healing than any priest or psychiatrist or aspirin. I cook because I love to, because people say I'm good at it, and because over time I have depleted the resourcefulness you need to make up lies. I have opened and closed that door so often there's very little I believe in anymore, other than that I know how to cook.

Have you ever looked at yourself in the mirror and wondered whether the life you're living is worth it all? I have, of course, but that's not the point, is it?

3.

I'm just another chef. A pretty good chef who has been at it for so long now that at this point, I can honestly say that being a chef is my whole life. And you know what? It's a life I love.

I was born in 1977, the year of uprisings and repression in Italy, the appearance of left-wing sidewalk tribes like the Metropolitan Indians, the shenanigans of the murderously brutal Magliana Gang, the spate of movies starring the Cuban-American actor Tomas Milian, and Elvis Presley's last concert. The popular Italian TV ad show *Carosello* ended in 1977. Not long ago I was struck by a headline in the Italian newspaper *Corriere della Sera*: Italy's unemployment rate is the same as it was in 1977. It must have been a shit year. The world lost Maria Callas and Charlie Chaplin that year too. And turtleneck sweaters, the ones that made your neck itch, were all the rage. How can anyone possibly have warm, fuzzy memories of that year? My parents probably knew nothing of Maria Callas or Charlie Chaplin, let alone the *Carosello* show, or maybe they did but just didn't care. They were living in India at the time, and as far as my mother is concerned, that year never ended, with her and dad's revolutions, counterculture, and kids born during their travels. She genuinely cherishes warm, fuzzy memories of 1977. So initially, before I became a cook, I was the son of two real-life flower-power-love-is-all-you-need hippies, who gave up Rome and Italy's economic boom to live in India. And that is where I was born, in Dalhousie, Himachal Pradesh, the tip of Himalayan India squeezed in between Kashmir and Pakistan. After that, back in Italy, I was a teenager growing up in the boonies, one of those kids who cared far more about living (on and off their motorbikes) than school.

In 1981 Franco Battiato was topping the Italian charts with *"Cerco un centro di gravità permanente"* —which translates as, "I'm searching for a permanent center of gravity." My parents, having returned to Italy after seven years in India with a four-year-old in tow and my brother on the way, could no longer endure living in a big city. They found an old neglected schoolhouse nestled in the rolling hills of Umbria, one of those buildings with a huge central room that housed all the classes and a smaller room off to the side with a bed for the teacher when they were snowed in. The local council rented it out for 20,000 lire a month and it was okay for a while. It would be okay, my parents said, until they decided to move on. Meanwhile, we could grow a few vegetables. Dad turned down a job in a bank and started to paint, channeling an urge to commit his stories to canvas, and coaxing the world into accepting who he was.

At the end of the day, it's how people recognize the difference between an artist and a sociopath. The difference between a chef and a sociopath? I don't believe there is one.

Someone eventually decided that my father's paintings were worth money, and so Dad stopped being a dabbler and became an artist. That was his job, while Mom took care of selling his paintings to fancy art galleries on Via Margutta in Rome and raising me and my brother. I just didn't get it. Or more to the point, I couldn't explain it. What does your dad do? they used to ask me in elementary school. And I, a bit ashamed, would say, "He's a painter," after having heard the likes of "farmer," "mechanic," and "policeman." When I was in junior high, I discovered that a classmate of mine was the mayor's son and fell into a silent depression that lasted a whole week. Every now and again they wouldn't quite understand, and would say, "C'mon, a painter?" or "Great, we're painting the house right now, we might call him," and I wouldn't clear up the misunderstanding. At least that kind of painting was a real job. In the meantime, the old schoolhouse we were living in felt more and more like home, and my parents would end up never leaving it. In 1992, while Italians were singing along to Giorgio Gaber's "Qualcuno era comunista" (Some of Them Were Communists), they bought it for 20 million lire. They bought their permanent center of gravity and lost a piece of their wandering hearts. It was the year before Dad died, on the day of his fortieth birthday, of leukemia. My dad died as he had lived, a hippie to the bitter end.

Coming from a family of Italian hippies can produce one of two consequences: either you become a second-generation Italian hippie or you rebel, albeit lovingly, against your past. Well, I ended up in the latter category, so alongside school, girls, booze, travel, and drugs, work has always been my way of seeking independence, freedom, and prospects for the future. I have always felt that I was working to make it on my own and, if possible, to support whoever was with me—not least my flower child of a mom.

My mom had all the shortcomings, but also the strengths, of a sweet, unabashed egomaniac, and she was that way with food too. When my brother and I got home from school, she would greet us enthusiastically: "Guess what we're having for lunch today, boys! Pasta with a tomato and cream sauce!" or "Fried eggs!" and we'd both be ecstatic. Her absolute and utter joyfulness was so contagious she managed to convince us that she really was a good cook. The only dessert she ever made was sponge biscuits soaked in red syrupy Alkermes liqueur and alternated with layers of custard cream. She would serve it at every birthday as something new and exciting, maybe because she'd made the custard using the egg whites as well as the yolks that time, or replaced the Alkermes with a different liqueur. I thought you could buy real custard cream only in pastry shops and that was why it was so good in my friends' homes, because they bought it. My mom's was the way it was because it was homemade. In fact, I think she gave me this explanation herself. Mom simply didn't know the first thing about cooking. Dad cooked only on special occasions, but he put a great deal of care into preparing dishes. He loved mixing things, baking bread or maybe pizza in a wood oven; he loved tending the fire and looking after the vegetable patch. I was always quite happy with whatever my mother made for us, but I so admired the way my dad was able to turn cooking into pleasure. Mom fed us; Dad delighted us.

The day of my dad's funeral, Mom was wearing one of her long flowing skirts, her hair tied back with a colorful scarf, and she was smiling. In the years that followed, whenever anything worried her, she would chant, *"Om Namah Shivaya!"* a Hindu mantra that translates as "I bow to Shiva," or "May the Lord's will be done," or simply (as this pissed-off son might put it), "Whatever!"

She was often out, sometimes returning home late at night, but she always left something for me and my brother, Francesco, to eat. But without her there to make a rousing presentation, the food became monotonous and boring. And so I would add my own touch. I had free rein, and what drove me was the fervor of a sixteen-year-old and memories of the food fests prepared by my dad, whom I wanted to emulate. I would sauté something in a pan, add a sauce here and a caramelized crust there. I got hooked on simple dough made with flour, water, and yeast, the basic elements in any good restaurant. Mixing flour and water, and turning those simple ingredients into complex food, left me in total amazement—and bliss. I discovered the potential of discerning flavors and learning how to reproduce them. Then I began inviting friends home for lunch, first just guys and later girls too. I was the only teenager who cooked for friends when they came over. Right there it hit me that food was power: An empty house and knowing how to cook meant there was an astonishing chance I might just learn what sex was all about.

The first present I gave my first real girlfriend was a loaf of still warm freshly baked bread wrapped in a napkin with the four corners tied together, like something out of a Mickey Mouse comic strip. Her name was Michela. She was petite, wore her black hair in a bob, and was painfully shy even when we stole kisses far from prying eyes. The loaf she eventually got was my fourth attempt, after three that hadn't turned out exactly how I wanted them, either overcooked, not quite done, or entirely the wrong shape. I'll never forget the look on her face. Polite, rather than surprised, it was an expression of someone struggling to process an unfamiliar situation. We tore a few chunks out of the loaf and ate them right there, in the middle of the main square of the village. We didn't finish it. "A bit more salt, maybe?" was her only comment. Had I overestimated the power of food? Or misjudged Michela? I never saw her again, and she married and settled down with her next boyfriend.

The year 1996 was a puzzling one for Italy. An up-and-coming politician named Umberto Bossi proclaimed the independence of Padania (the northern Po valley region) from the rest of Italy, amid a litany of swear words and rude gestures, vaguely inspired by pagan rituals of baffling Celtic origin.

Marcello Mastroianni passed away in Paris, depriving us of a certain refined Italian ideal. My life, on the other hand, was quickly depriving me of money. I had been working as a waiter to pay my way through high school and was nearing graduation when I discovered that if I managed to get an A in my final exam, with no dad, no assets, and an unemployed mom, I would qualify for a relocation scholarship if I moved to Rome. Seven million lire a year sounded like an excellent reason to relocate. The other reason was Matteo. I had met him a couple of years earlier. He lived in Rome and descended from the other category of flower children from the '60s, the ones who had stayed put; needing something to drift toward, they had chosen local politics.

"Hey, Matt, how about I crash at your place in about a week's time?"

"Sure, cool."

"I was thinking of staying awhile."

"Sure, great."

"Yeah, awhile. Maybe a long while."

"Oh."

"How about five years?"

"Okay, I'll just run it by my mom."

Matteo had an instinctive elegance about him, a few well-disguised nervous tics, and was content to still be playing with Lego blocks at seventeen years of age. It's fine to play with Legos at twelve, and there's nothing wrong about playing with Legos at thirty. But to be playing with Legos at seventeen, with hormones raging and a teenager's typical craving for independence, is epic. Or the sure sign of a sociopath. Together we listened to the Police and Pearl Jam, played with Legos, and enrolled at the university. I left the untamed hills and ventured into the untamed postcapitalist urban fringe of the capital, with its pockets of homegrown hippies. I was coming full circle, in a gesture of affection mixed with rebellion, by returning to the city my parents had fled. The only things I took with me that belonged to my father were his old Nikon Reflex camera and a vague idea of what the word "good" meant when it referred to food. I started to connect the dots on the map of my life, and to smoke pot. *Om Namah Shivaya.*

I continued to study with sporadic confidence, met some people, and moved to Via Placido Zurla, in Rome's not-yet-hip Pigneto quarter, renting an apartment on the same floor as my aunt. Matteo moved in with me. Before even buying a mattress, I stocked the fridge and started cooking for two days straight, inviting over everyone I knew. My identity revolved around food, cooking, and good company. It was my passport, and I needed it to get by in Rome. I needed money too. My scholarship didn't cover even my basic expenses, so I went to the first restaurant I heard about that was looking for a waiter. Its name was Sessanta. Sandro was the chef and Giovanna worked front of house. Only as many days as I need to pay the rent, I thought. Yeah, sure, I mused, without much conviction. Two weeks later, the sous chef had a fight with Sandro and stomped out in the middle of service, leaving him in the lurch with a French knife and an overflowing pass. There were three of us servers in the dining room. I cracked open the black door that led to the kitchen, stuck my head in, and piped up, "I know how to cook a little." That evening I crossed the threshold into the kitchen. And I've never looked back.

4.

Sandro met Giovanna in Paris in the early '90s. At that time, he was as thin as a rail. He sported a Mohawk and was heavily into punk rock. He wore a tattered uniform with his favorite knife dangling from his apron strings. Giovanna fell madly in love with him. She was studying languages and had been living in Montmartre for a while, making ends meet working as a waitress. Sandro had been in Paris for a year in a rented loft in Pigalle and had just entered the kitchen of Paul Bocuse. When I met them in Rome, ten years had passed since their first meeting and Sandro was sporting a prominent beer belly and had lost the tough-guy look he said he once had, but they were still together. All he ever wanted to do was enjoy himself cooking at the expense of the owners. As far as everything else was concerned, he didn't give a shit. When the fresh yellowtail arrived, the first thing we'd do was make a beautiful carpaccio or tartare and gorge ourselves on it, nothing but the best parts. Then we'd freeze what was left. Sandro ordered cheeses that cost an arm and a leg and were impossible to sell (leaving us feeling obliged to cut some sizable wedges for ourselves, just to taste them), and bought a mountain of top-of-the-line kitchen utensils with all the bells and whistles, and silver platters to serve them on, the likes of which I had never seen before. His menus were outrageously extravagant, and his techniques were imaginative as well as precise. Not that I was in any way involved; I was the lowly pantry chef in charge of making salads.

Sandro carried on as if he were still in the snobbish Parisian culinary school he taught at before returning to Italy. Sessanta was a fun and useful stopgap, but it couldn't go on for much longer, we all knew that, even Sandro. The financial drain perpetrated with clinical precision by the chef exasperated the owners, and the self-congratulatory attitude of Sandro and Giovanna was always one short step away from reality. I took a few exams at school without attending any classes, mainly to keep my grant. I spent weekends working, but even though I learned a great deal from Sandro, I was looking for more than a career making salads. I left the restaurant in June 2001.

In July, they caught Sandro with his fingers in the till and fired him, charging him with theft. He got so mad that one night he punctured all four tires of the car of one of the owners. Except it was the wrong car, and someone saw him, and so Sandro and his beer belly ended up spending a night in the slammer. He asked his friends for help, but when you're in hot water, your so-called friends are the first to disappear. Giovanna apparently returned to Paris and hooked up with someone else. The thing that pissed off Sandro the most was the fact that this someone else was a dull, middle-aged sales assistant. A sales assistant? *Che cosa?* After experiencing the ecstasy of an artist like him? I lost sight of Sandro for a while, but his cooking was way too good to keep him down. And if Giovanna is still with that other guy, then that's her bad luck.

My only satisfaction at this stage of my life came from the fantastic dinner parties I threw at home. I was living well above my means and engaging in a certain level of culinary experimentation. When I went into a supermarket, I'd switch on my Walkman, put on my headphones, and turn the volume up to the maximum, but without putting in a cassette. When passing by the cash registers, if I heard the white noise change from *zzzzz* to *zzZZZZzz*, that meant the shoplifting alarm was on, otherwise it was there only as a deterrent and was probably either fake or off. That day I didn't hear anything.

I did my shopping, adroitly slipping the most expensive items into my backpack: a bottle of Barolo, a slab of Scottona beef, pine nuts, French cheeses, Venezuelan chocolate. This enabled me to play around with cuisine that was worthy of the name. A steady stream of friends and acquaintances came over and stuffed themselves at my dinner parties, these events being anything but commonplace in cash-strapped student circles. Word got around that you'd always get a great meal at Leonardo and Matteo's place.

I started calling myself a chef—and allowing myself to be called one—much, much sooner than I should have. But other people's confidence defines you (at least I've always let it define me), and context is the measure of everything.

5.

In July 2001, I returned from Genoa, where there had been violent clashes between antiglobalization protesters and police during the G8 summit, my head bursting with ludicrous journalistic ambition and countless photos of the riots, a few of which were purchased by Italy's moderately left-wing daily *La Repubblica* and a couple by the way more left-leaning *Il Manifesto*. No one paid for them or even suggested my sending any more. What else could I do but get back into a kitchen? But this time around I needed a plan. Giulio's restaurant in Rome's colorful Trastevere quarter was looking for a station chef, and I diligently put together my résumé: detailed and jam-packed with blatant lies. I listed working in real restaurants that I had never set foot in, plus a brilliant but entirely phony five-year career that started in Umbria and saw me excel as both a cook and sous chef. Giulio, who had given his name to the place, didn't make a single phone call—they seldom bother to check out résumés. "That looks fine, great, you're hired."

He showed me around the kitchen, told me his plans and ambitions, how his restaurant was state-of-the-art, and what he demanded of his kitchen staff: coordination, consistency, and courage—his three Cs. Plus a fourth, cunt, which he definitely was.

The chef was a young guy brimful of coke and debts, with a ginormous ego. He personified the innate human drive to create, combined with a massive degree of assertiveness and more than a slight proneness to snap. Skillful, for sure, compared to me. The other chef was a Japanese woman with a teenage son living in Tokyo. For a year after her divorce, she had survived on a booze-only, no-food diet. Her exact words. She had survived, no question about that, but not without consequences. If her skin was anything to go by, I would have put her anywhere between twenty-five and fifty-five, not to mention her belly, bloated with sorrow. Her saving grace was a distinctively exotic touch that she gave to both menus and sauces. Not much, really, but as far as I was concerned, a flair worth its weight in gold.

I would work one day with her and the next day with the other chef, after fessing up to both of them about my phony résumé. You might be able to dupe the owner, but you can't fake it with chefs, even total imbeciles. You can recognize right away the ones who know their way around a kitchen, from the way they clean and put the cutting board away after using it, to how they carry a knife, always back to front, with the blade along their forearm to avoid stabbing anyone. If you handle knives tentatively, you're not a chef. If you handle them carelessly, you're absolutely not a chef.

So I came clean about my past as a lowly salad maker and my ambition. I put up with anything. I was the first to arrive and the last to leave after soaping down the pass and giving the dishwasher some help with the dirty dishes and the floors. Blinddrunk chefs, deranged owners, bullying, quarrels that defied comprehension or even classification—literally any working conditions. All I asked for was that they didn't unmask me to Giulio and that they give me the chance to finally really learn something. They agreed with unexpected enthusiasm, and I very quickly understood why: They hated each other profoundly. They never missed an opportunity to discredit each other even though their paths rarely crossed in the kitchen.

He was engaged to one of the waitresses, who, like the majority of waitresses in Rome, was an aspiring actress who moonlighted as Giulio's in-house spy, pointing out to him all the Japanese chef's shortcomings. The Japanese chef always wore the weary expression of someone called on to clean up other people's messes. She would drink just about anything that came her way, and by the end of the dinner service was totally wasted. One time she sneezed so loudly and with such force, swaying uncontrollably, that she hit her head against the counter and fell to the floor unconscious. We were all extremely concerned, especially Giulio, partly because she was working there illegally, like me, the kitchen hand, and most of the wait-staff. Coke was readily available and stashed all over the place. I, however, stayed away from the stuff. I knew I needed to concentrate on becoming good at what I was doing. Not that I was on a whiz-bang career path, but just so I would not feel uncomfortable there or in any of the other places I would end up in, at least until I graduated from the university. Becoming good at something boosts your confidence, no matter what it is. I had met only a few chefs, but the thing that surprised me the most in all of them was their chutzpah, their bravado, and their self-confidence in dealing with things. In dealing with everything.

At that time, I didn't even smoke cigarettes on the job. I had two days off a week and I spent them with my girlfriend, Valeria, taking capoeira classes at the local gym and cooking special dinners at home. Valeria was determined to get ahead at school, and we had just started dating. Like any other guy in his late teens with a still unformed personality, I was vaguely in love and wanted to better myself, as if I owed it to her belief in me. Sure, I'd learned a few things, but only a very, very few.

6.

The evening of the Incident, the Japanese chef had been off work recovering from her fall. In the dining room there was a new girl from Venice, Lucia, with whom I would later connect very closely. Her knees were double-jointed and she had already had two abortions. She had just told me she was pregnant again but didn't seem to give much importance to it. However, that wasn't what was on my mind. Rather, it was the fact that the young-dude chef had suddenly decided to reward me by elevating me to the rank of sous chef, hoping, in so doing, to rid himself once and for all of the Japanese chef.

"Tonight I'm not going to do a thing. I want to see how you cope managing the dishes going out," he said.

Thinking back, I shouldn't have been so nervous, but being a bug under the microscope does that to you. Giulio was dashing in and out of the kitchen, creating more havoc than anything else during a dinner service that was already frenzied. The dishes weren't complicated, but the plating was quite detailed, some I had barely glanced at being prepared, and the baked sea bream with cherry tomatoes and thyme in a potato crust was one of them. I could have cooked the dish my way, of course, but that evening I was the clone of the young-dude chef and had to perform every movement exactly as he would. I knew I had to respect the hierarchy that exists in every restaurant kitchen (no chef wants a helper taking the initiative; all they want is people to do as they're told), but I also wanted to win his trust and maybe a little more independence. The young-dude chef was standing there with his arms folded firing away orders and correcting me the whole time. Basically, he wanted to get away with doing as little as he possibly could.

"Have you checked that the sea bream fillets are properly deboned?"

I was pulling the fish from the fridge to rinse it under running water and dry it, and looking at the long line of tickets on the rail above my head.

"Yes, Chef, I deboned them yesterday."

"Have you sliced the potatoes?"

I was already reaching for the gastronorm full of julienned potatoes that had been left to soak in water.

"Here they are, Chef, I prepared them fresh as soon as I arrived."

"Careful with the pan, if the heat's too high the oil will burn."

I took the pan off the heat although I had barely lit the gas and was just pouring in the olive oil.

"And the cherry tomatoes?"

"All ready, Chef. Cut in half and draining on the wire rack." Out came the tomatoes from the fridge.

I added butter to the spaghetti with bottarga fish roe and stock to the surf-and-turf risotto that a table of ten of Giulio's friends had ordered quite a while before. I was screaming at the kitchen hand for the appetizers because he was taking too long threading the shrimp and bacon onto the skewers.

"Careful with the skin. It must not come off and it's got to be crisp."

"Of course, Chef, crisp."

"But don't overcook the fish."

"No, Chef."

"Is the oven hot enough?"

I leaned over to look in the oven; it was always on during service and therefore obviously hot.

"Three sixty-five degrees, Chef."

"Put it up to three ninety."

I turned the temperature dial up just a fraction, to 390°. "All done, Chef."

I was still calling for the appetizers, the risotto was ready, the spaghetti was done, and the four baked pasta dishes needed to be pulled out of the oven before they started to burn. Everything had to go out at the same time. I lifted the sea bream with a silicone spatula, gave the potatoes a shake in the other pan to crisp up and brown them a little.

"Go, go, go! Get that bream into the oven, you're falling behind, shit, you're in the weeds!"

"All good to go, Chef."

I took the fish off the heat with the tomatoes, a handful of capers, some grated lemon rind, a pinch of thyme, and a dusting of salt, then laid the potatoes over the top and shaped them quickly with my hands. I licked a finger to taste for salt, then put the pan in the oven and started plating the other dishes. Out of the corner of my eye I could see the kitchen hand was still behind with those fucking appetizers. I was ringing the bell like a lunatic to call Lucia.

"Hey, Luci, start taking out the baked pastas and the spaghetti and then come back here and I'll give you the others."

As Lucia called Giulio for help, I ran to the appetizer station to pull the shrimp broth out of the fridge, pour it into a bowl, cover it with plastic wrap, and put it into the microwave.

"Grab the kamut croutons!" I shouted to the kitchen hand, who finally seemed to have stirred from his listless torpor and was scattering croutons over dishes on the pass, and drizzling them with parsley-infused olive oil.

"Come on, Leo, get a fucking move on, the bream is browning, come on, it all has to go out together!"

I could see the wrap balloon over the soup in the microwave. It wasn't supposed to get too hot. I was screaming at the kitchen hand to load it on the pass with the skewers, the sauces, and the two salads. I grabbed the pot holder above the oven and pulled out the pan with the bream, placed it back on the burner to crisp the skin, stretched over the counter to get a serving plate, and started to decorate it with two thin lines of mayonnaise, some aromatic herbs, and ruby paprika. I couldn't find the carrot curls.

"Where are the carrot curls?" I asked. "Where are they? Hasn't anyone prepared them?" Damn it, it was me who hadn't prepared them.

"I'm sorry, Chef, I forgot them! Can I plate the dish without them?"

"Come on, come on, *move*! Of course you need the carrot curls, but it's too late now...just get on with it!"

I looked over at the pass: The plates were still all sitting there, Lucia was at the door waiting for the bream, the young-dude chef had finally stopped breathing down my neck and was getting the toasted sesame seeds to sprinkle over the salads. I turned off the gas and bent down to grab the pan out of the oven. Without a pot holder. A searing pain split my brain in two like an apple, leaving nothing but the big red numbers on the temperature display: 390°. I lifted the pan from the oven as the heat burned through every layer of skin right down to the bone, and from there to my eyes, setting off a powerful spasm, but I managed to place the pan on the pass near the serving dish that was waiting for it. My right palm was shiny and dry like a pane of glass. But I used it to pick up the steel palette, delicately remove the fish from the aluminum pan, and place it in the middle of the dish. I cleaned the edges of the dish with great care using the cloth I kept tucked in my apron strings and drizzled a few drops of smoked oil over the top. I glanced over the dishes confidently and then, finally, uttered the magic words: "Take it out!"

"In here, I'm the one who decides what goes out."

"Sorry, Chef."

"Take it out!"

Lucia left carrying three plates, followed by Giulio with the other two. I inched back toward the ice machine, plunged my entire right arm into it, grasped a handful of ice cubes and lifted it out, keeping my arm behind my back. I could barely distinguish between hot and cold. I could hear the water dripping onto the floor but did not utter a sound, not wanting to appear the complete dickhead I genuinely was. Then I got some butter and rubbed my hands with it, like it was some kind of miraculous medication. Nobody realized what had happened. I finished service wearing rubber gloves, my hand throbbing as if it had a heart of its own in a state of permanent fibrillation. The dishes had to go out and they had to be perfect, immaculately presented, and all at the same time. That was how it had to be and that was all that mattered.

On the way home that evening, I stopped at an all-night drugstore and bought a tube of burn ointment. My palm sported a massive blister, plus four more on my index, middle, and ring fingers, and pinky. Only my thumb had been spared. They say humans evolved larger brains after developing opposable thumbs, and not vice versa. I had saved my intelligence and my reputation. What a dumb-ass idea to put a pan in the oven. I'd never have a crappy dish like that on *my* menu.

7.

The unmitigated madness that reigned at Giulio's came to my rescue, when almost overnight, in a nonstop, daily procession, first one chef and then the other barged into the owner's little Ikea-furnished office to complain about the other's ineptitude. Unbeknownst to each other, they both adopted the same strategy, which was to show how much better, defter, and more trustworthy I, a mere chef de partie, was than their rival, who was a pathetic joke of a chef. Giulio ended up firing first the Japanese chef (not even two months after my arrival) and then the young dude, who got his revenge by dragging his former employer into a labor dispute—but not before thoroughly cleaning out his pantry. And so I ended up in charge of the kitchen, and I was the only chef. I never really cared what happened to those two. I believe the young dude went on to become a second-rate stage actor. All that mattered was that once there were two chefs above me and now there were none. The oven-baked sea bream disappeared from the menu and I had a say in who got to work in the restaurant.

"Hey, Matt, how about coming to the restaurant tonight?"

"Sure, are you offering me dinner?"

"Nope, work."

"Oh."

"The waitress is a hottie."

"I dunno, let me think about it."

"Well, bring a clean shirt with you, you'll be working front of the house."

My future is within my reach. This is an unhoped for stroke of luck. I have no degree, no one wants my photos, I have no actual skills to speak of, but I am in charge of a restaurant.

A couple of weeks later, Lucia's voice, coming from Matteo's room, wakes me up: "Chef, it's nearly eleven, will you come down and have breakfast with us?"

"Don't wake me up, it's my day off! And don't make a mess, you pigs."

I'd cleaned up the house the night before after getting back from work, and my capoeira instructors were coming over for dinner, because I was royally pissed off at being ignored during class. I knew only one way to get a bit of attention, what else could I do? The menu included three cold and three hot appetizers, with a skillful interplay between soft and crunchy textures; two entrées; a fillet of Piedmont beef with myrtle sauce; and a small selection of desserts. Matteo and Lucia went out and I cooked all day. I was even late getting to the gym, and by the time I arrived they were in the showers, so all I did was tell them how to get to our place. By the end of the evening, I had become "*o cozinheiro*," the chef, and I was now officially "someone" at the gym.

One of the instructors I invited that night was a guy named Giangi, and before leaving he asked if I'd be interested in organizing dinner parties with him, events consisting of samba, cocktails, and good food. I, of course, would look after the food side of things. Not right now, he hastened to add. It was only an idea at this stage, but he wanted to start talking about it. I was still up to my neck in problem-solving at Giulio's and trying to understand whether I really liked that lawless world that seemed prepared to let me in out of nothing other than deep-rooted pathological negligence. Nonetheless, I asked Giangi to stay back for a drink, and we spent the rest of the night discussing his plans. I listened and made a few suggestions, as if I were ready to start whenever he was. I have always opted for remote possibilities rather than outright refusals, a tactic that has often borne sweet fruit.

In the meantime, I was starting to realize two important principles: Be wary of establishments that bear the name of the owner, and always distrust a career that takes off abnormally fast. Not that this kept me awake at night, because being trusted and appreciated by Giulio fanned my pride, and a sense of responsibility in some way did actually make me a better, more competent cook, simply because in his restaurant I was the top dog. And nothing else mattered at the time. Of course, there was that niggling doubt that if I was held in such high esteem by an asshole, then it was safe to say that I was one too. But apart from the owner, Giulio's could potentially turn into something of real worth, even though it was not a sophisticated place by any stretch of the imagination. Observing the restaurant from this side of the kitchen door, all I saw was a monument to overinflated egos and cocaine, but from the outside it didn't seem any worse than so many places just like it: pastel walls, soft lighting, a burnished timber bar counter. We served shrimp skewers with a sweet-and-sour sauce, clams au gratin, baked sea bass coated in mint-and-chervil breadcrumbs, steamed beef ravioli, desserts topped with luscious Fabbri syrups and store-bought wafers. Uninspired fusion cuisine interspersed with a handful of stand-out dishes.

Yet the work made me surprisingly happy. The kitchen is the sultanate that rules over the whole restaurant, and I was its benevolent absolute ruler. Happy even when still serving brunch an hour past noon; happy an hour past midnight. The tasks were mindless and repetitive, the clientele made up almost exclusively of Giulio's friends who, after a while, took turns disappearing into the restrooms only to emerge sniffing conspicuously. Night after night, Giulio became increasingly consumed and dispirited, all alone behind the long dark counter at the bar. He didn't even wait for the end of service before the effects of the coke started appearing. He would shout abuse at the two chefs who'd ruined him, whine loudly about overheads, and curse at the wages of the bloodsuckers he had to pay, but most often he'd laugh mockingly at his own bad juju.

A little more than a year after I started working at Giulio's, every table, every pot, pan, and plate exuded the unmistakable stench of tragedy. There was only one thing left for me to do, which was par for the course in our line of business: abandon ship a minute before it sinks. Land the final blow just after you've been paid your wages, when the owners still trust that fate will step in and rescue them.

Giulio was in the grip of overwhelming panic, snorting more and more coke, thrashing around in a state of unbridled agitation, and spewing out a steady stream of preposterous solutions devoid of logic or coherence and pathetic attempts to patch up a situation that was beyond salvation: fixed-price menus, midweek closures, cocktail hour, aperitifs with free finger food, ethnic dishes, themed evenings, and regional cuisine.

"You know how to make pizza, right?" he blurted out suddenly one evening, his jaw jutting and his gaze unfocused, while I was on the doorstep ready to go home. Even the last remaining regulars had become suspicious and moved on. Lucia hadn't been around for a while and Matteo stayed for a few only weeks and then bowed out to write his dissertation. The waiters were just kids, a new bunch every week, all of them clueless. By now I was embarrassed to see my friends coming to the restaurant. And to top it all, my new status as "chef" did not come with a raise. It was still just €1,100 a month, cash in hand, always late and always grudgingly. The time had come to pull up stakes. Actually, it was probably too late already and, worse, I had no plan B.

"Giulio, I'll be out of here in a couple of weeks. Can you pay me my last salary before then?"

"What? And I should pay you? For pissing off and leaving me in this shit!"

"I'm not leaving you in any shit, I'm handing in my notice..."

"Well, as soon as the place picks up, I'll pay you, damn it. Whatever happened to loyalty? What am I supposed to do? Pay everyone and call it quits? And be the only one who gives a damn if the place keeps going or falls apart?"

I thought about what I should do. It was only about one month's wages, after all, less than €1,000.

"You know what, Giulio? As of tomorrow I'm done, you can keep your cash."

Freedom.

Lightheartedness.

Fuck you.

I started working out at the capoeira gym three times a week. I felt revitalized, like at the end of a violent and prolonged scream, and went back to school. But with no money flowing in, my savings quickly ran out. I started speculating: How about suing Giulio? What about Sessanta —would they take me back? Washing dishes was out of the question. Working in a fast-food joint? No way, too depressing. I began to seriously consider setting up my own business, importing secondhand cars from Germany. Or working as a carpenter with my brother.

One evening on my way to the gym, I stopped at an ATM to check my bank balance: €1,500, enough to survive a couple of months. There had to be a solution somewhere. I tossed the receipt and continued walking toward the gym, taking a slightly longer route. Giangi was in the dressing room. "You remember those samba evenings we talked about? Well, I've found a place over in the Testaccio quarter that might be interested. How busy are you right now?"

8.

It was past ten on a balmy Roman night, and I was changing my clothes in a broom closet at the venue where Giangi and I were now organizing samba parties. I never found out his real name; everyone called him Giangi. That evening I left earlier than usual, still feeling a strange urge to cook. Maybe it was because Barbara, the hot new waitress with a mop of curly hair, was coming over for a late-night snack of blue cheese and bubbly as soon as she finished polishing the cutlery. It was the first time I'd asked her out, and she accepted right away. Nothing was more exciting than the prospect of starting a new relationship. I'd just finished work and I was really buzzing.

Just outside the venue, I noticed an old white Fiat 850 Westphalia camper van. A thing of beauty, instantly recognizable. I knew it well. Vincenzo had bought it to go to techno parties and ended up living in it. I, however, had decided that I would have nothing more to do with him for a while. Or rather, for as long as possible. I'd met him in Sandro's kitchen. He was from Lucca, short like me, and skinny, but with the physique of a fat guy who's lost a lot of weight, and they introduced him to me as Ciccio—Fatso. Nicknames can conjure up memories like nothing else in this world. Names tell stories of exploits, bring to mind anecdotes, and in my case remind me of someone's eating habits. Ciccio was still Ciccio even after shedding the seventy pounds that earned him his nickname. Now he had stick-thin arms attached to sloping shoulders, sinewy hands covered in burn marks, and the black stuff under fingernails that comes from kneading dough every day. He appeared out of nowhere one New Year's Eve to help prep the appetizers.

Vincenzo was a born liar and for that reason people liked him; they felt at ease when he was around. When I became the chef at Giulio's, I asked him to come along and give me a hand and then decided to let him stay—or, rather, he decided to stay. His tumultuous presence had a soothing effect on me. Because this junkie, this erratic, affectionate liar, worked magic when let loose in the kitchen. He was always cooking and experimenting with food, at the restaurant, in his own kitchen, or at friends' places. Mainly mine. One joint after another, we would stay up until the early hours of the morning waiting for the dough, an outlandish mixture of rotten apples, various types of flour, sugar, water, and oil, to rise just so. We knew it was ready by its aroma.

Making bread was our common ground. His was incredible. A profoundly gratifying fragrance would fill the house when, after an hour and a half in the oven, we would take the loaf out and, with a puff of steam, let the flour-dusted crust crackle between the palms of our hands. He could determine, by sound alone, exactly where the air bubbles created by the yeast were located: if they had settled on the bottom of the loaf; if there were any hollow spots; or if, as was more often the case, the bread was perfect. The smell of that bread has stayed with me like verses tossed away by a despondent young poet. Five months later the only thing on my mind was how to get rid of him.

Ultimately, Vincenzo's irresistible acts of generosity and charm couldn't make up for me having to be his nanny, his ATM, his analyst, and his latrine. So one day, completely out of the blue, I simply said to him, "I'm letting you go tomorrow." Vincenzo was the dark hero of those carefree days: sensitivity shattered by greed, greed sustained by sensitivity. A real chef.

I'm out of here, I said to myself. Fuck yes. I'm going home, I murmured, convincing myself it was the right thing to do. Only, when you have to convince yourself to do the right thing, it's never a good sign. I thought about Barbara's curly hair, the heat. I froze, with the motorbike lock in my hand, under the yellow streetlamp. For a split second I was in a Gregory Crewdson photo. "Hey, Vince, it's me, Leo. Open up."

The van's small white, arched door opened with a click. Behind a pair of glasses I saw a slightly bug-eyed gaze, just like I remembered it from way back.

"Leo baby! It's been ages, what the fuck are you doing here?"

"Let me in. What are *you* doing out here? I work here."

"Here? But isn't this place a club?"

"Nah. On Saturdays they have live bands, but during the week I organize samba nights and theme parties. Hey, will you let me in?"

"Goddammit, Leo baby, of course I'll let you in. Come on, have a joint."

I knew it.

I was right back smack in the middle of it and thrilled to be there. So when he said, "Hey, Leo baby, why don't we go over to my friend's place? She's a pastry chef. There'll be other people too, it'll be a fun night, and great wine...c'mon it's been more than a year since we hung out. We can take the bike. How about it?," I didn't hesitate.

The next thing I knew I was texting Barbara, who had probably left the restaurant and might even be at my place by now, blowing her off with a pathetic excuse, all the while hollering, "Okay, let's go!"

Fuck. I'm a moron. Farewell creamy blue-veined cheese, goodbye hands running through Barbara's curly hair. An absolute moron. We ate mint-scented arancini and kamut-and-cumin bread sticks.

"Leo baby, take a look—I make everything in this!" He pointed at a tiny oven not much bigger than a toaster.

"You're a fucking genius, goddamn you."

I told Vincenzo what I'd been up to since the last time we met, my words filling the narrow crevices of the landslide of descriptions and stories he buried me under. Then it was on with the jackets and helmets, he grabbed his backpack, and we climbed onto my motorbike.

"So, where are we going?" I asked.

"Get to Piazza Conca d'Oro and I'll tell you where to go from there."

My old Honda 250 started on the first try. We arrived in this smart residential part of town and parked the bike. Vincenzo was still talking, and so was I, when I could get a word in edgewise. Elevator, top floor. The penthouse. Jesus. Sara, the owner, welcomed us in. That is, the daughter of the owners, who were out. They won't be coming back tonight. I recognized her. I had seen her at the occasional techno party but never spoken to her. I now discovered she was the pastry chef Vincenzo had mentioned.

The pastry station isn't really part of a professional kitchen. It's an area unto itself, usually physically separated from the other stations. There you don't use scoops of sugar, guessing roughly at amounts, you don't measure things by the handful, you don't check how things are cooking by looking through the oven window. The pastry station is that secret place where the alchemy occurs: different kinds of flour, butter, oil, cocoa, coffee, thermometers, electronic scales, cooking times that are exact to the minute and temperatures that can't fluctuate by even half a degree. It's not that far from a science lab, and the preparation and cooking of sweets and desserts requires a certain understanding of chemistry and physics.

In confectionary art, the better you know how those processes combine to develop aromas, compositions, consistencies, and balances, the better the outcome. In short, almost anyone can learn to cook well, many even manage to become professional chefs, but only a few, a very few, are good pastry chefs. It's such a specialized field that many pastry chefs do nothing else—they never set foot in other parts of the kitchen. They have their own ovens, their own fridges, a separate pass. Seeing Sara use a credit card to scrape the ketamine off the bottom of a frying pan after it has just crystallized makes it exceedingly hard for me to imagine her putting the finishing touches on a Saint-Honoré. As the evening progressed, I declined invitations to partake of the harder stuff, being more than happy to stick with pot. I opened a couple of bottles of decent wine and munched on some aniseed pralines, which were quite good. Hmmm—homemade.

"Hey, Sara, did you make these? Vincenzo tells me you're a pastry chef."

"Yeah, we learned how to make them at the Gambero Rosso cooking course. Do you like them?"

"I do, yeah...What cooking course was that?" These pralines weren't the kind an amateur whips up for a bunch of friends. "It couldn't have been just a weekend course..."

"No, it was one of those new ones, for professional cooks. I mean, I've got a master's in food and wine writing, 'cause my parents were sick of me goofing off, and I always got a kick out of cooking. I met Maurizio Santin there by pure chance and I did his pastry-making course."

"Wow, cool... It's pricey, though, isn't it?"

"Yeah, a bit. But I really dig pastries and desserts and all that stuff. I like to jumble things up, play around with different ingredients. Sometimes it's a god-awful mess, but every now and again I hit a home run."

The food-writing course, learning pastry making under Santin, that's a lot of ladder to climb before one could ever step into the great Santin's kitchen or Andrea Besuschio's chocolate-lover's haven. Sara seemed quite nice but way too laid-back to become a pastry chef. Or even grasp the wealth of experience she had at her fingertips. Seeing opportunity going to waste gets on my nerves and makes me feel ineffectual. The sight of Sara curled up on the Alcantara sofa with her shoes on made me green with envy.

The house was enormous and so was the deck. I slipped out to get a breath of fresh air while, indoors, joints were still being passed around and the piano was getting a light dusting of white powder. In the end I sensed that I didn't fit in with the offspring of these well-to-do Roman families, with their dim-witted, indulgent parents. I stuck a hand in my pocket and grabbed the small container that I always have on me. Inside there were two grams of charas, four papers, some filters, and a few cigarette tips. I rolled a joint, basking in the privileged position of being able to look at the others from the outside. I had my own personal space. Who gives a rat's ass if it's a sign of being disaffected that I was out here smoking alone, while everyone else was inside smoking together?

And what about Vincenzo? He reached into his backpack, chatting all the while, and pulled out a block of hash. It's what they call a ball in Rome, seven ounces exactly. I'd finished rolling my joint, there was no wind, my lighter worked on the first try, my corner of the terrace lit up momentarily, and the window became a mirror. I inhaled slowly, then it was dark again, the mirror disappeared, and I looked inside. A wave of fury engulfed me—maybe I was angrier with myself than with him. The dickhead, he'd brought a block of hash without telling me. Fuck, you don't carry an illegal substance with you if you're riding on the back of someone else's motorbike without telling him. Especially if that someone is me.

They got out the scales, a cutting board, and a carving knife—my favorite—and Vincenzo lined the blade up about an inch from the edge of the block, pressed down clumsily, and knocked a slice of about half an ounce to the floor. I decided to go back inside. They continued doing what they were doing while I sat on the sofa. Vincenzo collected about €150. He didn't seem overjoyed. I was thinking to myself: This is the last time he rides with me. This is the fucking last time that he and I go anywhere together.

I took Vincenzo to one side. "Listen, I'm splitting. What about you? Are you coming or staying?"

"Why don't we have one last joint and then go?"

"No, I'm going now, you do what you want."

I should have added—but didn't, dumb ass that I am—if you decide to come with me, do me a favor and leave the block here. In the end, Vincenzo gave in. Picking up jackets, helmets, and Vincenzo's backpack, we said goodbye and took the elevator. You could hear the music all the way onto the street. We got back on the bike. This time it took three pushes on the pedal and a quite a bit of cursing to get it started. It was cold and I was thinking about Barbara and her curly hair, goddammit. I drove really slowly. Finally Vincenzo shut up, and so did I. I turned down Via Delle Valli toward the loop. There wasn't a soul about.

The traffic lights giving onto Viale Etiopia were red. I slowed down, looked right, then left, changed gears, and was about to run the lights when a car approached from the right, windows down and three people inside. The driver looked at me and mouthed something as he passed. I saw the scene as if in slow motion, in the muffled silence of this deserted part of Rome: my Honda groaning, me pulling on the clutch and the brake, the car passing. I saw, very clearly, the lips of the driver forming the word "PO-LICE." Then he was gone and time went back to normal speed. I looked down the street, to the right. At the gas station about three to four hundred yards away was a police car with its lights off. No one else. I stayed put. The lights were red. I was just slightly over the white stop line. I'd stopped at a red light.

Car stationary. Me stationary. Vincenzo, who had seemingly missed the whole scene, was quiet. Me too. The traffic lights seemed to stay red forever. Time was slowing down again. The only sound was the *vroom vroom* of the Honda's motor. Then, finally, the lights turned green. I exhaled, realizing I had been holding my breath. I put the bike into gear and started moving. Turning into Viale Etiopia on the left, I checked the rearview mirror. The blue police car had left the side of the road and was following me. Shit. Were my headlights working? Maybe I was just being paranoid, c'mon, maybe they were just going somewhere. I drove on, almost to the on-ramp to the loop, slowly, but not too slowly.

Suddenly, I remembered there was a stretch of the loop that you can't drive on at night. I always forget from where to where. I forget because I always drive along it anyway, because the chances of getting caught are one in a million. But now, with a police car behind me, what should I do? At the very last moment

I veered right into Via Tembien. I checked my rearview mirror again and the police car had turned right too. Fuck. I continued along Via Tripoli, unfamiliar with this part of the city, a neighborhood that was fuzzy in my mental map of Rome. I didn't have a clue where I was. I put the indicator on, turned right, and looked at the sign: Via Cirenaica. I checked my rearview mirror again, the police car turned right too.

I turned my head around slightly and said to Vincenzo, "Listen, you have to keep cool now, okay? There's a police car following us."

"Jesus, that's why you've been going around in circles, I was wondering why... What are we going to do?"

"Nothing, that's what we're going to do; maybe they'll just stop us to check our ID. That's all, what else? Oh yeah, one of my headlights isn't working, that's probably why."

"Fucking hell, Leo baby, you should have gone through that red light. They must have gotten suspicious when they saw you stop. Who stops at a traffic light at four in the morning?"

"Okay, let's just behave and keep going a little farther. They might just ask to see our documents. Do you know this part of the city?"

"No"

"Great."

In front of us, the traffic lights on Via Tripolitania were green; I went through and then stopped at a red light in Viale Libia. The police car drew up beside us and stopped. I kept looking straight ahead at the traffic lights, pretending there was nothing amiss. I held my breath. Green. I started turning right into Viale Libia — where the hell were we? The police car turned right into Viale Libia. We came to the next traffic lights, this time red. I stopped. This time the police car stopped behind me. I looked right and left, trying to fathom where to go. On the right, the sign said VIALE ETIOPIA. Fuck! We were at the lights in Piazza Gondar; in front of us was Via Delle Valli. The same traffic lights where the car had passed me and warned me not to go through the red light, only now facing the opposite direction. It was clear that we were not going anywhere in particular. It was clear we knew they were following us, and that's why we were wandering about aimlessly. So obviously we have something to hide. And it wasn't the broken headlight.

"Vince, I'm turning right now. Get ready, they're going to stop us now for sure. Don't fuck things up."

Green. I moved off. I accelerated a little, arrived at the first place you could do a U-turn, turned around, and drove past a closed newspaper kiosk. I felt Vincenzo make a sudden movement. The police car switched on flashing lights and siren. I accelerated a bit more and tossed the small container I had in my pocket. I realized that Vincenzo must have thrown the block of hash behind the kiosk. The police car overtook us and stopped sideways, across the lane. I slowed down and killed the engine. Two uniformed cops emerged.

"Stop! Get off the bike! Keep your hands in sight!"

From slow motion, time suddenly shifted to fast forward, narrowing like an esophagus just before vomiting. Everything happened in a split second: yelling, being pushed, hands—mine—on the hood of the police car. Hands—someone else's—delving into my pockets and patting me down. More flashing lights, more sirens, three more police cars arrived, all of them screeching to a halt. In the middle of Piazza Gondar.

"We're not doing anything wrong, we're cool, we're not resisting arrest!"

"What else have you got on you?"

"Nothing, nothing at all, no need to worry, everything's fine."

One minute I was racking my brain trying to decide what to say, as we handed over our documents. The next we were sitting in the back of a squad car, with our hands handcuffed behind our backs. I discovered that the seats were hard plastic shells, that they weren't padded. How about that. Sitting next to me, all Vincenzo could say was, "I'm sorry, I'm sorry, Leo, I'm so fucking sorry, man."

And I, almost to myself but moving my lips, whispered, "I can't believe it. I can't believe this is happening."

For a moment, in my mind's eye, I was sitting on the sofa at home with Matteo. The time was now, the place far away from here: "It was Vincenzo or Barbara, and you chose Vincenzo. That's what worries me the most, Leo."

"But you know how my mind wanders. I start thinking I can have it all, maybe not right now, but maybe tomorrow."

"Yeah, but today you chose Vincenzo. And tomorrow you can't choose Barbara because you'll be in the slammer." Was it really going to end this way?

The police station was half empty, sparsely furnished, and filled with a musty smell. It occurred to me that working here must be depressing, no wonder they're always so pissed off. There was a female officer and two male officers, one of whom was really big. They exchanged pleasantries with the cops who'd brought us in.

"Hi, guys, what have you got?"

"Possession. A block of hash."

They took us into a small room.

"Take off your clothes."

I stripped, down to my shorts and socks.

"Everything."

The boxers came off, as did the socks. My arms dangled loosely at my sides. What was the point of trying to cover up? Lately I'd been hitting the gym, a bit of fitness training as well as capoeira. I wasn't embarrassed at being naked, quite the opposite, in fact. Let the female officer get an eyeful of me and maybe she'd be shocked that a chef could be so ripped. I let my thoughts get out of hand, as they often did. The female officer left, taking my clothes with her and without giving me a second glance. The burly cop said, "Turn around. Bend over." I didn't ask why, just turned around as instructed and bent over doggy style, with my butt in the air and my hands touching the floor.

Then the questions started.

First, the usual ones: Where were you this evening? Where did you get the cannabis? Where were you taking it? Where's the bit that's missing? Did you sell it? Where's the money? Where do you live?

And then more questions that I wasn't expecting.

How many of you were at the house? How many women and how many men? Do you remember if you ate anything? What was the house like? Did you smoke? Did you drink? Do you remember how the others were dressed? Were you the only one eating the chocolate or did Caffi eat it too? (Vincenzo Caffi, that's his full name.) And other things like that, to see if our stories matched, I suppose. I gave my answers calmly, everything I said was the truth, I didn't have to make anything up. The whole time I was being questioned, I was bent over, with my butt in the air. Were they trying to intimidate me? All I could think about was please, just don't search my apartment, please let this interrogation last as long as possible. At home I had one and a half ounces of weed and a few hundred euros: payment in cash from dinners at the Testaccio venue, but try explaining that to them.

Then it ended.

The policewoman came back in and handed me my clothes, almost kindly. "You can get dressed now."

I put my clothes back on. They made me sit on a wooden bench in the corridor, and after a quarter of an hour Vincenzo arrived and sat down beside me.

"Well then."

"Yeah."

"Did they have you bend over with your butt up in the air too, Leo baby?"

"Yep."

The two officers who arrested us entered a small room at the end of the corridor, along with the burly cop. I could hardly believe what I was seeing through the half-glazed door. They were chatting and laughing. I caught a few words here and there but missed most of it. The huge policeman made a movement just like the one I saw Vincenzo make at Sara's place, the one with the cutting board and the knife. Only this time it was smoother. From where I was sitting, it seemed like a surgical incision, of what I had no idea. Nobody paid us the slightest attention. Then the oversize policeman bent his elbows wide, pulling a face from the effort, and suddenly let go, like when you're straining to break something and it suddenly snaps. I even imagined hearing the snapping sound. One of the three was saying, "Come on, what the fuck are you doing?"

"Shut your trap, you know I can't sleep otherwise." And more laughter.

I turned to Vincenzo, questioning him wordlessly: Did you see that?

He was poker-faced, concentrating on his next move. He scared me even more than the cops. You never knew what Ciccio was going to do next. Fuck, these guys were cutting weed, now what? What the fuck would happen now?

The public prosecutor arrived in jeans, a white shirt, no tie, a tan jacket, and a weary, displeased air. He climbed the stairs with the three officers who had just emerged from the booth. Footsteps filled the air, then a door slammed and voices faded away. Our breathing was slow and shallow. It felt like the oxygen was getting thinner. Outside you could hear Rome awakening, giving a big leisurely stretch. Then one of the officers came over to us by himself. It wasn't the big guy.

"Sign here, you're free to go. This is the report relating to tonight's arrest, any further communications will arrive by mail," he said. Just like that. No small talk. A piece of paper to sign. Three ounces of hashish, 4:38 a.m., Piazza Gondar. Lucarelli and Caffi.

We thanked everyone, said goodbye, and shook hands. Vincenzo's thanks were particularly heartfelt. People said goodbye back, and a few officers even smiled. We signed out, put on our belts and shoelaces, got back our things and the keys to the motorbike.

Outside it was a glorious morning. Six forty-five and the sun was already warm and energizing, the sky a freshly painted azure. We wondered if we'd looked a tad too overjoyed. After all, we'd been charged with possession with intent to sell, not a thing to be sneezed at. Parked outside the police station was my bike, delivered to the door, no less. We headed home, the pandemonium of rush-hour traffic in Rome yet to erupt. I stopped in front of the camper van. It was all over.

Little did I know that in actual fact it had only just started. But to us this wonderful morning had been a gift. We didn't talk about anything serious, no mention of lawyers, court hearings, fines, anything. We relived the events of the night before and congratulated each other on our steady nerves and balls of steel. For a short moment we were allies again, just like old times when we used to bake bread together in the middle of the night. Then I drove home alone, repeating the same promise, over and over: I will never hang out with Vincenzo again, not ever. My work wasn't paying enough. There would be legal fees and I had no idea how much they would be. I'd worry about that later. Right now the sun was shining. I changed my mind and went over to Testaccio and headed straight for the kitchen. I pulled out my favorite bowl, the ceramic one that my grandmother gave me when I moved to Rome, and filled it with flour, without measuring, then added some water and started to knead, gradually regaining my composure.

Giangi and I hadn't yet drummed up the guts to admit that our dinner parties were not going well; perhaps we should have. He took care of the invitations, the music, and the beverages. I put together the menus—a different one for each event—and bought the food. Sometimes we lost a little, sometimes we made a little, on a good night we might make a couple of hundred euros each. Permits, licenses, food safety rules—you're joking, no way. These were private dinner parties, like cooking at home for friends. Only we were not at home and the friends paid for the privilege. Perhaps they were not paying enough. Perhaps there were too few of them. I couldn't work it out. The dining room always seemed full, mouths were munching and glasses were clinking. Why weren't Giangi and

I making a fortune? How much longer would it take? I was nearly twenty-six, not that old but not that young either. And last night I could have ended up in jail and then before a judge in a fast-track trial, and instead here I was mixing flour, water, and yeast, following Vincenzo's recipe. I called Matteo and told him what happened. I left out a lot of the details, but I had to talk to someone.

I escaped all too often into my own little dreamworld, where I'm Leo, the star chef or the acclaimed artist, living in Rio de Janeiro or Bogotá, with women throwing themselves at my feet. I can do and say whatever I want. I dreamed of having more money than I knew what to do with, that time would stand still and I'd never hit thirty, that I wasn't earning peanuts in a crummy makeshift eatery in a working-class neighborhood like Testaccio, and that curly haired girls like Barbara would say they loved me. Instead, Barbara appeared with Matteo, said a quick hello, and went off to work.

I looked at Matteo. "What's she doing here?"

"She turned up last night and rang the bell. You weren't here, but I was."

"So while I was getting myself arrested, you were banging Barbara."

"It's just that you make such stupid fucking choices, Leo."

"You did the right thing. Barbara's cute, isn't she?

"Yep. She thinks you're a dickhead."

"What do you think I should do?"

"Open your own place."

"Are you joking?"

"The truth is that things aren't going half as bad as you're making out."

He was right. I did have my own place, sort of, just as I'd had a mother who always let me do whatever I wanted, yet I longed for something else, and I didn't know what.

I was a twenty-five-year-old with a passion for cooking and precious little experience, but I did know I liked being called a chef. If I'd had the money, I would have been well on the way to opening my own restaurant. Thank heavens I didn't.

There are only two reasons for opening a place of your own: Either you're a genius with a brilliant idea, lots of drive, and loads of family money to spend, or your ego is completely out of control. Giangi and I were well-endowed when it came to egos and a desire to work, but that's all we had. But we couldn't afford to let things slide downhill for much longer.

Very, very few restaurants make a profit. There must be some reason why so many hopefuls still believe that being a restaurateur is an easy job, but I haven't discovered it yet. That night, after everyone left, Giangi and I split a measly €250, net of expenses, and finally admitted that maybe it was time to call it quits. Too many things had come to a boil in a very short space of time. When I got home, I buried my head in my pillow and fell asleep wishing my bed would turn into sand and I'd awaken in Copacabana.

9.

The noonday sun streaming through the half-opened shutters woke me up. It crept under my eyelids without knocking. Leaden eyelids. A throbbing headache. The usual sour taste in my mouth. Had it been a late night? Another one? But then, it's hard to decide what constitutes late. It's like overeating. Like you have to plan ahead, know when to stop. It's something you should know, but you don't, because if you did maybe you would stop before it was too late. Or before eating too much. You eventually get it, but by that time it's over or your belly is exploding. Or you've lost count of how many drinks you've downed. Or all three. These are the half-baked thoughts that run through your head when you've been out too late and drunk too much.

I turned over and slowly got onto my feet, to the sound of rustling and scrunching. There were scraps of paper covered in scribbles all over the bed, and on my pillow lay the thick red pencil I'd used on paper, sheets, furniture, everything—I must have tossed and turned quite a bit last night. Scrawled sentences followed by question marks, words that seem to have tumbled onto the paper from a height, few of which I could decipher. Did someone else write them while I was lying there quiet as a mouse, with my eyes half closed, halfway between too late and too early? I disregarded anything that looked like mindless doodling and retrieved anything that made the slightest sense, trying to piece them together: lasagna/lasagnetta? sauce, basil-tomato, no-cook? appetizers? mixed? fried (?) NO—maybe/veggies, meatloaf/mini meatloaf/veggies/meat(?), bread home-baked/shop bought—any oven???, what pasta? Eggs, kamut flour? Things like that. With the big red pencil. Because that's how I am: too sloppy to do it any other way.

Spring was definitely in the air in Rome, with temperatures above 70 degrees, visibility nearly 7 miles, average humidity 62 percent, and crisp clear skies. I picked up the phone, cleared my throat, and tentatively stretched a couple of limbs. I was parched, but the fridge was too far away to bother, and someone seemed to be in the bathroom. Fine, no water, I could manage without. I was adept at making others believe that mine was not the voice of someone who'd barely dragged himself out of bed. Especially at one in the afternoon. Who would think that anyway? It had been more than a year since I last spoke to Sandro. I'd heard that Sessanta was his now. Who knows what he used for money, or how deep in debt he had gotten himself. Rumor also had it that he was doing quite well. I dialed his number, hoping it hadn't changed in the meantime.

"Leo!"

"Hi there, Sandro, my man, it's been so long, is this a bad time?"

"Hell, no! How are you, what are you up to, besides going to bed at seven a.m. as usual?"

"I'm still cooking, Sandro. Have been since I left Sessanta."

"Yeah, I heard... Are you still at that place, what's it called, Giulio's?"

"Nope, I left a while back... I've been doing dinner parties over in Testaccio, and now, guess what, I have to put together a party for about two hundred and fifty people on a riverboat on the Tiber. Actually, that's why I'm calling you..."

"Wow! Good for you... What did you want to ask me?"

"Buddy, I need some advice on the menu. I have to work out if what I've put together is okay. Can I pass by the restaurant?"

"Whenever you want. Today? I don't have too many book-ings tonight..."

"Perfect, I'll see you at six. Oh, and thanks, after all this time."

"Cut it out. See ya later."

I turned on the TV. William, our smart-ass cat, would be back in a while. He'd sit in front of the main door of the apart-ment block waiting for someone to open it, then pad up the stairs to our landing on the first floor and start meowing out-side the door. One of us would hear him, or sometimes my aunt next door would let him in. Today it was me. I got some chicken out of the fridge and a packet of rice. Small pot, water, stove. When the water came to the boil, I threw in some rice, then the chicken, cut into little strips, no salt. Salt is bad for cats. And it's criminal to give cats leftovers. William was by no means a spoiled cat, it's just that I like to cook for those I love. More than anything, I like cooking at home. I'd been out of work about a month and was starting to fret. When I'm jobless and fretting, cooking soothes me, so here I was boiling rice and chicken for William.

Christ, 250 people are a crowd. But I can trust Sandro, and at the end of the day, all I need is for someone to say, "Yep, can do." It's what I always say, it's my default setting, even when I don't actually know—or even dare hope—it can be done. Besides saying "Yep," Sandro might even give me a few tips on how to pull it off.

The gigs in Testaccio were over, but an unmissable oppor-tunity presented itself to Giangi and me: the annual Capoeira Batizado. Every year capoeira members from groups all over Brazil and Europe host an enormous get-together. In a few days, between two and three hundred people would be converging on the RadioRock boat anchored on the Tiber, behind the Gasworks. During the Second World War, the old Canadian vessel, three stories high, transported troops and military vehicles. During the '60s, it was turned into a private merchant ship that sailed between Ponza and Ventotene. Eventually it was purchased by Carmine Gammella, who had it towed up the Tiber to the bend in the river where it is still moored today. Carmine spent a lifetime on this river, dreaming of turning it into another glamorous Via Veneto. But la dolce vita never budged from downtown Rome and never made it onto the Tiber. Too many trees uprooted by floods, too many bags of garbage, dirt, and mud floating by whenever it rained for more than three days running. Is bad weather what makes the Tiber so nasty? Or is it the twenty-first century that's spitefully casting up three thousand years of history? Rome was born on the banks of the Tiber, and Rome was now slowly killing it. Young kids don't give a crap about the river, or its history, or Via Veneto. Carmine's riverboat was simply a place that hosted private functions and dinner dances for teenagers blinded by raging hormones and craving booze.

The boat's name was the *Nestore*—I noticed the letters way up high, near the dock line that moored the boat to the riverbank, one evening while I was pissing against a wall—but everyone just called it the RadioRock Boat because the Roman radio station organized all its events there. And in about ten days, for one night only, it would be my boat. Chef Leonardo Lucarelli's sensational menu would tickle the taste buds of at least 250 jubilant capoeira enthusiasts.

Turning on the radio, I rustled up a ring cake using the old beige electric mixer my grandmother gave me, back when kitchen appliances weren't all unrelentingly white. I tried to concentrate, swallowing an aspirin. The eggs were past their use-by date, but only just, and for a simple cake they'd be fine. If your eggs are past their prime, this is what you have to do: bake a cake or a quiche. Anything else and you can taste the eggs are old, especially in custards or sabayon, and you risk sending people to the ER.

I was listening to RadioRock, as it happens, and had time to take a leisurely shower and get my act together while the cake was baking. Right now, there was only one reason for me to get my ass out of the apartment and it was to deal with the Capoeira Batizada shebang on the riverboat. Sandro would save me. Sandro would tell me two or three dishes to wow the customers and I'd know exactly how to make them. Everyone would eat. And they would all eat well. It was past five o'clock and outside the light was sheer magic, the kind of Roman light that knows exactly how to cast itself upon ancient Roman walls. It's a joy to see. As I turned on the shower and opened the bathroom window, air and sunlight poured in and my headache vanished. I said to myself, Wow, I am one good-looking stud. But I said it with a sigh.

"So, two hundred and fifty guests?"

"Yeah. I think it's doable, but I'll have to prep everything in advance so I only have to heat it up when I get there."

"Is there an oven?"

"I don't know. Actually, I don't think there is. But they told me there are griddles."

"And what about a boiler?"

"I don't think so."

"I can give you a pot with four baskets."

"Get outta here! Perfect. And what about the menu, Sandro? What do you think? Can I base it on things we did at Sessanta?"

"Are you joking? Sure you can! But I can't let you cook any-thing here, I'm afraid."

"No, that's fine. So look here." I pulled a notebook out of my backpack. "Do you think a menu like this is feasible: mixed appetizers, maybe olive pâté crostini, fried eggplant-and-carrot balls, tomato boats, and salad? I'd have these on the tables as the diners arrived. Then I'd go with a choice of first courses. Vegetarian lasagna, precooked and served at room tempera-ture, with a hot fondue, and while they're eating that, I'll be boiling the orecchiette pasta, one basket after another, with a sauce—yours, the one with raw tomatoes and basil, whizzed in the blender with some sea salt and oil and nothing else. Then, while I'm draining the first two pounds of pasta, I'll add the sauce and plate it, and move on to the next two pounds and then the third, and so on. For the main course, a vegetarian quiche with spinach sauce and beef meatballs with yogurt sauce. For dessert I was thinking of biscotti and chocolate cake. And a big fruit salad. What do you think?"

"Well, the menu's a bit demanding, but I think it's manageable…"

"And what about quantities?"

"What I usually do is calculate the amount of food I'll need for the number of guests and then take away a bit…"

"What? You take away a bit? You don't add more? I mean, what if it's not enough?"

"Oh, people usually eat less than you think, especially when it's a big crowd. You know, they get up, wander around, get dis-tracted, there are kids running around…take away a good fif-teen percent from the total. And think about where you'll be doing all the cooking, you'll need a fair amount of space. And a big fridge…"

"Are you sure I can't do any cooking here?"

"No, not possible, I need the whole kitchen to myself."

"Okay, I'll get by...and thanks for the pot. And the friendly advice. Oh, I was forgetting something important: your Metro Caterer's supplies card! Can I do the shopping on your card?"

"No sweat, just don't overspend, because they'll be invoicing my restaurant. And another thing: Break a leg."

10.

I just love those massive wholesale cash-and-carries. I love Metro, shelves stacked sky-high with food, the fish counter ablaze with live red and European lobsters crawling over one another and then tumbling back down, enormous cold rooms that you have to enter wearing a windbreaker, vegetables sold by the crate. Not to mention all those fantastic spices, sauces, and powders. I invariably end up getting lost. Those vast amounts of food make my mouth water and fill my head with ideas. I create fantasy dishes as I stroll past shelves and fridges. Spanish pata negra cured ham, veal shanks with mashed potatoes and a demi-glace sauce, lamb chops with escarole Roman style and mint sauce, radishes in clarified butter, braised rabbit legs, roast suckling pig with a vanilla-enhanced tomato reduction and crispy skin on a bed of... enough already. It was time to calm down and check the shopping list hanging from the six-wheeled shopping cart; I could buy only the bare essentials and could not under any circumstances stray from the task at hand: Parked outside was my motorbike, and it had to carry me and the shopping. So, roughly speaking, 250 people would consume around 220 pounds of food.

Frozen puff pastry and lasagna sheets, tomatoes, lettuces, zucchini, eggplant, cream, milk, Grana Padano cheese, basil, butter, oil, salt, marjoram, dill, mincemeat, bread, spelt, honey, and everything else all piled up in the cart, while my shopping list became a list of words crossed off in red pencil. At the checkout I filled plastic bags, two at a time for extra strength, paid by EFTPOS, and cleaned out my bank account. This party had better be a success, there would be no second chance.

I tied the crates of tomatoes and vegetables to the back of the motorbike using a cargo net; I crammed the meat, the lasagna, olives, and a heap of other stuff into my backpack as I leaned for a moment on the hood of a Milan-gray Mercedes: If I had a car like that, just imagine the groceries I could be loading. I was ridiculous and I couldn't help laughing. Plastic bags dangled precariously from the handlebars, two on each side.

Crushed up against the gas tank, I struggled to steer the bike and brake as smoothly as possible. A few drivers honked as I overtook them in the hectic Roman traffic as the bags brushed against the side of their cars. "Sorry!" I yelled over and over again from under my helmet, but I was so bent forward that no one could hear me. Wobbling on my overloaded motorbike, I was as happy as when I'd get into mischief as a kid and do something I was absolutely not allowed to do. However, I made it home, and had hardly turned off the motor when a bag burst and everything spilled out onto the pavement. Thank God the bottle of oil didn't break; that's bad luck. The crates of vegetables were leaning dangerously to one side but didn't fall because they came to rest against the muffler. So that's where the smell of scorched plastic came from.

First things first: clean up, unpack the groceries, divide them up, and put them away. The big four-way cooking pot would have to go to the riverboat too, and all on my bike. I'd worry about that tomorrow. At the moment my fingers were itching to start. I turned on RadioRock, washed my hands, tied on my apron, took a deep breath, and lit the stove. I had one wooden cutting board, all the wrong knives, no scars on my hands, and nowhere near enough experience to organize a function this size, so it all seemed pretty easy.

By midnight, the pasta sauce was ready, the mixture for the veggie balls was resting in the fridge together with the raw appetizers. Sliced vegetables were all over the place, a few of the lasagna sheets were already cooked, the others waiting to be. The ground beef was mixed with the bread that had been soaked in milk with spices and grated orange peel. I was getting ahead, so I cracked open a cold one and went out onto the balcony for a smoke.

Two whole days went by. I filled up my grandma's and my aunt's fridges.

On Friday I went to the riverboat to inspect the place. Tomorrow there would be fruit salads galore and two long tables seating more than two hundred happy people, all gorging themselves silly. Kids would be running wild, beverages and crisp white napkins would be offered by smiling waiters, as samba blared from the loudspeakers. Everyone would put away their cares and woe and enjoy the meal and the party, then they'd come charging into the kitchen to thank me. I'd be worn-out and hot and sweaty, and I'd down an enormous cocktail. Wow.

I walked along the gangplank and boarded the vessel.

The place was big and cold. It was spooky seeing it so empty, I'd only been there for parties. The rickety trestle tables were covered in rust. At the back, toward the stern, was the door to the kitchen, oval shaped and hovering about four inches from the floor. Inside, nothing but a gas cylinder connected to a large stove, the only one, perched perilously on some sort of patched-up metal tripod. Next to it, on the floor, a rubber hose for the water, which apparently was safe to drink. I took a closer look and rocked the stove from side to side. No cursing, no profanity, I was simply stunned. Tragically stunned. Reality can do that to you sometimes. And there's nothing you can do about it.

I picked up a stick, broken off from God knows what, lying on the floor and wedged it under the stove—no more wobbling. Sometimes you can set things right with relative ease, other times you can't. I found Giangi in the main room fixing up the bar area. Put simply, there was no kitchen. What there was, was this weird squarish space with one dirty window overlooking the river from the butt-end of the boat, metal walls coated in peeling white paint and droplets of moisture, a grimy, rusted floor, a wooden table, luckily large, and a crappy swinging door giving onto the dining room. Yikes, it was going to be tough, all right. Now might be a good time to curse, silently, and to myself. But no, I had everything ready. It was only a question of getting here early and roping in some kids to help. Setting the big pot on the stove and filling it with water, bringing it to a boil, and then it's all good. A brilliant plan. The image of the fridge overflowing with food calmed me. I went onshore to untie the pot, which was in a big plastic garbage bag, from the seat of the bike.

Saturday arrived. Everyone was still at the gym in Via Bocea. I was not. I was putting on the finishing touches at home. All the food went onto cardboard trays and then into the polycarbonate gastronorms that Sandro lent me. "Just wash them and give them back to me on Sunday." Giangi managed to get hold of an old Peugeot station wagon for me to use. My bike, which I'd left at the riverboat, would take me home tonight. I left at 4 p.m. with the car loaded and the phone numbers for a couple of kids who'd be giving me a hand.

The dining space already looked a lot better. Green tablecloths matched the green-and-gold flags bearing the motto ORDEM E PROGRESSO hanging here and there, seeming to herald a surefire success. It was nearly dusk, the artificial light was not as merciless as the sun streaming through the filthy windows.

I'd say I was almost calm, just buzzing slightly in anticipation but without the churning stomach that comes with sheer terror. The day before, I'd bought a new chef's uniform, which I now put on, fastening the round buttons with deliberate calm and tipping my chef's hat jauntily to one side, like a beret. Then I wound the strings of my ankle-length apron behind my back and tied them at the front. I also had a new cotton side towel, white and thick, that I folded carefully and slipped under the apron ties, just a little to the right of my thigh. In my pocket, a joint, already rolled, and my lighter. I took a deep breath. For a split second, time stood still. For a split second, everything seemed to be waiting for me. With satisfaction, I saw a chef with my face staring back at me, serious and confident, in the reflection of the dusty window. I was waiting for me too. Okay, let's rock and roll.

First, get the bread out of the big paper bags and slice it evenly on the cutting board lying on the big wooden table. Big, sure, but not big enough to accommodate too many tasks. Okay, one thing at a time. Start with the bread, then the appetizers, then the trays of ingredients for the orecchiette pasta sauce, the piles of plastic plates, bottles of oil and salt. For the time being, the vegetarian quiches were lying on the floor in the gastronorms. I'll slice them as soon as the last two pounds of pasta have been served, I'm thinking, and we'll continue like that, one step after another. While the dishes are being cleared, there will be enough time to slice the quiches, so they'll stay warm. It will run like clockwork. The kids arrived. I liked the tone of my voice.

"Can you help me with the bread? We have to slice all of it and put it in breadbaskets, one for every four diners."

"All of it?"

"Yeah, because later there won't be any room to slice it. If there's any bread left over, slice it and put it back in the paper bags, but be careful not to put them on anything damp."

One of them started slicing (there's only one bread knife, shit, hell, I'm thinking to myself). I grabbed the big four-way pot, noticing the slightly lime-scale-encrusted holes in the triangular baskets, and filled the pot with water from the hose curled up on the floor. I went into the dining room to check: All the flatware was where it should be, the napkins too.

There was a breadbasket every four settings. In the kitchen, the water was boiling, already salted. On the table were the appetizers ready to be placed on serving platters. We were truly ready to go. It was seven thirty; dinner service was due to start in half an hour. I straightened the napkins, brushed a few crumbs from the tablecloths, and returned to the kitchen. Time to smoke a joint. Before putting my hand in my pocket, one of the kids rushed up to me.

"Hey, Leo, people are starting to arrive, some of them are already sitting down, they want to start with the appetizers."

"What do you mean, people are already here? Everyone has to be served at the same time. That's no good at all!"

"Yeah, but there are families, with kids, and I think they want to start eating..."

"Right, then, we can start serving the appetizers. They have to go on those platters, one for every four guests, just like for the bread. The meatballs in the center, a little salad inside the radicchio leaves, the skewers with the tips pointing toward the center, and on the other side, the tomato boats, all lined up. Make sure you get it right. You guys, start putting the platters on the tables, that way we'll speed things up."

There was nowhere near enough space. Even with only three people it was difficult to move, and my helpers had never handled a dish in their entire lives. I organized an assembly line: me plating with a chubby girl who had just arrived, another kid taking the platters to the door, and the third ferrying them to the tables. We were incredibly slow. By the thirtieth platter, just about everyone had arrived, and by the sixtieth, the first guests to arrive had already been waiting a good forty minutes for the orecchiette. Children were running all over the place, completely out of control.

Time to start boiling the pasta. It was a disaster. Half of the water had evaporated. Intent as I was on the appetizers, it never occurred to me to check the water level. I added more from the hose, but it was freezing cold, naturally, and the water came off the boil. This was a serious problem—a really, really serious problem. Boilers of the type used in a professional kitchen deliver a continuous flow of (boiling!) water. Whatever evaporates or is absorbed by the pasta during cooking is constantly replenished. Here I had only one big pot of freezing water and forty-four pounds of pasta. There was no option but to wait a few minutes before tossing the first two pounds of orecchiette into the water. I asked the kids to start clearing the plates, but in slow motion, giving me a bit of extra time. Even an experienced maître d' would be hot under the collar at this point, with a dining room in such a state of turmoil, let alone these newbies. The first kid comes running into the kitchen, flushed and breathless.

"The bread's finished! They want more!"

"Fucking hell, that bread was supposed to last through the mains too. What are they going to eat with the meatballs?"

The Brazilian master of our capoeira group, the organizer of the batizado, the Big Boss, strode purposefully into the kitchen.

"Hey, how is it all going in here, *cozinheiro*? Do me a big favor, can you serve the Capoiera Mestres right away? It's *muito importante*, the masters are my special guests. *Significa muito para mim.* It means so much to me. Is good? *Está bem?* You want me to be *tranquilo?*"

"*Tranquilo*, yes cool. The first plates of pasta will be for them. All good with the appetizers?"

"*Tudo bem*, all good, it's okay, so we wait for the pasta."

He turned on his heels and left.

I noticed an edge of discomfort in my voice, but only for a millisecond and then it was overwhelmed by a mountain of despair. The joint lay forgotten in my pocket. It was all-out war. Bread gone. How stupid, I should have served it later, and there wasn't any more. The water was boiling, I tossed in the first two pounds of pasta and waited three minutes, strained, then added the next two pounds. Three more minutes. Two more pounds. Three more minutes, the last batch. I stirred the first basket. The pasta was still raw. Someone came to the oval door: It was Barbara, her face framed by her curly hair.

"Need a hand in here?"

"Hell yes, I do. While I drain this pasta, can you start plating the rest?"

I turned to the pot, then turned back around to her.

"Thanks."

Following the fateful night I dumped her to go and get myself arrested, our relations had been somewhat frosty. But now I didn't have time to ask myself whether she was insulted, indignant, indifferent—or just taking pity on me.

Food had to start flying out of this hole, right now, and there was a lot of it. Flying out at the speed of light, if possible. And it had to be good too, of course.

I sent out what was ready, best-laid plans to hell. I ordered the kids to get the lasagna plated and out the door, just get it out. Meanwhile, I drained, stirred, sweated, and completely lost track of what was happening in the dining room. I added water to the pot, but only a little at a time because it was cold, drained more pasta, sweated, tossed another two pounds of orecchiette into the first basket, then another into the second, without waiting three minutes. A sudden realization hit me, switching on like a neon sign thrust violently inside my head: Orecchiette has the absolute longest cooking time of all dried pasta shapes, more than fifteen minutes. It was crazy to think I could cook orecchiette to order in one pot for 250 diners, an impossible task. It should have occurred to me, but it didn't. An hour later, I was still at it, with unfamiliar faces traipsing in and out of the kitchen, some to holler and others to lend a hand, including a dad begging for a plate of pasta on the run for his little daughter. Everyone wanting something. No flow, no rhythm, just a relentless stream of demands, while I fell farther and farther behind. The drums of the invading barbarian horde were drawing ever closer: What I wouldn't give to be the fearless Pope Leo right now, raising a hand to turn back the Huns.

"Hey, when the fuck is this pasta gonna be ready?"

A voice echoed around the kitchen like a club striking metal, fiercer than any of the other complaints seeping through the damp oval door. Here comes Attila the Hun, I said to myself, and I'm up to my eyeballs in pasta.

"We've been waiting over an hour. There are five of us, we've already paid, and we will not wait a fucking hour for a plate of pasta. Some people have had theirs and some haven't. There are people eating lasagna, and all we've had are the cold antipasti. What the hell is going **on in here**? You *will serve the five plates* of pasta we paid for *right now!* And after that, everything else that's on the menu!"

I raised my head, continuing to stir the orecchiette, and mopped my dripping brow with a filthy side towel.

"Listen, you're right, I'll try to get you served immediately, we've had a few delays, but you'll get your pasta right now."

"*Now means now!* I'm not leaving this kitchen unless a waiter follows me with the pasta for my table!"

"Look, I'll send it out to you right away, I swear. I don't know what to say, I'm sorry."

My submissive attitude only seemed to fuel the rage of the belligerent diner, who was not budging, but I feared this was merely the tip of the iceberg and that the atmosphere in the dining room was incandescent. I continued to apologize profusely, but the flow of abuse did not abate.

"Shit, man, you can't run a kitchen like this, it's insane!"

I realized that the damned orecchiette were sticking together, so I gave another stir to each of the four baskets in the pot and started to drain the pasta, without uttering a word, because there was nothing more to say. I didn't need words, I needed food. Another diner peered through the door, wearing a furious expression.

"Hey you, is this pasta coming or not? It's been a fucking hour…"

One thing at a time, one thing at a time. I had to get rid of these two, then send out everything else immediately. I had to halt the invading Huns.

"Yeah, yeah, sure thing, it's going out right this minute. The pasta I'm draining now is for you, gimme a break, guys, otherwise I'll never get on with it, please..."

In the meantime Barbara was stirring the tomato-and-basil sauce into the orecchiette, and starting to plate. I looked at the plates, wiped the edges clean with the same filthy side towel, placed a useless basil leaf on top, and then said to her, utterly defeated, "Can you please take these to the two who were in here just now, but serve the others around them as well, because I don't want anyone to think that to get your food, you have to barge into the kitchen and start swearing at everyone, otherwise we're done for."

Adding, as she turned away, "And don't give a damn about what order the dishes are in. *We have to get food on those tables, pronto!*"

An ugly clump of orecchiette lay on one of the plates that was about to be served. Boil pasta in too little water and it sticks together in the pot and stays that way, forming a mass of gluey, undercooked dough. I hoped the angriest diners didn't end up getting them. Forget Pope Leo. I was Napoleon Bonaparte and this was my Waterloo.

I drained, stirred, sweated, and crammed more than two pounds of pasta into each basket. The water was barely on the boil now. Everything was taking longer and longer, but I kept on draining the pasta and trying to fish out the clumps of orecchiette, sending them flying all around the steamy iron-walled enclosure. I stirred, plated, and crammed more pasta into the pot, never raising my head. Barbara was joined by the two kids and the plump blonde. Someone told me the capoeira masters were demanding their quiche; they'd finished the meatballs more than half an hour ago. Many of the other diners were still waiting for the pasta. I forced myself to get into a rhythm, no point letting uncooked, poorly prepared food go out. Slow maybe, catastrophically slow, but at least let it be good, for Christ's sake! If you make someone wait an hour and then serve a second-rate dish that's inedible, cold and undercooked, well, you'll soon find that someone in the kitchen wanting to break everything in sight. My plan had changed: All I wanted was to get out of there alive and cut my losses. If retreat it is, then at least let it be a dignified one, no fatalities and no smell of burning. A few casualties, undoubtedly. We'll lose some customers who will get up from the table and furiously fling their napkins to the floor, but let's save the others, let's at least save them!

The kitchen was steamy, sweat was trickling into my eyes, blinding me, while I struggled desperately to preserve what was left of my dignity. Mine and the food's. I'd lost all control of the dining room, by now everyone was serving; kind of them, for sure, but who knows what they were telling the diners, many of whom were visibly incensed. My fingers were blistered, burned by the flames shooting out at least eight inches around the bottom of the pot. In the meantime, I was nearing the last eight pounds of orecchiette. The light at the end of the tunnel! There was pasta all over the floor, grubby and slippery. But I was so in the zone that the blisters weren't even hurting.

Exactly two hours had elapsed since I tossed the first two pounds of pasta into boiling water. Meanwhile, the guys had begun slicing the vegetarian quiches and the lasagna, and anyone near enough to hear my orders was plating as best they could. Out of the corner of my eye I was checking the dishes that were going out, while I hurriedly took out the meatballs. Then I just gave up. Surrendered. I let whoever was handling the food get on with it, hoping they had some idea of what they were doing. Partly because it was obvious that I had lost it and didn't have a clue what I was doing anymore. Every now and again I'd pathetically try to say something.

The big aftmost window was completely fogged up over a thick layer of dust, creating hideous thick black streaks; good thing too, because there would no longer be a cocky face smiling back at me under the jauntily tilted chef's hat, now soiled with tomatoey red splotches. I wasn't shouting out orders anymore, I was begging with a whimper.

The Brazilian master showed up again two or three more times. Two or three? I lost count. The last time, he didn't say a word, nor did I, we just looked at each other. The first plates went to his fellow masters. They—albeit excruciatingly slowly—had eventually been served everything, including fruit salad and dessert.

The meatballs and quiches were polished off, empty gastronorms were strewn all over the place, on the floor, on the table and on the still steaming pot over a now mercifully cool stove. I was ladling fruit salad into red plastic cups while Barbara put together the desserts, in the end all jammed randomly onto platters, a few on each table. By now only a few diners were still seated; half past eleven had come and gone. I was soaked to the skin. My uniform was spattered with sauce and starch from the pasta water. My side towel was nowhere to be seen, my hands were red and sweaty, and in the kitchen, it looked like a huge arancini kamikaze had blown itself up. And we were the victims.

I managed to pull myself together and started to plate the last desserts in the correct order, cleaning off smudges of chocolate with a paper towel, in familiar movements that brought me back—at least somewhat—to my senses. Because even when you're drowning in shit, when the service is unsalvageable and has arguably gone to the dogs, when you have wall-to-wall dockets that seem to be written in Sanskrit, you must never give up. You have to grit your teeth and keep on going. In the end, somehow, you'll make it out of there. These were sayings I'd heard before, many times, but it took until this evening for them to start making sense. I was exhausted, but it felt as if only an hour, at most an hour and a half, had elapsed. In fact, it had been more than four hectic hours.

A tall, frizzy-haired fellow appeared in the kitchen, nice regular features and a candid, slightly boyish expression. He smiled at me.

"So, you're the chef who organized the function."

"Yeah, so what?"

"Well, earlier I was royally pissed off with the dickheads who were putting out dishes at a snail's pace after the antipasti, which were good, by the way. Then I snuck a look in the kitchen and saw you were doing it all single-handed! I couldn't believe my eyes. I even asked the curly haired waitress, the cute one, if you were on your own with no help. Anyway, I gave the servers a hand out there, but I didn't want to leave without meeting you and congratulating you."

"You really mean that?"

"Look, I'm not bullshitting you. I'm a chef too, and I've seen you at a couple of training sessions."

The oxygen started flowing again and nourished my aching muscles, and even though I was fully aware of the dimensions of tonight's fiasco, I basked in these words of praise. I thanked him a little tepidly, grateful that at least his orecchiette weren't all glued together. Dog tired, I started tidying up, suddenly remembering that I still had a joint in my pocket. Reaching in all I found was some brown gunk. Crap. Barbara, just as weary, smiled at me wordlessly, then came up, planted a kiss on my cheek, and headed off to clear up the dining room.

Another guy wandered into the kitchen. Forty-something, longish wavy gray hair, a boxer's squashed nose, and good-humored eyes. I'd seen him helping out with the dishes and giving orders to the improvised waitstaff.

"Do you happen to have a joint?"

"Sure. Here."

He passed me a small metal box containing papers attached to the lid with some Scotch tape.

As I listlessly gathered up my kit, the joint hanging from my lips, words began pouring out of me.

"I shouldn't have put so much bread out on the tables at the start, I should have kept more sliced in the bags. I should have brought more pots so I'd have a steady supply of hot water, and then, shit, I should have chosen a different motherfucking pasta shape, anything but orecchiette."

"This dinner has gone the way it's gone, but you did it all on your own. I don't know any other chef who would have taken on anything like this."

And so, mellowed by the joint, the chitchat, the cocktail that actually did appear eventually, the tension slipped away. But I couldn't tear myself away from the kitchen. No, damn it, for me this evening was an outright disaster. One in four guests got up and left, so we had to give them their money back. And what kind of a fool did I make of myself with the mestre?

"Excuse me, are you the chef? I mean, still the chef?"

It was a girl's soft voice. I turned around. Cute too, very cute.

"Yeah... and you are?"

"Souheila."

"Hi. Did you enjoy the food?" I asked defensively.

"Yeah, it was really good. There was a bit of a wait between the pasta and the main course, but everything tasted fine."

Her head was tilted slightly, her gaze inquisitive. She seemed more than a little tipsy. Definitely drunk, I would say. Which disappointed me somewhat: so that's why she's telling me she liked the food. I could have served her river rat in an anthrax sauce, and after four of Giangi's cocktails she would have polished it off with glee. Maybe even the tall guy, and the other one, Riccardo, were trashed too and I simply didn't notice.

"Maybe I'll see you later, sweetheart, at the party upstairs, after I've changed my clothes. But right now I've got to tidy up."

"Couldn't I just stay here and keep you company while you work? I've never been inside a real chef's kitchen before!"

"What the... Souheila, are you kidding? A real chef's kitchen! This shit hole? Why don't we hook up some other time and I'll take you to a real kitchen. Where a girl has to duck for cover if she doesn't want to be hit by a barrage of testosterone bouncing off the walls and suddenly ending up in her panties... but here? Why are you hanging around here? The only thing left to do now is clean up. C'mon, we can meet upstairs later."

Souheila left, waving goodbye.

I stayed holed up for a while, licking my wounds and mentally replaying, in an endless loop, the film of what could have been and wasn't. Precooking. Of course, why didn't I think of that? Had I arrived with the orecchiette precooked, I would have plunged them in boiling water for sixty seconds and voilà, all done. Give or take a few minutes, all the pasta would have been cooked in twenty-five minutes.

Why didn't I realize that 250 people couldn't possibly all walk in at the same time? I should have been ready for the early birds and the latecomers, and instructed the servers accordingly. Shoulda, coulda.

The kitchen was empty, and so was the dining room, and my plastic cup was empty too. My stained uniform was stuffed into my backpack. I left the side towel behind, it was beyond repair. And it was hardly destined to become a lucky charm, anyway. It had had a pitifully short and wretched life. Amen. Pot empty, pasta scraped off the floor, wooden table more or less scrubbed, bags of garbage all stacked against the dirty window. Time to go. The party upstairs held no appeal; I was in a foul mood and thoroughly bushed. It was one o'clock in the morning. I virtually slunk out, looking for and finding Giangi. From his point of view, the party had been a success: The mestre was satisfied, all the capoeira masters were blind drunk and inundated by swarms of women. Of course, the money from the dinner, less expenses and refunds, didn't amount to much, but we'd make up for it, we'd recoup, we'd do something else together. Now it was time to samba, Leo!

No fucking way, I said to myself.

We're going to recoup what? For months we've been organizing things that have bombed, first in Testaccio and now tonight.

"Maybe next time we should put a little more thought into organizing things, learn from our mistakes," he suggested.

No, no more plans, that's it. Too much effort, too little returns. No success, no profit, everything just thrown together, improvised, makeshift, and random.

"I dunno, Giangi, why don't you think up some brilliant idea. I'm running on empty, I need to sleep."

So tonight it finally dawned on me: It was well and truly over. Sometimes it takes moments like these to get the message across. There's nothing left to do, nothing left to say. It's cold, the air is heavy and damp, foul smells are rising from the river, it's probably around fifty degrees, give or take, and thank God I remembered my gloves.

Through the Testaccio neighborhood, past the Pyramid of Cestius, down Via Marco Polo, nearly there now, the traffic lights on Via San Giovanni red, as usual. Finally, I arrive at my destination, Via Placido Zurla, Pigneto quarter, home.

Questions are buzzing around my head, clouding my mind like a gray sky in the middle of summer. Jumbled thoughts fade into the pillow as I drift off to sleep. Enough. That's it. This chef business has to end right here, right now. Whatever will be, will be. Then again ... what if I'm not ready to call it quits quite yet? Maybe, but I can't go on like this either. I want it to end here, I really do. I'd like to apply for another scholarship. I'd like to end on a high note, not like this.

My anguish and my dire misfortune were absolute. The sound of the key turning in the front door awoke me. Matteo knocked quietly on my bedroom door.

"Hey, you there?"

"Sure, man, come on in, I'm awake."

"Did your big bash go ahead?"

"Yep."

"Did it go well?"

"It couldn't have gone any better than it actually did."

"Let me know tomorrow if that means it went well. Did they eat everything?"

"Yep."

"So it went well. Good night."

11.

The music was too loud, and I knew full well I'd end up with ringing in my ears even in my dreams. Matteo was behind me, Silvia in front. She could really move it on the dance floor, whereas I, like everything else I did, was merely average. The smell of marijuana was intense, but I couldn't work out exactly where it was coming from. Silvia's short black bangs, catlike features, and wistful expression reminded me of Björk. Until last year she was with a surfer dude: she, a photographer and student at the European Institute of Design, he a video maker and the scion of a wealthy family. Then the surfer dude went to visit his father in Costa Rica and nobody heard from him again. At the time, I thought she was too good for the surfer dude. I'd love to have had a girl as pretty as her, but I was a humble salad guy, and I deserved her even less than he did.

Silvia floated around the smoky room. She was still gorgeous, maybe a bit whiny, every bit the brooding world-weary artist and not even thirty, making her much less desirable than I remembered. That evening I was particularly nice to her, even though I felt hollow and useless. Matteo was turning on the charm with a girl from Bologna, a newcomer to Rome. I liked the girls Matteo schmoozed. Glass after glass, I started feeling light-headed, slurring my words. "I'm okay, I can hold my liquor," I said to myself. "Stop drinking, you're not okay, you can't hold your liquor," said Matteo.

The alcohol got my thoughts drifting to kitchens, to the party on the riverboat the week before, and the €250 that Giangi and I split between us. My bike was parked outside my apartment building, its gas tank full, a bill, paid, lay on my nightstand, there was some ganja in my left pocket, and in my right, my last €50. The fridge came to mind, inside it an Époisses de Bourgogne that I'd bought as a treat immediately after getting paid for the riverboat party. I can't fucking stand people who call it Taleggio. Sure, to all intents and purposes, it's a classic French cheese sporting the usual mold, but the difference hits you the moment you cut into the sticky rind and get to the creamy, almost chewy heart. Époisses cheese is one of those flavors and textures that I got hooked on after meeting Sandro, and I met the only supplier of the cheese in Rome through him.

"Are you coming to the restroom with me?" Silvia whispered, bringing her lips to my ear, still dancing.

When we got home we were all pretty smashed, and the girl from Bologna immediately headed to the bedroom with Matteo. Good-quality coke doesn't take your appetite away, nor does it keep you awake. It generally does take away your sadness. Silvia's coke was excellent but left my sadness intact. I suggested tasting the Époisses and uncorking a bottle of Riesling, given that they're a match made in heaven. It's a cheese from Burgundy, in France, I tell her, and it's made only in a handful of communes in the departments of Côte-d'Or, Yonne, and Haute-Marne, and only four cheese makers export it.

While I was talking, I opened the small round wooden box as if the label said Tiffany's. She barely tasted it and said she didn't like Taleggio, but did like Riesling, but enough already with the geography lesson, let's go into the bedroom. I put the spurned cheese away without defending it or complaining. I told her to make herself at home. She stripped down to her bra and panties and then took them off too. I did the same. Some girls are more beautiful when they are clothed than naked, and she was one of them. She said she wanted to take a shower and it would only take a moment. As she closed the bathroom door, I started thinking that I liked her a lot more when she was the girlfriend of the guy who didn't deserve her.

Not even ten minutes later, a bathrobe was on the floor next to Silvia's wet footprints, the bedroom door was ajar, and she was lying up against the mirror nailed to the wall like a headboard. Weird how reality can turn ugly when least you expect it. I paused, turned off the light that showed off her stretch marks, kissed her on the neck, detached myself from her, and said I'd be back in a minute, don't run away. She gave a little whimper of surprise, shrugged, and then I heard her sliding down onto the pillows.

One second later, I was stretched out on the sofa in my aunt's apartment, the one next to mine, butt naked and with a lime green blanket wound around my waist, the TV on and my camera on the coffee table, which I had grabbed before absconding, because you never know. I mean, I didn't really know Silvia that well, perhaps in a fit of rage she might have smashed it out of sheer spite. I brought the Époisses with me too, not because I thought it might be in danger, but because it's always a good idea to have something delicious at hand. I smiled, trying to imagine that little Björk face, mulling over my sudden disappearance, and I fell asleep instantly.

Next morning the incessant ringing of my cell phone woke me up. I opened my eyes and grabbed it.

It was ten thirty and it said Caller Unknown.

"Hello?"

"Yeah, hi, I'm... Hey did I wake you? Do you want me to call back later?"

"Nah, don't worry... Who is this?"

"It's Longo Longo, we met the other night, do you remember?"

"Long... who? No I don't, sorry."

"Longo Longo, that's my capoeira name. We've crossed paths at a few training sessions, I spoke to you at the party on the riverboat. I came into the kitchen at the end of the evening. My name's Michele, by the way."

"Ah, Michele, of course I know who you are!" I was actually lying, but there was no use investigating any further.

"I wanted to tell you back then, at the riverboat, but you looked shattered, and I wanted to be sure first..."

"Sure about what?"

"Of getting you involved in a project of mine! Are you busy now, are you working anywhere?"

"I'm in negotiations about a job at a restaurant that's opening soon," I lied again, because it's always best not to show yourself too willing or too desperate.

"Have you heard of the Verve?"

"That renovated farmhouse where they hold a jazz festival?"

"Exactly. In May they're opening a restaurant there and later the summer festival season begins. They've taken me on as chef, and I need at least one other person in the kitchen with me."

"Ah. And when do you need an answer by?"

"Tomorrow. Mauro, the sommelier in charge of the restaurant, is interviewing for staff at around four. If you're interested, I'll get an appointment for you at three, that way maybe you guys can work something out. See, I'd rather have you than a complete stranger... How about it?"

"Sure. Will you be there too?"

"Yeah, I'll be in the kitchen getting things ready."

"Oh, by the way, Michele, thanks."

Click.

Time to take stock: not a dime to my name, a probable court appearance, which—glass half full—might cost me as much as €7,000. I needed to study and pass some exams in the July and September sessions at the university; I wasn't ready to give up capoeira or photography just yet. I did not feel like being stuck in a kitchen all summer long. As things stood, the only real options for survival were: slip on a white polyester jacket with the name of the dry-cleaning service stamped on the pocket and work in some dive in Rome's working-class Torpignattara quarter, or consider the possibility of becoming a professional drug pusher as a profitable enterprise, since I now had a police record anyway. So, tomorrow at three o'clock I'd be at the Verve, freshly showered and with my hair neatly combed and parted, wearing my best smile and hoping to be hired.

My aunt's apartment was empty; she and my cousin must have left already. Before going next door to my place, I peered outside to see if Silvia's car was still parked there. It wasn't, which was fine by me.

Sometimes it takes little or nothing to turn things around, sometimes a random phone call pushes you down a certain path. This random phone call suddenly placed the world at my feet. The fog had lifted and the sun was blazing.

12.

Monday, April 28, 2003, day broke at 5:11 and found me wide awake, convinced it was still the night before. The sun would set at 7:04 p.m. and I might still be at the Verve, talking with Mauro. I dozed off again, hoping the dark pouches under my eyes would go away, and slept through lunch. As I was leaving, I caught the news that the Italian comedian Ciccio Ingrassia had just died. Shortly afterward, I was standing in front of the Verve. The converted farmhouse looked amazing: elaborate stonework, terra-cotta jars, low walls, and an old barn, in a beautiful country setting. All around, but hidden by the trees, was Rome. I decided that I really liked the place even on this dull, gray day with the threat of a storm in the air, like a promise you have no intention of keeping. Like when you swear you'll do something knowing full well you won't. But you don't give a damn because at that precise moment all that matters is the promise, not the fiasco that is bound to follow, or the deception.

The iron gate was half open. I asked a guy carrying a ladder if he knew Mauro, and he said he did but had no idea where he was at the moment and told me to ask the girl sitting over there on a wooden bench. She had big dark eyes, a '30s-style bob, and great tits, which I noticed even though she was wearing a sweater. An unlit cigarette between her lips, she was rummaging about in her handbag, pulling out an assortment of odds and ends including an elegant corkscrew. I sidled up, offering her my Clipper lighter. She thanked me and smiled. She worked here and her name was Giusy.

"Mauro is in the restaurant back there." She pointed with the cigarette between her index and middle fingers and blowing the smoke to one side.

No rain yet. Mauro was sitting inside waiting for me, looking relaxed. As I approached him with my hand held out, I quickly sized him up. Thinning hair, a ginger mustache, an oversize knot on his necktie, not much older than me, maybe a little over thirty. He smiled, with cheery and oddly watery blue eyes, and started to talk. Better that way, it would give me time to adjust and adapt to his demeanor. His eyes never wandering from mine, he asked a few questions, we made small talk about kitchens, our likes and dislikes. He informed me immediately that he was aware Michele and I already knew each other, which was a good start—it helps to know whom you're working with. The season would be brutal because with the concerts, the restaurant would be fully booked every night. No days off.

Best to come clean, no fake résumés or trumped-up jobs. I told him the truth. I had no culinary qualifications, I had no hotel school diploma. After finishing art school, I enrolled in an anthropology course at the university and had only three more exams to go to finish. I'd worked as a dishwasher and at an appetizer station. I'd run an entrée and main course station in a down-at-the-heels dump in Trastevere, before being promoted to chef due more to the deranged temperament of my colleagues and bosses than to any ability of mine. However, the food that came out of that kitchen was undeniably worthy of mention. I'd worked as a salad prep, organized parties in Testaccio, and put on a dinner for 250 people on board the Radio-Rock riverboat. If given the choice, I would rather cook meat than pasta, and I could bake a mean loaf of bread.

"But are you prepared to work every day of the week, at least ten hours a day, for the next four months? This is a straight question and I want a straight answer."

"Yes, absolutely. That's what a chef's work is all about."

"Look, Leonardo, I don't care about hotel schools or culinary courses. I've worked in the hospitality industry for twelve years and I've seen it all: aspiring chefs, kids wet behind the ears unable or unwilling to learn, starry-eyed thirty-year-olds lured by the fantasy of tinkering with caramelized shallots and white Alba truffles, all the losers and dreamers who go to cooking school, and the others, the ones who can truly cook, who find their way into kitchens and work their butts off.

"The most expensive diploma from the most prestigious school is nothing compared to hands-on experience in the kitchen. Good chefs, before mastering the techniques of low-temperature cooking and fancy vegetable shapes, have to be able to run with things, without breaking balls or developing delusions of grandeur. They have to respect the head chef, make themselves useful when necessary and, amid the pandemonium, enjoy themselves. If you've washed dishes for at least a year without cursing too much or getting yourself fired, then you might well become a decent chef. Do you know why I never hire Italian kitchen hands?"

"Why?" I asked, looking rapt but thinking he could have kept the sermon to himself.

"Because Italians are not up to it! Making sacrifices, I mean, or considering washing dishes in a restaurant to be important and essential, and as an opportunity. Italians are big dreamers. They want to be valued, their egos need stroking, they don't want to serve the kitchen, they want the kitchen to serve them. Whereas for foreigners, maybe illegal immigrants, the job means everything to them—to them and to their family back home in Bangladesh. You bet it's important and essential.

"A Bangladeshi doesn't get depressed washing dishes, doesn't collapse after ten hours with his hands in water, doesn't get pissed off when he's nearly finished for the night and another table of ten walks in, and doesn't have a life waiting for him at home. This, right here, is his life."

"And... as far as wages are concerned, what were you thinking?"

"Fifteen hundred euros a month, no overtime, no penalties if we close some days or go home early. No written contract, my word is good enough."

"No contract"—that made no difference to me, I didn't give a damn about contracts, all I needed was the money. And I kind of liked Mauro. Sermons or not, I agreed with him. We shook hands. We'd start in a week. Michele appeared as well, and I recognized him. He was the tall guy, the first one to poke his head in the kitchen at the end of the party on the riverboat to congratulate me, with his cheery, candid expression and admiring comments. And so much taller than I remembered! We said hello, and I strode up to him, laughing, my nose only inches from his chest; there was quite a distance between the top of my head and the tip of his chin. Mauro joked about the difference in height, declaring that it was all for the better, we'd fit in more easily between the flattops, the fryer, the oven, and everything else. So that was that, I was officially a member of the team. A handshake was all it took.

On my way back home, the promises I'd made to myself the previous night and even that very morning vanished into thin air. I'd get back to capoeira eventually, too bad for the July and September exam sessions, there would be others, and I didn't have the scholarship requirements to maintain any longer either. Nothing else mattered, except maybe the photography, but that was a private thing. There was the lawyer to pay, of course, but from May to September I'd earn €7,500, exactly the amount I needed. The rent was, all things considered, reasonable, and as far as food was concerned, I'd be eating at the restaurant. It didn't matter if this was my calling or not, whether it would be for a season or the rest of my life, if it was a stroke of luck or a nosedive. I was ready and raring to go, and it was more than I deserved. Safer not to think too much about it, or let in even the merest shadow of a doubt. It had to be like the dream that floats away when you suddenly wake up. All I wanted was to get to work on time on my first day.

13.

I returned to the farmhouse a few days later for a meeting before work was due to begin. The place was buzzing like a bee-hive, and just as chaotic. There must have been more than thirty laborers going about their business in small groups, swamped by piles of building materials. The deck leading to the outdoor stage for the jazz concerts was still a bare frame, there were yards and yards of electric wires lying around everywhere; light-ing fixtures to be installed, plaster and wooden boards around what would eventually be the outdoor grill for the self-service area, carpets for the dining room still wrapped in cellophane, and everywhere chairs, tables, boxes of glasses and flatware. It seemed impossible that the opening was only days away. Yet everything had a reassuring air of commitment about it. I felt like I was in the right place, a moment before the right time. Michele's hair was as scruffy as last time, and he wore a chef's jacket over Bermuda shorts and a pair of wacky flip-flops.

The kitchen was large and square, accessed by a door open-ing onto a sort of corridor that gave onto the dining room. Crates of wine and mineral water were stacked in a corner, along with two chest freezers and a fridge display for cakes, as well as a rusty, discarded pass left over from what the place had probably been in a previous incarnation: a pizza restaurant. The pizza oven was gone; in its place was shelving crammed with tablecloths, glasses, napkins, trays, rolls of paper towels, gastro-norms in all shapes and sizes, everything covered in dust, and heaps of other stuff in random piles.

In the kitchen, over to the right, was Mambo, an olive-skinned Bangladeshi with gleaming white teeth, and his two kitchen sinks, a huge hood-type dishwasher (the kind with a bar that you raise and lower to start the cycle), and a garbage bin for food scraps. The dishwashing area occupied around a fifth of the total kitchen space. In the middle was the pass, a stainless steel table with a sizable space underneath for storing plates, and on the left, the work area for entrées, two adjacent refrigerator counters, and immediately next to them, a nonrefrigerated counter with drawers, a ten-gallon boiler, a stove top with six decent-size burners and plenty of shelves below for stacking aluminum frying pans, the hot plate, a deep-fryer and, last, the gas grill with lava rocks, where I would be working.

Behind the cooking area were two double-door fridges, one for the meat, fish, and cheese, the other for the vegetables. Next to these was a smaller chiller, for all the cooked food during prep, and right next to that the glass door leading outside, near the stage where the concerts would be held. Along the wall between the grill and the fridges stood, in all its glory, a six-tray convection oven, with a rack underneath and two side shelves jutting out to hold smaller utensils and equipment. So, no blast chiller and no vacuum sealer, but pretty much everything else needed to work comfortably and prepare and store food for a pretty big crowd.

Mauro took me to the locker room and handed me two black uniforms: I'd never seen uniforms this color. I got changed, tied the apron firmly around my waist, fastened the buttons and turned back the cuffs: clothes really do maketh the man. I felt like a bizarre lay preacher or a homegrown version of Neo from *The Matrix*. Anyhow, I felt awesome and you can't make good food unless you do.

I saw myself reflected in a shiny surface, and once I'd stopped staring at the uniform, I looked myself straight in the eye and asked myself what the hell I was doing there. No, that's not true: I'd glimpsed a lost soul in eyes that didn't seem to be mine. I don't know if everyone's brain works this way, but here's what happens to me: I home in on one small detail that gradually swells and expands and obliterates whatever else is going on. There is always a whisper of uneasiness at the back of my mind, a foreboding. I continued doing what I was doing—I'd never step back or jump ship at a time like this—but for a split second my gut told me something meaningful, which was gone as fast as it had come.

I still wasn't too familiar with this world, but it seemed clear to me that résumés mean nothing, they're asked for as a matter of form and then not glanced at. What matters is that you're proactive and relatively cheap, and all the better if you're a fast learner and have little experience. Experience, as we know, is an asset, a commodity, for those who promise they'll give it to you. No experience translates into fewer headaches for the "informally" hired, and it means that not having a contract is the least of your worries. After two days of chitchat and goofing off, it transpired that everyone (and I mean everyone!) in here was working cash in hand.

We were a bunch of guys who wanted to help get this slow-moving multiheaded monster off the ground so it could start spewing out the best jazz music on the planet and gobbling up more than two hundred people a night. No one was tied down by a family, no one owned a home, and no one imagined making headway in the job they were doing here and turning it into a career. Everyone lived in the here and now, had a life, had plans, and had a desperate need for cash. Peddling drugs would be a viable option if it weren't so damn dangerous. So instead of drugs, they peddled cheap labor and did what had to be done.

Michele and I did too, but we identified with that semi-legal world, and with the job. We arrived at ten in the morning and left long after midnight. Everything else got put in stand-by mode, it couldn't be otherwise. Or at least, that's how we were with the others, as if everyone except us was just messing around. I never get whether it's the environment that shapes people or people who shape the environment around them, or whether it is awareness or inertia that dictates how we view others. The thing is that nobody ever suspects that a chef might have another life—as a waiter or a barman, for instance—probably because, if you really think about it, they never do. The chef is, for all intents and purposes, the restaurant. Deep down, I enjoy this role-play. I like being entitled to top-dog status, and it's one of the reasons why I'm always finagling my way into restaurant kitchens.

I passed the bug on to Michele, who ever so slowly began taking on some of my habits while I acquired some of his meticulous manual skills and knowhow. I started getting to know this shy and intelligent guy, who was awkward, unhurried, and methodical, who measured his words before speaking, did not have an impulsive bone in his body, and was utterly engaging as well as hypersensitive.

Michele became famous at the venue for his slightly affected way of doing things and a disturbing propensity to waffle on seemingly senselessly. He cooked with the dreamy expression of a person always one step behind you or one step ahead of you, his head in another place, and for this reason displayed the utmost composure and clearheadedness. As he swayed imperceptibly to distribute the weight of his tall frame, and julienned vegetables in a Zen-like state, I feared he would be torn to shreds. Because if kitchens were the vaguely cruel and violent places I had so far found them to be, then he'd soon be obliterated, there would be nothing left of him.

He's harmless enough, I told myself. I could crush him whenever I wanted. And as this new and unfamiliar sensation descended upon me between the pans and stove tops, this lack of conflict, resentment, or rivalry calmed me down. Not only was he harmless, he'd be useful too. His laid-back approach would give me an opportunity to grow.

Up till then I'd managed to disguise my shortcomings, always nudging what needed to be done into familiar territory, and using other people's weaknesses to hide my own. Maybe here I'd have the chance to turn those weaknesses into strengths. Learn how to make a brunoise the proper way, following Michele's precise and unhurried example until I found my own pace, but with the same precision. In the kitchen there would be just him and me, plus Mambo, who earned his nickname when he arrived at the Verve for a job interview with Mauro wearing a white T-shirt emblazoned with LET'S MAMBO! front and back.

This saddened me a little, reminding me of a modern-day version of Robinson Crusoe's Friday. But there you go. I never could remember his real name, and Mambo was quick and easy to pronounce. He was always laughing and always cheerful. He had a job, his "bosses" (seriously? Michele and me?) treated him kindly, and €700 a month cash, under the table, was a more than decent salary. He was an illegal immigrant, and this job was his only link to his adopted country, giving him a measure of dignity in a place whose language he still hadn't mastered. Of course he didn't have to because he needed only the basics, which he mangled uproariously: uggplant, baseball (basil), shopping (chopping), fush (fish). This became an excellent source of amusement during those long hours of drudgery in the kitchen.

He taught us obscure phrases in Bangladeshi—no doubt rude and offensive—and hooted when we tried to memorize them and repeat them as accurately as we could to the waitresses. Mambo, on the other hand, practiced saying, "Can I whip your ass this evening?" or "You would be an excellent sheath for my huge Bangladeshi dick." So, as I was saying, I don't know whether it's the environment that dictates roles and behaviors or vice versa, but I do know that restaurants have their own crude linguistic code. Outside, relentless sexual innuendo is not my thing, and the same waitress chuckling to herself as she exits the kitchen would probably slap my face if we were in street clothes.

I would never ask Mambo whether Bangladeshi dicks are more like black men's or Europeans'. Dicks, tits, and gang bangs just don't feature in my everyday conversation. However, the minute I cross the threshold into the kitchen, my native language changes to a different vernacular. Every industry has its jargon, and in the world of restaurants, it's an uncommonly foulmouthed one. There's no pretending in there. You don't pussyfoot around food, you just dive right in. You can't clean a fish without yanking out its guts with your hands, and human relationships and dialogue are treated the same way. We handle the basest instincts with our bare hands: Either there is quality or there isn't, either you love your coworkers or you piss one another off; there is no middle ground. In the end there's always someone you take a liking to and someone you despise.

In those early days, Mambo worked the hardest of us all. He mopped the restrooms, the floors in the dining room, and the indoor concert space, mowed the lawn, set chairs in front of

the outdoor stage, cleaned and polished all the various accou-
trements. Mauro had said it—we needed a Bangladeshi kitchen
hand, and we had one. Already so enmeshed in all the most
demeaning but essential tasks, he was far more part of the
machinery than we were. Guardian of the nooks and crannies,
unconditionally dedicated to his job, light-years away from the
Bay of Bengal and yet closer to his family with the money he
was able to send them every month.

There were no hitches in the first few days. We had about
twenty covers a night, the prep work took a very long time but
was doable, and with Michele at the wheel we could afford to
waste time on decorations, swapping advice, and experimenting here and there. His julienne was much more precise than
mine, his touch neater and more even when spreading sauces,
and the consistency of his purees was far smoother: He was
simply more methodical. I was by far sloppier but faster and
more practical, had a clearer picture of the contents of the
fridges, and could see more clearly what was happening (and
was about to happen) in the kitchen.

The fact that I was officially the sous chef and he the head
chef suited both of us. We learned from each other, merging
our individual capabilities into a single organism whose movements and words never got tangled up. I was content to be working for a chef so far removed from the norm, who didn't give
a rat's ass about power, was unpretentious and cheerful, and
whom I had obviously beguiled. Because he probably needed
someone just like me. A less experienced cook would be useless; Michele wasn't domineering enough. Someone with too
much experience would eat him alive. Neither of us pretended
to be what he was not, and very soon we became close friends.
Often in the evening we would stop and have a drink together at

one of the tables outside. Mauro would appear from underneath the stage with a bottle of French champagne or some classy Italian sparkling wine, and entertain us with interminable insights into subtle scents and flavors. He impressed us, and bored us a little too. But on such a journey of discovery, every taste is worth savoring and warrants the utmost attention.

I loved learning about wines, about which I knew absolutely nothing at the time, and I loved finding fault in the bullshit dispensed by this little man with his mustache and dramatic pauses. Mauro was a master wordsmith, and with those words he sold his wines, notably the most expensive ones. Words are more than just language: Language is a code for communicating, words are myths, enigmas, talismans. Words are limits, lucidity, arrogance, traps, distance, seesaws, charm. Words are, above all, games. And alcohol plays a big part in those games.

In my opinion, most of us are sorely lacking in both logic and irony. That's why we call winemaking an art and golf a sport. We're happy to let ourselves be made fools of by expert crap-mongers. Which explains why we don't mind spending €50 on a bottle of Brunello di Montalcino, one of the nine, ten million bottles supposedly produced every year on the hillsides around Siena. It doesn't take a genius to work out that the numbers don't add up, because the quantity of Sangiovese grapes grown there can't possibly produce millions of bottles of wine. Even so, we happily fork out good money for a bottle of Brunello. If there were no sommeliers, chefs would be out of a job.

14.

I was sitting in the dining room, a long rectangular space with the tables arranged in two rows with an aisle down the middle; some of the lights were already off, and only the ceiling lamp in the center of the room was still on. Patrizio was wiping down the coffee machine, Michele and Mauro were with me. Two beers and a glass of champagne sat in front of us. The clock said eighteen minutes past one in the morning. Outside, workers were dismantling the stage where Cat Power had just finished performing. A short, fat guy plunked himself down at a table near ours and took a crack at getting a free drink by whining loudly about the shitty, cheating world he was condemned to live in. At the same table sat the last lingering clients, an ineffectual young fellow and a blonde girl wearing all the colors of an impressionist's palette. The fat guy was still droning on, his strident voice colliding with their silence like a moth against an incandescent bulb. The young fellow and the blonde ignored him, clearly irritated by his presence, until the young man went ballistic.

"Will you do me a favor and just go away?"

The fat guy turned toward us and slithered over to our table. He looked at us with sad eyes. I offered him my beer and said he could have it, as long as he stopped jabbering, because this had been a bad enough night already. He was about to sit down, but Mauro said no, he can go drink his beer outside. I looked at the guy and decided he'd be better off hating it when the lights were on instead of hating it when the lights were off, as he had declared in a long rambling speech. Without missing a beat, he grabbed a chair and went on yakking about concerts costing too much, music should be free, lightbulbs burn out way too fast, which never used to happen, lightbulbs used to last for years but now they design them so they burn out instantly, nowadays engineers are paid to design things that break right away, it's called planned obsolescence. He pointed to the ceiling light above us, with one bulb burned out. I was bone tired. Michele was listening to the guy and agreeing with him, one softly spoken word coming gently to rest upon the next, and Mauro was dialing a number into his cell phone. The security guard from the main gate, without so much as a how do you do, strode in, lifted the fat guy up, and threw him out.

The couple near us got up and walked over to the cash register to pay, he grumbling, she checking her makeup in a round mirror she retrieved from her purse. By now it was thirty-seven minutes past one, and Mauro took a sip of champagne.

"So what happened this evening?"

"Nothing. I mean nothing went well," I replied.

"Oh, come on. It's not that that nothing went well. We just have to fine-tune a few things," Michele said.

"Seven tables got up and left after waiting more than half an hour for the antipasti, one table refused to pay because they waited from eight to ten thirty for their dinner, we had to let it go and apologize, and there were complaints from everyone else. Everyone else complained," Mauro added for good measure. Then he looked at me searchingly. Michele didn't say a word.

"What can I say, Mauro? This was our first real test, I guess we should have imagined it, with a draw like Cat Power. I did my best, and so did Michele. Yep, it was a disaster. We'll have to take steps, but at the start of the evening we only had six tables booked, and we've never had more than twenty, twenty-five customers all at once. Who knew we'd have a hundred and fifty covers?"

"We should have, Leo, we definitely should have expected a crowd that size. Actually, you guys should have. Twenty minutes into service the pass was crammed with orders, dishes were practically falling on the floor, and you two were in the weeds—you should have got your ass in gear. Why didn't you?"

I was stunned into silence, sweat trickling down my back and my hands aching. There was no use denying it: There was an air of foreboding when Giusy entered the kitchen with news that the concert had sold out. But we felt we were in control of the situation and could handle anything, without knowing exactly what "anything" was going to be—stations ready, fridges stocked with the right ingredients, all properly portioned, tables clean, plates stacked neatly next to the pass, the boiler steaming away and the grill incandescent, dozens and dozens of skewers piled high next to it, steaks sliced evenly, resting in the fridges and ready to serve more than a hundred dinner guests. When the orders started arriving, three or four at a time, Mauro was manning the pass, calling out a code that was still foreign to me.

"Fire off 92! Three gnocchi arugula, one mixed app, one crispy lasagnette, two mixed grills, and one sirloin with yogurt. Fire, Leo! Slam it out! I need 35 on the fly! Close table 21! 42's dying! Fire up 60 and push it out with 15! Cancel 12 in the stalls! Close 42 for God's sake!"

The grill was packed with meat and the orders just kept on coming. There was no more room for the fish, and I had to take up one of the burners with a portable cast-iron grill. I was starting to send out dishes that were only half cooked and putting skewers in the oven to finish cooking, but they were drying out and taking too long. Michele's station was swamped with pasta, gnocchi, sauces, and dirty pans piled one on top of the other. There were peppercorns flying, sauces splashing, and wall-to-wall wreckage. Orders started going to the wrong tables, haphazardly and incomplete. New orders took the mayhem to a whole new level, spiraling uncontrollably into a black hole.

I no longer gave a shit about the plating or the salads, tossing dishes on the pass any fucking way, hoping that Mauro would fix them (he didn't), and continuously asking, "What the hell goes with the salmon? Four steaks are ready, can they go out?"

Was the chicken in the mixed grill or by itself? Mauro was no help. Every time he'd read the orders over again from the beginning, getting me even more unglued. I tried snatching the dockets closest to me and doing them myself, but they might as well have been written in cuneiform. Some I'd randomly pass on to poor Mambo, without warning, and get him to plate the meat. Without a word, he would haphazardly throw meat on plates and race them over to Mauro, letting the mountain in his sinks grow exponentially. Meanwhile, the servers had given up scraping the dirty dishes and were simply piling them up the way they were. A disaster, a genuine out-and-out, definitive disaster. At the end we were shattered, just like the servers, and probably the customers too.

"Perhaps"—and I was only hazarding a guess—"two of us might not be enough for all these people?"

Mauro looked at me and shrugged.

"Tonight there were a hundred and forty-three customers. And according to you, the two of you weren't enough. All right. Let's call someone else in, another pair of hands. Do you think you'll manage? Is that the problem? And when we have two hundred people? Will we get someone else? And if someone else isn't enough? I hired you guys because for me, you two are enough. What do you think of the menu, is it too complicated? Is that the problem, you can't cope with the menu? Is that it?"

Michele shook his head and didn't say anything. No, it wasn't the menu, I said to myself. If anything, it's the guy expediting the orders, but I neither shook my head nor uttered a word.

"The menu is not complicated. There are six first courses and seven mains, all grilled except for the oven-baked savory strudel, and that is precooked. Three sides and three desserts, one mixed and three oven-cooked appetizers, plus a raw vegetarian one. So?" Mauro said, laying into us.

At this point I stepped in. "Well, Mauro, we need to find a way to get the food out fast and good. The workspace is too cramped. I think we need at least another chef, and I have to work the outside grill. The other chef stays inside to help Michele. And we have to find a better way of organizing the orders."

"You're just about right, Leo. You have to get the food out fast and it has to be decent. Not necessarily excellent, not even great. You want to know the whole story? We don't need to be creative. McDonald's are masterminds, their philosophy is a stroke of genius. You're out and about, in a train station, an airport, what do you eat? A sandwich that tastes of plastic and costs four or five euros, or McDonald's. You get a good choice, it's hot, tastes nice, and you pay less than for the plastic sandwich. You don't go to Mickey D's yearning for a hamburger; you go because you're waiting for a train and in the meantime you munch on something familiar and filling. It costs you four euros and you don't miss your train. This has to be our philosophy: We're feeding people who are only here for the concerts. They want to enjoy the music, and while they're here they want to eat something DE-CENT"—he underlined the syllables with the tone of his voice—"and they want it fast and cheap. That's why I've got you two in the kitchen, and not chefs with God knows what pipe dreams."

This got Michele to his feet.

"Are you serious, Mauro? How can you give us McDonald's as an example? Do you want us to stuff diners with nothing but empty words? Are you worshipping at the altar of deceit?"

"Don't lose your cool, Michele. You're not here to create but to execute. Everything has to be preprepped," he said. "That's your big mistake—thinking you could cook to order tonight, with a full house."

Michele shook his head, but he sat down again.

"We have to have everything ready so we only need to heat it up and plate it, that's the solution. As of tomorrow, you come in earlier, and as soon as you finish prepping, you start precooking the meat and the pasta, then store everything in the gastronorms and keep them handy. And yes, okay, you can look for another chef. If you know anyone who can start immediately, good, otherwise I'll find someone myself."

Mauro headed toward the bottles. He'd said what he had to say, his task was done, and there was nothing left between him and another drink. It explained the watery eyes I had noticed the first time we met. Michele and I pulled ourselves to our feet and shuffled into the kitchen. It was twenty-four minutes past two, and I was so tired I didn't even feel tired anymore.

"C'mon, Michele, you know he's right. And to tell you the honest truth, I don't mind a Big Mac from time to time."

"You must be joking. He's turning us into canteen cooks. And the sommelier also being the manager is getting on my nerves. What does Mauro know about running a kitchen?"

"Don't take it personally," I said, wiping down the filthy pass with a cloth. "I think you're both right. For now we'll preprep and see how it goes," I suggested, spraying the oven with oven cleaner and covering my nose and mouth with the same cloth.

Michele gathered the pans and washed them in the left-hand sink, Mambo was still washing dishes, four big garbage bags full of scraps were lined up against the glass door, and under one of them a small puddle of putrid liquid was flowing like a stream toward the grate in the middle of the floor.

"Hey, Michele, I think I know the chef we need."

"Hmmm. Is he any good?"

"Yeah, Paolo's a nice guy. He works out at the Tuscolana gym, you must've seen him at some batizado, and he was there the night of the riverboat party."

"Paolo, right, the one with the ponytail. But doesn't he work in a library? Is he a chef as well?"

"No, but he sidelines. He's just finished a culinary course, and a few days ago at the gym he asked me if we needed a hand. He works at the National Library, I believe, but he's off over the summer. How about it, should I call him tomorrow?"

"Call him, sure, that's perfect."

Michele had a ready smile. We continued to wipe down the doors, handles, and insides of the fridges.

I went over to the stereo and cranked up the volume of Chumbawamba's "Enough Is Enough." Cleanup time has a weird charm all its own. There's something inexplicably gratifying when a filthy kitchen, food splattered on every surface, stained, greasy, and cluttered at the end of service, unfailingly turns into a shiny, new, perfect kitchen with everything in its place. I too was in my place, in a clean, tidy kitchen where a solution is found to every problem. The song lyrics seemed strangely appropriate: "Open your eyes, time to wake up, enough is enough is enough is enough." And screw jazz concerts, screw Mauro, and screw orders. It's only for the summer, I reminded myself—that will be more than enough.

The solution that Mauro came up with was crap. It worked for a few days, but it certainly wasn't the secret to serving up memorable meals at the Verve. It worked because we didn't crash and burn like we did that first, woeful night of the Cat Power concert. The orders came in, and in five, ten minutes the dishes went out. In part this was because Paolo was such a nice guy and working with him was a breeze. He'd never be a chef, but he worked like he was one. And we didn't rub his nose in the fact that he was slow, late getting dishes out, and talked bullshit about truffles from Alba and hazelnuts from the Langhe district of Piedmont. Nor did we complain about the Fridays he took off to compete in capoeira rodas with his girlfriend. It worked because after a couple of nights, Mauro left the pass and started helping the girls in the dining room, more or less the same way he did in the kitchen: telling them which tables were waiting for their dishes and which ones still had to order, but, better still, he actually started doing his job, which was to recommend the most expensive wines. Only it was tough to match expensive wines with shoe-leather steaks or overcooked pasta. No one was hailing the solution as some kind of miracle, but no one was getting up from their table in disgust, throwing down their napkins, and demanding to speak with the manager either. And so we overcame our first hurdle. What's more, with Mauro out of the kitchen, we could hammer out new ways of doing things and come up with our own solutions, laugh more, and add or remove things. Now at least we could feed two hundred diners quickly and without complaints. But what we really wanted to do, deep down, was leave these two hundred people absolutely wowed.

15.

All around, silence clung to the walls as thickly and tenaciously as gluten skin over dough. Everyone had left, Mauro's last bottle of wine was still standing on the small round table, lit only by the wan glow of the kitchen. It was just me and her, but all I could see in my mind's eye was the dinner for the mayor at the Verve the following week and the vagaries of life. She was the result of my first try at interviewing candidates for the weekend dining staff: the food runners, the workers you need on really hectic days.

I had to choose my own personal food runner, who would be picking up my main courses. There were two girls: one was a pint-size brunette, good figure, amazing tits, a slight overbite, a bit of a scatterbrain, and about as useful as an origami flower in the rain. No experience as a waitress. The other was a pocket-size Sardinian with short, wiry hair, a flat ass, no boobs to speak of, and a lot of restaurant experience, on the ball. Food runners don't do much. They set tables, serve meals, and clean up afterward, no responsibility and nothing much to worry about. At most, you can ask them to try to carry more than two plates at a time. The brunette could carry only two plates at a time. I can teach her, I said to myself. And I chose her.

This was her second weekend. The concert had finished earlier than usual that night, and the rest of the staff had somewhere to go. Worse, Patrizio had left, and when he was gone and the bar was closed, the buzz subsided dramatically. While I was mulling things over in my head, I realized that she was about a foot away from me, saying that men always feel they have to make promises. She doesn't believe their promises and says that women promise things only if they're in love. I imagined her brain like a still, shallow Swiss mountain lake and tried to concentrate on her nipples, which were just visible through her top. I politely took over the conversation, hoping to steer it anywhere but into the differences between men and women. When you talk about things in general, it's impossible not to be reasonable. That's the path we go down when we're looking for safe, run-of-the-mill banter that lets us make a show of our boring and banal common sense. I ask her if she wants some wine, but no, she doesn't drink. I jabber on about photography and college, confident that my clichés are less clichéd than everyone else's. She's wearing her hair up, exposing the curve of the nape of her neck and her perfectly round head. I've just finished rolling a joint and pass it to her to light it. She comes closer and lays her head on my shoulder. She's saying something about travel and luck, and dreams and aspirations, and something about virtue, in the classical sense, perhaps.

I was no longer listening, all I could feel was her warmth, her breast resting on my arm. My heartbeat started accelerating out of control. Was it her or the joint? I wondered. And then I saw her lips part and felt my mouth on hers. That's the way it's supposed to go, isn't it? I was riveted by this precise moment, the instant at the beginning of a kiss and the landslide that immediately follows. A kiss is the green light, the checkered flag that is suddenly waved, the feeble excuse for my hands to make a beeline for her boobs and all the rest. Everything that a moment before was out-of-bounds, after a kiss is fair game.

"I liked you right away, d'you know? When I came for the interview. I sensed that you lived in your own secret world, all ready to be discovered."

"Do you have a secret world?"

"Sure I do, but not everyone does. I'd love to see your photos."

"I'm not really a photographer, I'm a chef."

"You know what I think? That in this life we have to have courage. I believe you should be what you dream, not what you do..."

She was turning serious. Then she came closer again, purring like a cat. I decided I'd had enough of the kissing and clichés. The price for screwing this girl was getting way too high and, besides, I was dead tired.

"I think what you do is exactly who you are, that's the only way to survive and keep your dreams tucked away where they're supposed to be," I replied.

You're a jerk who thinks with his dick, I told myself. I regretted not hiring the plain Sardinian girl who could carry five plates at a time. I thought about how hard I'd worked today to get every meal out in the correct order, and what challenges lay ahead of me tomorrow. It's not the brunette's fault I can't stand her; it's my fault. I told her I was calling it a night. She frowned and said she was going to bed too—by herself.

Walking home, Matteo texted me.

"Coming home?"

"On my way."

"Alone?"

"Alone. What about you?"

"No. Be quiet when you get back, she's shy."

I put my phone back in my pocket. It rang again, another message from Matteo.

"You're getting soooo old."

Long story short, Mauro stopped calling the brunette, to everyone's great relief. (This is how shift workers are fired: First you don't get the roster for the following week and then the restaurant's number stops coming up on your phone.) He'd kept the Sardinian girl's contact details, and by the end of June, she'd become my food runner. The kitchen was running more smoothly now, and that's what really mattered. And yes, I am getting soooo old.

16.

June 28, 2003, Saturday. The clock says 4:28. In actual fact it's 4:23. I moved the hands forward five minutes in an attempt to avoid—or at least lessen—my chronic tardiness. I'm getting the aubergines ready for the side dish of mixed vegetables on an electric slicer, the blade set open at point three of an inch.

4:42. The aubergine isn't sliding smoothly through the aluminum slicer; it keeps flipping back as soon as it comes into contact with the blade, and the pronged pusher isn't holding it straight. I decide to use my hands, and with care, ramp up the speed.

4:58. Mauro passes by, pauses, and looks at me with a serious expression before speaking, slowly and deliberately: Watch out, Leo. With no thumb guard, you could very well lose a finger.

5:06. Giusy passes by: Oh my God, Leo, what the hell! You're freaking me out with your fingers so close to the blade.

5:12. Paolo calls out from behind me. He wants to know where the bread knife is. I turn, all the while slicing, and tell him it's over there, on the pass for the entrées...

5:12. My thumb starts to sting. I look down and see blood spurting onto the slicer and then all over the sliced aubergine. The blade continues to turn with a soft metallic hiss. My thumbnail is the shape of a crescent moon with exactly point three of an inch missing from the tip. Instinctively, before saying a word, I close my thumb inside the palm of my hand. My first thought is for all those aubergine slices, and that if I cover them in blood, I'll be throwing away all the work I've done. That's the tragedy that comes to my mind. Only after moving the aubergines out of the way with my left hand and discarding the three slices actually spattered with blood, with my right hand closed in a fist held out in front of me and with blood dripping onto the floor, do I turn around toward Michele.

"Hey, Miche, will you help me look for a piece of my thumb? I've fucked up."

Paolo keeps stirring the pastry cream. Giusy has started cutting the bread. Mambo is chopping the parsley. No one has noticed a thing.

I feel a little light-headed and am aware of the pallor that is spreading over my face. Michele, as unruffled as ever, sits me down and starts searching for the tip of my thumb. Shortly afterward, he helps me into his car, holding a bag of ice. I say nothing. It's Saturday night, damn it, every table in the restaurant is booked, and I am on my way to the hospital with a chunk of my thumb in a plastic bag.

6:15. I'm in the waiting room of the emergency department of the San Giovanni Hospital, my right thumb bandaged and my left hand clutching the bag of ice.

I am alone. After dropping me off, Michele went back to the kitchen and all the others are still at work. The thing in itself isn't serious: I expect that my piece of thumb can be sewn back on. If Michele hadn't found that bit of thumb, if it had gone through the meat mincer, it would have been much worse than this. More than anything, I'm fretting about my job, fuck it, my new job. I've only just started, I can't be out of the picture so soon. No contract, no holiday pay, no sick pay.

I look around, read all the posters on the walls: flu shots for the elderly, HIV tests, visitors please wash your hands, health-care workers' disputes. Then I gather my composure and breathe in the medicinal smell of the hospital. My thoughts branch out from a central core—the eggplant slices I managed to save from the blood—toward different parts of my mind, and then a question forms—What do I do now?—but remains unanswered. I know what I have to say, though: I cut myself at home. I pass the time counting the people going by. There are heaps more women than men. They're staring into space, listening to their inner silence. A shriveled-up old lady on a gurney, her form virtually invisible under a sheet, is all alone. Someone's taken her false teeth out and her lips have sunk in, she's wearing one shoe, who knows where the other has ended up. I feel lost, stupid, and vulnerable. My inner silence is making a worryingly loud noise.

7:18. Finally, a doctor pokes his head through the steel doors and calls my name. As I get up from the bench and move toward him, I mentally go over the explanation I am going to give for the sliced thumb, to avoid hassles.

A big beefy male nurse holds my hand still and squirts anesthetic over the wound from a syringe a few inches away. Then, while the doctor swabs the blood and puts in the stitches, he asks me how I hurt myself.

"I was at home, putting a loaf of bread through the slicer, and I got distracted..."

"At home?" This raised an eyebrow. "And you were cutting a loaf of bread with a slicer?"

"Yes. Why? I had people over for dinner tonight and I wanted the bruschette to all be the same thickness. Only I was going too fast."

"Yeah, sure. Relax. We don't give a shit how you ended up cutting yourself. It's your business. But you sure didn't give yourself this cut with a knife, and if you say you've got a slicer at home, then you do. We couldn't attach the tip back to your thumb, but you're lucky, you came this close to the bone. The cut was straight, so it only took a few stitches. The top of your thumb will be flat for a while, then it should gradually go back to the way it was."

"Thanks. So there was no point looking for the bit."

"No, but you did the right thing to bring it along. Listen, you have to go home now. And I mean home. You stay off work for at least two weeks, okay? Are you working someplace, do you need a doctor's note to take time off?"

"No, thanks. I'm unemployed, so I don't need a note. Thanks."

"No problem. The doctor will write you out one just the same, for the minimum days you should take off. People usually ask us for more. You make sure you stay home for a while. The slightest bump to your thumb will set off the bleeding, and if your stitches burst, it's a pain in the ass. That friend of yours, the tall one in the chef's jacket? he said to call him as soon as you leave. Make sure you tell him he'll be in the kitchen on his own tonight, understood?"

7:41. I leave the hospital. The shriveled-up old lady is still on her gurney, her eyes closed. My bandaged thumb is huge and round like a Mickey Mouse cartoon, the pain's bearable. I start thinking about tonight: The restaurant is fully booked, not a single empty table. I'm thinking that Michele will have finished slicing and grilling the eggplant, they'll be in the gastronorm with the dressing, all ready to go, like the meat—sliced, seasoned, and waiting in the lowboy fridge.

Everyone must be wondering where I am and when I'll be back. With a latex glove on my right hand I could still work, maybe if the bandage was less bulky. The job's illegal, for crying out loud. If I go back to work right now, I'll be a hero in everyone's eyes. I'll save the service—they probably think I won't be back for days. My coworkers will heave a collective sigh of relief. In stoic silence, I'll accept their proffered respect and trust. I take my cell phone out of my pocket to call Michele and see who can come pick me up. I go out onto the street, turn the ringer back on, and see there is a text message. It's from Michele: "Sorry you hurt yourself, but everyone has to take responsibility for their actions. Try to remember to say it happened at home. Call me when they let you go. Longo."

7:43. I'm really upset. Still holding my phone, I reread the message. Why on earth did Michele send me that message? Yeah, I know he's the chef, but I might have expected something like that from Mauro, not him. No, the truth is that I wasn't expecting it from anyone. And what hurts the most is that I'm reading it now, after already saying that I cut myself at home, slicing the bread. Because I know full well how things work. You don't have a job, so you can only hurt yourself at home. And yes, I am taking responsibility for my actions in this game I've decided to play. But I was hoping for a hero's medal, or a pat on the back, or even a mumbled "Thank you." Instead, nothing. Worse than nothing, it's all taken for granted. And the excuse I just gave to that churlish male nurse isn't even my own. All that matters is that I said I cut myself at home because that's what I was asked to say, what I had to say, and what else could I have said? So we all have to take responsibility for our actions? Why doesn't that go for the employers? They get invisible people to work in their kitchens, and if they hurt themselves it's a hassle. A hassle for the employers but not the workers who slice off their fingers. Fuck the rules and responsibilities. I very nearly go back inside and tell that giant nurse that yes, it's true, I work cash in hand in a shit hole where, if you injure yourself, they dump you at the emergency department and all they care about is that you don't squeal on them. You know what, maybe I'll report them to the police.

And then I remember the chunk of thumb I lost and Michele picking it up, and my rage dissolves into a flicker of affection.

I call Michele and don't say a word about any of this, only that my thumb has been bandaged and if I wear a rubber glove I can go back to work. If he comes right now, I'll be ready and raring to go, in my uniform, at the grill in time for the evening onslaught, and not to worry, everything's okay. In the end, I guess what upsets me the most is that it was Michele himself who sent me the message.

11:58. I open the bottle of aspirin and pop another tablet. The grill is smoking because of the burned fat, but the last steak has just left for table 46, the one with the lady who is so fat that we had to get one of the armchairs from the lounge bar for her to sit on. It feels like there's another heart stuck to the tip of my thumb, it's throbbing so hard. I leave the outdoor kiosk I've been working in for the last few days and head for Patrizio's bar.

"Hi, Patri, how's it going? Are you hungry, do you want something to eat before I clean the grill?"

"Ah, Leo, I should be asking you the same thing! Don't worry, I'll have an ice cream later on. You must be feeling like crap."

"Nah, who's going to miss a piece of meat? From the grill, I mean, not from my thumb. Come on, seriously, what can I make for you?"

"I dunno, you decide. As soon as the concert finishes, all hell will break loose in here. Make something I can get down fast."

"Fine. How about a kebab and some grilled vegetables?"

"And how about I make you the usual, a mojito? Or are you on medication?"

"Only aspirin."

"So, no mojito."

"Says who? The only side effect is that you get drunk quicker! Actually, if you want a cheap way to get drunk, just take a couple of aspirin before you go out, that's what a Sri Lankan dishwasher used to tell me."

"You're terrible. Go on, I'll bring it to you."

This symbiotic relationship between bar and restaurant is a classic. The bar serves free booze to the cooks, and the kitchen gives the best food to the bar staff.

What's more, Patrizio and I feel an admiration for each other that eventually evolves into camaraderie. He manages to cope with two hundred hands waving dockets in his face without misplacing a bar spoon or a slice of lime, without ever getting caught off guard. I never leave my station without first scrubbing the grill to the same high gleam as when it came out of the factory. Not even when I've sweated over it for five straight hours of nonstop cooking, and before, at least three hours of prepping. This is what impresses your colleagues. If you work your butt off, you're a good guy. That's not all, of course. At the end of the day, everyone is equal in a restaurant, except that a good barman and the head chef are a bit more equal than everyone else. Or the sous chef, who's usually the one carrying most of the work on his shoulders. The food runners are on the fringes, the waiters are the skivvies, but the chef and the barman are the artists, the organizers, the ones who really matter.

Something really terrible has to happen—more serious than an underage sister left pregnant at the altar—for a cook and a bartender to fall out. They are far too useful to each other.

Patrizio is the quintessential barman. Reserved, polite, a lover of first-class spirits, and a teller of tall tales and legends that add body to the drinks he mixes without a shred of tetchiness. He blends ingredients as formidably as he intuits moods. It takes him no time at all to size up the clients, and he always knows how to deal with them.

I've never once seen him even the least bit tipsy. He's a rock, a pillar of strength, and sooner or later everyone falls into his trap. People forget he's neither a priest nor a lawyer and that he is not bound to secrecy. We come, we drink, we relax, and out pours our shit. Like the odd bottle swiped here, tips falling into pockets there, and contempt for the crazy demands of a professional kitchen. It's no different at the Verve, it's just how life is for a barman. Who usually ends up munching on a fillet of prime marbled beef so rare it's still mooing, while filling in the chef, who's sipping a cocktail, on all the latest gossip. That's how I find out that our two bosses have a weakness for high-stakes poker, which they play in their office late into the night.

Patrizio has done the rounds of dozens of places all over Rome and is used to enjoying the same status as the chef. He controls the cash register at the bar, the stockroom, and the orders. It's standard practice for him to offer a free drink every now and again to his favorite customers. The business doesn't suffer; rather the opposite, since those customers usually leave sizable tips.

In theory, the chef is one step above the bartender in the pecking order. The chef defines a restaurant's identity, his wage is higher, and he controls the food costs, beverages included. But usually, there's a tacit agreement whereby a good chef turns a blind eye to the cocktails that a bartender offers and to whom, and in general, to how relationships with customers at the bar are conducted. Partly because there is a very good chance that the chef is also a customer at some other bar. And most times, the bars that chefs frequent after closing are the ones where former colleagues work. So this is our grubby little world, in which owners are merely a necessary appendage. Because we can't afford a place of our own and, if we could, we would be paying our staff cash in hand and they would be pilfering eye fillets and drinks while trading gossip about our vices and weaknesses. That's the way the cookie crumbles and that is fine with everyone. You cut your finger, it pisses you off, it shouldn't happen but it does, so be it. And I'm here, cleaning the grill and drinking. Michele ambles in, already in his street clothes. I'm still in my sweat-stained undershirt, my glove is greasy and blackened, amid the fumes from the degreaser. I'm mellow, the alcohol is doing its job.

2:04. I return home, worn-out. William saunters up the street to meet me and jumps into my arms, purring, to hitch a ride upstairs. I scratch his head and enjoy this rare display of feline affection. I don't turn on the stereo or the TV. I crumble some weed into the palm of my hand, roll myself a good-night joint, lie on the sofa, and stare up at the ceiling with William spread-eagled across my chest and ask myself which part of the slicer I touched by mistake, at what precise moment. The pain finally starts to subside and I trace letters with my finger over the dark canvas of my thoughts. I look, and see that I've written my own name. At last there is silence within me, and it's reassuring.

17.

July rolled around and the concert season reached its peak. One day, Mauro, fired the previous week, came in to visit as if nothing had happened, dressed like a teen in cargo shorts and a Billabong T-shirt. No tie, no suit. He said that if they wanted to work with dumb-ass kids, he knew how to be a dumb-ass kid, and wore a suit and tie only to look more professional. Something that had obviously been neither recognized nor appreciated. It was early, but he seemed hammered, or maybe high. He asked for a drink at the bar, and Patrizio insisted he pay for it. I felt sorry for him, but he reeked of failure, and the stench of failure is contagious so I kept a low profile. He poured out a sob story: They had robbed him of his position and left him jobless. I wondered if he expected us to chain ourselves to the gate as a sign of solidarity with our guru, because all he did by coming in was discover that the place was humming along just fine without a sommelier or even a manager. We didn't need him at all, and that was a bitter pill for him to swallow.

It was really quite simple. The owners needed a front man and they chose Mauro, a sommelier who fancied himself a floor manager because compared to everyone else, he had a smidgeon more experience in the restaurant trade. He'd been lucky enough to come across two willing and able chefs but not smart enough to earn his position by becoming indispensable for the day-to-day running of the business. He gave us free rein, we got better, and he made himself redundant. Mauro's big mistake was letting the owners realize it. Without intending to, Michele and I became the cause of his being fired, and now we held absolute power over the restaurant.

We added new dishes to the menu and removed some that for him were set in stone. On weekends an old friend of Michele's came in to give Paolo a hand in the pastry station. We went berserk, recklessly concocting insane desserts the likes of which the world had never known, like chocolate-and-eggplant strudel, prepared with such guileless passion and optimism that when Joe Zawinul, the Austrian jazz musician, tasted it at his birthday party, he exclaimed that it was better than the best Sacher Torte in the whole of Vienna. Conquering uncharted territory makes you bold and arrogant and pumps up your energy levels. We weren't out to wage wars, but it became clear that life in the restaurant business was a constant battle. There is always a loser, and it must not be you. When success happens, you've got to have deserved it.

The umpteenth dinner service finished uneventfully, not without effort, of course, but uneventfully nonetheless. I was on my way home on the bicycle Paolo had lent me and I was sober. When I got to Via Prenestina, Michele's Opel overtook me. I raised a hand to wave and then saw it pull over. Seated next to him was Vanessa, a girl who worked in the dining room with Giusy and the others. A few days after she arrived, she hooked up with Michele and moved into his pad in the elegant Balduina quarter. Before that she'd been with Patrizio, which is how she ended up working at the Verve. But Patrizio told her he wasn't in love with her, and she wasn't the type to hang around and lick her wounds. For Michele—and this is what he confessed to me—it was the first relationship he'd been in where he was untrammeled by plans and promises and heartache; she, on the other hand, had much more experience in such matters. She was an art history student with a passion for jazz. She'd lived in Rome for many years and knew loads of people in the city's theater and music scenes. Since getting together, Michele had let his hair grow into a curly unkempt mess. Vanessa and Michele were in love, and there was no need to make a big deal about it, just as they didn't need to confess it to each other.

I rode over to the car, took off my earphones, and leaned in the open window, slightly out of breath.

"Where are you off to, Leo?"

"Home, where else? You guys heading over to Balduina? You're an item, aren't you, eh?"

"Yep, we're going to my place, wanna come with us? We can fill up the plastic swimming pool."

"As long as I can take a shower. I'm all sweaty and I stink of roast meat."

"We like it when you're sweaty, Leo," Vanessa said with a giggle, "and we'll be taking a shower too."

"What about the bike?"

"Leave it here—have you got something to tie it up with?"

"Just this crappy lock, let's hope it'll do."

The Balduina neighborhood wasn't that close, and we chatted about everything except Mauro with his stench of failure.

At Michele's place, nothing much happened. We cracked open a couple of beers, I rolled my usual joint, and in the end we didn't inflate the plastic swimming pool—the water would've been too cold anyway. The air was weirdly tense, but I couldn't decide whether it was in my head, or I was feeling anticipation. Vanessa was wearing a T-shirt that did not quite cover her shapely ass. She also had on burgundy panties with navy blue stitching. When we called it a night and said we were tired, I asked Michele if I could crash on his sofa, because the guest room was so damn hot.

"Why don't you sleep in our room, there's air-conditioning. We can grab a mattress and put it on the floor."

"Yeah, sure," I said, and so we grabbed the mattress and put it on the floor. We turned the lights off and said good night.

Wide awake, my heart was thumping, and every minute movement they made broke into the soft hum of the night. My breathing seemed too loud. I waited until they started to kiss before stretching out my arm in the darkness and brushing Vanessa's. As she kissed Michele, she lightly stroked my fingers. This went on for a few seconds, and then I climbed onto the bed. They made room for me. Michele sat up as my lips found Vanessa's mouth, and he kissed the nape of her neck. I closed my eyes and let myself go. She smelled of spices and her skin was taut and damp. She took off her T-shirt, then mine and Michele's, and wrapped herself around him. My eyes were adjusting to the darkness, and I could see them now: They were kissing, almost meticulously, neither of them wanting to take control, searching for and avoiding each other at the same time. I wondered if I was just a plaything: Was I their chosen one, or would anyone else have done? Vanessa broke into my pointless ruminations by folding her legs around me and rubbing herself against my stomach. Michele wore the same expression as when he was cooking something for the first time and I thought he was taking it too frigging slowly; yet his calm, measured pace had saved the service time and time again. I seemed to be doing all the moving, still entwined with Vanessa, and like Michele, I was contemplating the situation that up until a few hours before had been no more than wishful thinking.

No one was talking. Vanessa turned over and lay on her back, parted her legs, took my head between her hands, and pushed it down toward her belly. It was exciting and perfect in every way, but I had to be sure they were both okay with it. So I got up, leaned over, and gave Vanessa a quick kiss, ruffled Michele's hair, said I had to go to the bathroom, and left the room.

I stood in front of the mirror for a couple of seconds, wiped my forehead and chest with a T-shirt I picked up from the floor, then went out onto the balcony to enjoy the cool night air. When I returned to the bedroom, Michele was lying on top of Vanessa, moving rhythmically. She turned her head and looked at me, the bedside lamp now switched on. "Come over here, Leo," she said, chuckling, "there's nothing to be embarrassed about." So I sat on the floor next to the bed and basked in the joy of nature taking its course, from the somewhat unnatural perspective of a very close observer. As I rolled a joint, Vanessa reached over and gently touched my face. I got up and opened the window above the bed to let some air in and smoke out. Michele's ass continued bobbing up and down, then he stopped and sat up; Vanessa crossed her legs, still lying on her back. My gaze lingered over the curve of her breasts. Of the three of us, she was the only one who knew exactly what she wanted. I passed the joint to Michele, who took a quick puff and offered it to Vanessa, who inhaled deeply, filling her lungs. Her eyes became small as the smoke swirled around us. Vanessa said that men don't understand women, they have a distorted idea of them. I asked if she'd imagined this happening, and she replied, "Why? Didn't you?"

In the kitchen I knew exactly how things played out, whereas here I was just a puppet waiting for its strings to be pulled and afraid of breaking something. Michele got up and said now it was his turn to go into the bathroom, and he'd be back in a moment, leaving the room reeking of naked bodies and longing and shyness. I took it to be a signal, meaning that before the three of us could go at it together, we had to loosen up, one step at a time. Before it was me who'd got up and left Michele some space, and now he was returning the favor. As soon as Michele padded out, leaving the door ajar, I flicked the roach out the window and climbed back on the bed. I clung to Vanessa with all my strength. She tasted just like my recipes and made me feel like I was falling and floating at the same time. She smelled of cut grass and forests. Her taut body guided me, adding salt to the narrative of my dishes. Her sensuality clawed at my heart, and this time I really felt the pain.

She told me to thrust harder, and I was happy to oblige, but after a while, once you've given as much as you can, you can't anymore and I couldn't. My mind wandered to Michele: Maybe he'll join in and why hasn't he come back yet? Vanessa sensed my discomfort and interrupted the flow of my thoughts by climbing on top of me and swaying back and forth until she gave a sudden shudder, froze for a fraction of a second, and let out a throaty groan, her body motionless and tense. Then she collapsed, her damp hair tumbling all around. The world went momentarily black and nothing else mattered but that precise moment, a pinprick in time, and I let go too. When I opened my eyes, Michele was standing there smiling, holding a bottle of wine. We left it at that. Vanessa laughed and covered her mouth and breasts.

I returned to my spot, on the mattress on the floor, and Michele to his, in bed with Vanessa. I sat cross-legged, cradling the bottle, and observed the two of them fondling each other. Sparks began to fly from Vanessa again; I gazed at them as they came, and perceived a vague and conflicting sense of sadness that, oddly, didn't detract from my pleasure. I felt astonished and incomplete, as if I'd had a brush with something that never materialized. Nibbled on a morsel of food that I could have devoured. And I sensed that this threesome was inexplicably related to the restaurant and the identities that had been forged there. As if without my being the sous chef of a chef like Michele there would now be nothing, and perhaps there was nothing. There was just the three of us and this fragile scrap of pleasure. The kitchen at the Verve had become the axis around which my emotional life revolved, a living entity that isolated every trace of unease and yearning and floated them in the limitless space of my mind. In the end, things are the way we remember them, and this is true for both promises and dreams.

I put these ruminations out of my mind and fell asleep. The next morning no one was in the least embarrassed. We passed by the pole I had chained my bike to the night before—nothing but the lock remained. No surprises there. When the three of us arrived at the Verve, we went about our business. I decided to cook a particularly sumptuous staff lunch. I needed a reason to celebrate, and announced that it was the theft of the bike. I mean, it wasn't even mine.

18.

It became clear that three of us were not going to be enough in the kitchen once the workload increased and the concert season got into full swing. Management sent us some résumés, and this time I was the one doing the interviews. I told the third candidate, Emiliano, to come back the next day for a week's trial period. He had cut his teeth in restaurants all over Turin, and his passion for writing was equaled only by his weakness for controlled substances. His speech was hurried, but what he said was well thought through and coherent. When he was high, it wasn't his clenched jaw that gave him away, nor was it his slightly compulsive habit of sharing his alarmingly exhaustive opinions of "people," "the world," and "eating well." What gave him away was his language: foulmouthed and funny at the same time. Between relentless ramblings, almost without pausing for breath, he would ask me to taste the sauce, did it need more salt? Was the garlic a touch too pungent in the salmon sauce? By that stage his taste buds were shot.

That was not the usual Emiliano, though. As a rule he was as high as a kite and much, much quieter. Sometimes it was methadone, other times he dampened the effects of coke with rohypnol, Prozac, Lendormin, or any of the other medications the doctor had prescribed for his mother, which he pilfered from her nightstand when he visited her. He didn't shoot up heroin; he smoked it. He'd stopped doing needles after he got hepatitis. Michele appeared to be oblivious. All he did was make jokes about how crazy Emiliano was and how I only ever trusted my gut when I chose people.

As I got closer to Emiliano, I began distancing myself from Michele. My brain seems to work exceptionally well on some levels, but on others it gets tangled up in pointless conflict with itself and slides into perilous bullshit. When that happens, my only escape route is to concentrate on something practical and precise that relieves the tension and wears me out. Cooking is a wonderful medicine, far superior to the benzodiazepines Emiliano took. In that sense the paradox is that my best moments in the kitchen always coincide with the most fucked-up times in my life. I don't know if that's why I tend to fuck things up so often.

Emiliano was a deep thinker, maybe the deepest I have ever met. It was just that when he got tired of thinking, he smoked so much heroin that in the morning you'd find him in the kitchen looking like a wreck, his pupils the size of pinheads. Naturally, instead of sleep he was looking for a state of enhanced alertness that transcended insomnia. He never wanted to switch off. People who think heroin makes you close your eyes and fall asleep don't have a clue. When his body told him to slow down, he stepped on the gas.

I admired his ability to live on the razor's edge—not only did he not fall but he left everyone else for dead, including me. My snap decision to hire him had been spot-on, because with him the menu took another massive and completely unexpected leap forward into brilliance and sheer genius. And it worked, fuck me, it really worked.

We talked more and more, and more and more we snorted a line of cocaine in the restroom before service. More and more I ended up at his place sniffing heroin between smoking one joint and the next, with thoughts that were strangely lucid and had nothing to do with tingling fingers. I sensed that the game could take over my life, and knew it could happen in a heartbeat, but I was convinced that my work would save me. Together, we fucked up our lives, distanced ourselves from the others, and turned the kitchen into a wellspring of miracles.

It was me who asked to shoot up together. Everyone chooses their own path to destruction, but Emiliano's strength and sensitivity would never be wrecked by a shot of brown, of this I was sure. Much more than he ever was. And, of course, he was right.

"Chefs reign supreme, Leo, but only in the kitchen," he told me, while heating the glass vial containing the little dark ball swimming in saline solution with a lighter.

When you do heroin, your thoughts stack up one on top of the other but remain lucid. You get a head rush and you become incredibly rational, which is hard to reconcile with the substance you've just injected. You rationalize and reach conclusions that you can transfer into your everyday life, yet you dig a trench between yourself and what it takes to understand them. And, above all, you believe that you are totally in control and no one will notice. You only do it now and again, after all, you think.

First times are sometimes last times—maybe that is why they stay so clear in your memory. When they are not, you stop thinking about them altogether.

19.

The season edged toward its conclusion, and I had learned lots of useful shortcuts. As usual I was sitting up in the circle, opposite Patrizio's bar, with neither beer nor wine in front of me. Luckily, as it happens, because although by this time he was usually gone or playing poker in the office, I noticed one of the bosses climbing the stairs. He knew we downed a few glasses nearly every night, but he hated actually seeing us drink. He grabbed an upturned chair from the table beside me and sat down.

He told me that the mayor of Rome was planning a meeting at the Verve, and this time he didn't want a buffet based around couscous but something more elaborate. If I felt up to the task, I could organize it all and there would be a bonus in it for me. The others didn't need to know about the bonus. I would put together the menu and look after all the details, and he would pass it on to the kitchen as if it came from the client, so Michele wouldn't feel that he was being pushed aside.

The boss was rewarding me with the prestige and confidence I had yearned for from the moment I set foot in this place. What I hadn't achieved slaving over a hot grill minus a piece of my thumb was now being offered to me thanks to the arrogance with which I had recently been laying into the menus and recipes. All this after consuming variable amounts of some of the craziest illegal substances out there, more often than not taken right there on the job. And Michele, who was clean, decent, and honest, was slowly being sidelined. And they call it a highway to hell.

I threw myself into planning the gala dinner and the menu, down to the minutest detail, with the frenzy reserved for a truly major event. The boss passed by the kitchen to announce that he didn't want this upcoming dinner to disrupt the whole kitchen, and that I could take charge of it with Emiliano's help.

In truth, there were heaps of things that Emiliano and I still didn't know how to do. We had never hand-rolled pasta, our ravioli and cappellacci were gnarled and misshapen, and we used lots of gelling agents and stabilizers, yet we still felt head and shoulders above the others. We spent hours immersed in frozen puff pastry, mini rice balls, and sauces thickened with agar-agar or xanthan gum, and all kinds of savory dishes set in aspic with no regard for the season, arguably displaying a flair for the bold and inventive. Black truffle and foie gras sauce—a match made in heaven. Igles Corelli's onion custard paired with a marinated egg yolk inspired by Carlo Cracco, raspberry mayonnaise with grilled baby octopus, pasta carbonara as finger food served in pasta shells and finished with béchamel sauce, chickpea crostini and bream, lumpfish roe, and trout burgers. In other words, a mishmash of everything I had garnered from my own experience, a few articles, and some books, all mixed together with a generous pinch of improvisation and much bravado.

We spent two straight days and nights in the kitchen, without ever going home.

The gala dinner was a huge success.

While I soaked up the satisfying sound of jaws chomping on food and basked in my boss's praise, a bald guy with dark circles under his eyes wearing a white jacket and tie and pointed dress shoes, also white, came up to me and asked if I was the one who had organized the dinner and made the savory finger food. I looked around. "Yes, that was me," I replied. The guy wanted to offer me a job. He would be opening a funky new place in Trastevere soon. It would specialize in Milanese-style aperitifs that would be the best in Rome. He'd heard great things about the Verve and about me and wanted to meet the chefs to find out if anyone might be free to work for him. Yes, I'd be free, but not right now, probably not till September. But I'd think about it. "Here at the Verve they're actually talking about extending our contracts," I lied. He already had a package in mind for me: €1,500 a month, a part-time contract for €1,000 and the rest under the table. Dinner service only, a smallish kitchen, but entirely under my supervision, minor arrangements to be ironed out at a later date. I countered with, "Not moving for anything less than seventeen hundred euros, which is what I get here, and I want at least the same amount." More lying. Fine, then, let's make it €1,700, and we'll meet next week to work out the details.

Unbelievable. God smiles down on assholes and drunks. I went upstairs for a martini at Patrizio's bar, and while he was mixing it I looked down at the crowd. Yeah, I made the food that all these people are eating. How about that.

20.

One evening Michele asked me why I was looking so glum. He should be used to it by now, since it wasn't unusual for me to wallow in moody silence, but today he insisted, and that wasn't like him either. So I told him about the time I had been arrested with Vincenzo, a watered-down version, without too many details, only how this screwed-up genius of a chef had landed me in hot water. Michele didn't bat an eyelid, he never did. He told me that his uncle was a lawyer. "Everyone hates him," he said, "but they also say he's a mean son of a bitch in court. He has a second job as a scuba-diving instructor."

Scuba diving was one of those things I had always wanted to learn, like hang gliding and chess.

His uncle was right: When you dive at depth with a respirator, you can experience a strange kind of euphoria that is sometimes called a rapture of the deep, because of the oxygen levels.

We were only in a swimming pool and there was no real danger, but in the open sea you have to take care, because being euphoric speeds up your heartbeat and can make you hyperventilate, which makes you consume more oxygen, and it doesn't take much to find yourself underwater blissfully giddy one minute and unable to breathe the next. You could tell his uncle thought he was a cool dude by the way he spoke. His explanations covered every minute detail and were excruciatingly verbose. Then again, none of us in the diving course had ever put on a respirator in our entire life.

"So what kind of attorney are you? Criminal or civil?" I asked as I stripped off my wet suit.

"Mainly criminal, but sometimes for friends I've taken on civil suits. You're in trouble, are you? Sent some diners off to the hospital with the runs, did you?" he said, laughing to himself.

"No, I'm in serious trouble. What I need is a criminal lawyer. Listen, are you as badass as they say you are?"

"A few months ago my law firm won a case before the Roman Rota."

"What, you won a case against the Vatican? Oh, then will you please take on my case? Please!"

"It depends what you've been up to, Chef. And no, I didn't win a case 'against' the Vatican but in their court. C'mon, we can talk about it later. How about you buy me a beer?"

Twenty minutes later we were sitting in the bar opposite the swimming pool. I told him the main points.

"When do you and Michele finish working at the Verve?"

"According to our agreement, the season ends on the thirty-first of August, but they're talking about keeping open through to the middle of September. Why do you ask?"

"Because my advice is to not think about it too much for the time being. Finish the season and in the meantime take a minute to fax your lawyer telling him you are relieving him of his duties, then pass by my office whenever it suits you and sign the papers. If your friend can't make it, tell him to give you power of attorney. Then take a little break. You sure need it, you look absolutely shattered."

I didn't take any more diving lessons. Instead of winding down, the workload escalated. Giusy went home to Policoro to look after her sick grandmother, and being one waitress short made it harder; there never seemed to be enough time. A new girl arrived to serve in the dining room. She was tall and her figure wasn't great, but she was not unattractive. Wide hips and

strong hands, a dreamy look about her, and a serious commitment to her work. In no time at all we found ourselves in the
same setup as with Vanessa. Michele, her, and myself at night,
in the inflatable pool on the big terrace of the apartment in
Balduina. Naked, in the water. The tall girl kept us at bay for a
while. The evening took an unexpected turn when she wrapped
herself in a towel and said, clearly but playfully, "Not with both
of you together, but since we're here, at least one of you will
sleep with me tonight, won't you? So I'm going into the bedroom and I'll be leaving the door open. Good night."

What the fuck! I like being chosen, and not as an after-
thought. Half an hour later, I was on the terrace with a beer and
a joint, thinking about the next day's menu and the court case
while Michele and the tall girl were screwing each other loudly
and enthusiastically inside. I wondered whether people have
any influence on how emotional attachments are formed. Or is
it circumstances, basic human needs (drinking, eating, defecat-
ing, fucking, talking) that lay down the law?

And so, the final days at the Verve slipped away. Patrizio closed
the bar and disappeared. I heard that he was working in London.
The jazz concerts were replaced by an open-air art house cinema
that was not very popular. Our menus turned into a sort of predin-
ner buffet for the few diners who continued to come. Emiliano
left as soon as he sensed that he wasn't needed any longer, no
questions asked. Paolo helped us turn out dishes from a secondhand cookbook he had bought for €10, and they seemed to be
working, for the little cooking we had to do. I was having fun concocting sushi-type dishes and experimenting with savory finger
food, also in view of the new job I'd be moving to in Trastevere.

A few days after the Verve closed, I had finished up and
didn't know what to do with all the free time I now had. When

Emiliano asked if I wanted to go to Scotland with him to visit a pastry chef friend of his in Edinburgh, I bought the airplane ticket in a flash. This was the little break the lawyer had recommended. During the trip, all I could think about was him and the court case; not working gave paranoia free rein to ruin everything. As soon as I got back, the first thing I did was contact him.

"Hello, hi there, is this a bad time? It's Leonardo and I just got back from Scotland."

"Hi, Leo, I was waiting for you to call."

"So, anything new? Should I drop by your office?"

"Well, the preliminary hearing judge was an old friend of mine. So, getting straight to the point, the whole thing cost me one phone call to a guy I hadn't seen in a while and a dinner invitation. Your case has been placed on file."

"Oh, good, placed on file."

Silence.

"Um, what exactly does placed on file mean? I don't think I know."

"It means that you had better come by my office as soon as you can, we can't talk about these things over the phone, you never know who might be listening."

The second after I hung up, I was on my motorbike.

The lawyer looked at me the same way he had every other time, with the expression of someone who's way too big for his britches. Needless to say, I was all ears.

"So, you were saying that the case has been placed on file, which means..."

"That you both are off the hook, you won't be pursued by the law. But watch out, for the next five years you had better not fuck up. And if you can, try not to brag or even talk about it. I don't know, say you and a friend fall out, or some girl decides to get even with you, they might ask for the case to be reopened, and the case would be reopened. Do you get it? So you and your friend, whom I have never laid eyes on, just relax. Keep on cooking, study, smoke a few joints, but do not go around with stuff on you. Oh, and as far as my fee is concerned, the secretary's got everything ready. It'll cost you seven hundred euros each, for a couple of letters I had to write, and for dinner. I couldn't very well take the judge to some dive in Pigneto; we went to a three-star restaurant, La Pergola, so you guys are paying for that too."

The kitchen giveth and the kitchen taketh away, I mused on my way back home to Via Zurla. One chef got me into this mess, which I'd had no idea how to get out of, and another chef, albeit through a completely different turn of events, had got me off scot-free. When I thanked the lawyer, saying that he was really good, he answered that to be a good lawyer you didn't just have to know the law, you had to know the judges. The world's not a fair place. And thank heavens for that.

21.

Déjà-vu should have opened at the end of October, leaving me just enough time to draft a plan of attack for setting up and organizing the new kitchen. I met with the architect, learned all about the laws governing exhaust ventilation, spaces, and licenses. We decided where to put the small convection oven (the only cooker I would have), the fridges, and everything else. I exchanged views with the interior designer and the two owners on the furnishings and supplies. I sweated over the notion of an entire menu, invented from scratch, made up only of finger food. This is what Déjà-vu was going to be: a place you could have a quick dinner or lunch, enjoy a drink prepared by a team of bartenders, and munch on finger food the likes of which had never before been seen in Rome (when the owners told me about it, I thought of the name they had chosen, and burst out laughing) — well prepared, well presented, and perfectly served directly by the chef. Me.

It was nearly Christmas, and Déjà-vu was still on the drawing board. From week to week and month to month the opening of the restaurant kept getting put off.

And what was I supposed to do in the meantime?

A whole lot of nothing. I drifted around in a constant state of anxiety over the imminent opening that kept failing to materialize. I mean, if you're starting up a whole new place in two weeks, does it make any sense to take up capoeira again? If in a week's time your head and hands will be completely tied up with running a kitchen, does it make any sense whatsoever to sign up for a Photoshop course? If in ten days' time, your only free time will be when you're asleep, is it worth studying for exams?

Nothing remained of the security that those months at the Verve had provided. Sometimes twilight creeps up on you just when you think the day will never end. I was bored, I'd stacked on the pounds, and pimples had broken out on my ass. After the first few days of living it up, inviting heaps of friends over for lunch and dinner, I didn't even feel like scrambling a couple of eggs. Most days I picked up a pizza or a Big Mac or invited myself over to my aunt's to eat. I felt like Bayern Munich the night of the UEFA Champions League final in 1999 at Camp Nou in Barcelona, when they were trumped by Sir Alex Ferguson and his Red Devils at the ninety-third minute of the match. The winning goal came thirty fucking seconds from the end of the game. In the last three minutes, Sheringham and Solskjær stopped the Germans in their tracks, with the Bayern ribbons already tied to the handles of the cup. That last fatal minute, the one nobody could possibly have foreseen, a misjudged play that brought with it an unexpected and sudden loss from which there was no return. Nothing was falling into place, or maybe I was the place that nothing was falling into.

How the fuck was it possible that only two months earlier I'd been the sous-chef-practically-chef of one of Rome's hippest joints, with all the attendant accolades and respect and power and money and sex and drugs and rock and roll, and now here I was struggling to stay afloat, grasping at an uncertain and completely random future? I'd hit rock bottom only to discover it was a trapdoor to an abyss. Even Mambo was doing better than me. He'd found work as an assistant chef at some Greek place in the Torbella neighborhood on the outskirts of Rome, owned by Bangladeshi friends of his. He was working less and earning more. When I asked him why they had set up a Greek restaurant, he told me, "Bangladeshi restaurant no good, too much like Indian, people sick of Indian, Greek better. Easy cooking, like kebab, but no call kebab, and people come and eat and happy."

Terrible decisions followed me around like a bad smell. The fairy tale had turned into a jinx. So there I was sitting on the sofa feeling sorry for myself, in the dark, when Matteo came home.

"Oh. Hi, Leo."

"Right."

"What the fuck are you doing in the dark? Can't we turn the light on?"

"No."

"Shit, the fridge's empty, how about doing some shopping?"

"No."

"Okay, why don't we go out, then?"

"No."

"How about dumping Déjà-vu and finding another restaurant?"

"No."

"How about dumping the job and becoming a photographer?"

"No."

"How about dumping Rome and moving to Bangkok?"

"No."

"How about ending it all and slitting your wrists?"

"No."

"Fine, then we haven't hit rock bottom yet."

22.

As it happens, another place like Déjà-vu was actually up and running and far better than anything I could ever have dreamed of. Matteo took me there. It was sleek and spotless, with an oval buffet table in the center. Waitstaff replenished the platters long before they were empty and might give the impression of the buffet being mean and stingy. It ran the gamut from classic Roman dishes like braised baby squid to rice balls, Scottona beef tartare with raw yolks placed on spoons as tradition demands, oysters both raw and au gratin, spaghetti with mullet roe bottarga, onions oven-baked in foil, veal liver with raspberry vinegar mayonnaise, braised beef tongue with Jerusalem artichokes, sea snails, clams from Goro, and deep-sea shrimp. Every tray sporting a label with the ingredients, vegan and gluten-free options, and the historical background of the traditions that inspired them. Specialties ranging from Italy's alpine Alto Adige region to Hanoi. I was dumbfounded. And I'd missed the boat, damn it.

Matteo and his friends fell over themselves with compliments, and so did I, masking my sorrow and gloom. Did they have a fucking army in the kitchen? Who could possibly lay on a spread like that and pull it all together into a coherent whole? I spied a smoking hot tray labeled "Roast goose, gluten free—a traditional dish from Assisi." I speared a piece with a fork and put it directly into my mouth, under the stern gaze of a waiter. Biting into the crunchy and slightly caramelized skin, the underlying fat dribbled from my lips. An explosion of sweetness and juiciness overwhelmed my palate and tongue, while the perfume of the thyme and rosemary fused together with the slight gaminess of the meat, which was moist and tender and perfectly cooked. This goose was my downfall well before the game had even begun. I'd never be able to make anything like that.

Matteo stopped to chat with one of the waitresses, and I had a hunch he wouldn't be coming home tonight. I'd be on my own. And so I was. A bit of TV. William curled up on the sofa, me on the floor. A thought crossed my mind, and action followed at the speed of light. I went to my room, retrieved the ball of brown I'd left in my desk drawer from the last night I'd spent with Emiliano, and went into the bathroom. I'm allergic to bee and wasp stings so there's never a shortage of cortisone and syringes.

I go about it methodically, with only the slightest sense of urgency and quite a bit of pride. I know exactly what to do, my movements are precise and confident: Break a bit off, place it in the bowl of the spoon, add saline solution, heat, pull back on the plunger, tap the side lightly, push the plunger just so, tie a rubber band around my biceps, open and close my fist, find a vein. A bubble of blood appears in the syringe—I've hit the right spot. I push the plunger down at least a third of an inch. I must have broken a blood vessel, because a faint blue bruise appears. Slowly I press all the way down. A smooth, sprawling sensation erupts in my temples, one that I instantly recognize but that never fails to surprise. Calmly I remove the needle, detach it from the syringe, throw everything in the trash, wash the spoon that just won't come clean on the underside, and return to the sofa. Then I get up again, remove the spoon from the cutlery drainer and hide it in the drawer full of kitchen utensils nobody uses. I have no idea why I don't throw it away, I really don't know. Something's not right, and the smack makes me realize it. Getting high gives you an incomprehensible emotional clearheadedness.

It wasn't just about the job being on hold. I'm a big man, with a bit of a belly despite the capoeira, and I was in a foul mood. Just like when I wake up suddenly and can't remember my name. I dropped to the floor again before it dissolved under my bare feet.

There I was, slouched on the marble floor, flabbier than I ought to be at twenty-six years of age, and brimming with melancholy and anger, my hands completely numb. My name's Leonardo, I'd told everyone that I was a chef and they'd all fallen for it. I'd fallen for it too because I'd said it so often, and now that I didn't have a kitchen to work in, I was nothing. I tried to get up and take a few steps. Bad decision. I slunk back to the floor, concentrating on my next move and focusing on every single muscle, on the exact impulse my brain had to emit to move one limb before the other. A movement. The same thing that can take a boulder or an earthquake thousands of years. William snoozed nearby. I was tired of being a boulder, so I got up again, successfully this time, and gave him a pat.

I opened the French windows. William purred and I wrapped both of us in the old lime green blanket. I stayed like that for a while, as if sleeping.

Valeria had been a fellow student at the university. We'd been together for a while, then I lost touch with her. She'd moved to Brazil and since returning had become my best friend. One day at capoeira class she waved me over to do the next set with her. I took my sweatshirt off and threw it to one side.

"What have you done to your arm? You're all black and blue."

I looked at my forearms: there were two big green bruises, as big as a fist, on my left one. The words gushed out of their own accord, without pausing to collect my thoughts. There were none to collect anyway, I was on autopilot.

"Shit. Yesterday I was playing volleyball with some of my cousin's friends but all they had was a basketball, and look what I did to myself!"

No raised eyebrow, I'd fooled her. If Valeria had doubted me for an instant, she wouldn't beat around the bush, at the very least she would slap my face, and not playfully. I loved this fierce and fragile woman. I'd always struggled to look her in the eye when I wanted to keep something from her, and I'd never been able to lie to her. As for the bruises, my answer had been ready long before I needed it. Fraud. The theft of a privilege of hers and a fragment of my life.

It wasn't the lie itself, it was the easy way it had come out. Valeria had always managed to catch me out, but not this time. That was the last time I ever injected stuff into my veins; her majesty Queen Heroin departed without a trace, without exacting a toll. Lying effortlessly to Valeria without so much as averting my gaze terrified me. A few months later, I told her the whole story and she burst into tears. That's all I have to say on the matter. It turned out okay.

I started feeling an urge to get moving again instead of hanging around waiting. As a kid I believed that airplanes dangled from a fragile, invisible thread. I preferred trains because they rolled on sturdy tracks. I was not an airplane, I was more of a train, and I wanted to run like a train. When an airplane veers off course, it doesn't take much to make corrections and bring it back to the right flight plan, but when a train derails, all you can do is pick up the wreckage. I always knew I could not afford to get derailed—nobody would pick up my wreckage. I've come across a lot of heroin addicts in restaurant kitchens, people you would never suspect. I can recognize them in a flash, and that's a huge advantage. I can tell whether or not they are going to be a liability. I was lucky, I didn't derail.

23.

When they told me there was a place looking for a cook, behind Vicolo del Fico, near Piazza Navona, I was tempted to say no, for the usual reasons. Déjà-vu should be opening soon, maybe in a week, two at the most. Instead, I wrote down the number, called Arturo — the owner — and the very next day I was standing in front of his restaurant. I hesitated for a moment before entering the dusky glass doors and decided there was no point putting on my interview face today. Then I stepped inside.

The place must have seen better days. A spacious room in a vaguely art deco style with a pretentious-looking mirror taking up most of the wall behind the bar. Old-fashioned beer taps, glass shelves groaning under an array of bottles, a somewhat glum air about the place, like an old wooden jewelry box with crumpled velvet lining, but not too bad. The restaurant area followed on from the bar, same chairs but rectangular tables rather than round. The place was utterly, wretchedly empty. And I don't just mean there were no diners, who at this time — it was about six thirty in the evening — wouldn't have arrived yet; I'm talking about the staff. You could hear a pin drop. No one setting up tables or sweeping, nothing other than a poignantly sweet jazz trumpet playing in the background. The only person in the restaurant was a gentleman of about sixty with a thick mane of pure white hair, combed straight back and falling onto his shoulders. He smiled and approached me with his hand extended. He had to be Arturo.

"Leonardo, right? Do you like this track? *All Blues* by Miles Davis, one of the best albums ever... listen, listen here..."

"Pleased to meet you... Arturo?"

"Yes, yes, that's me, come here, come over here, I'll show you around. Have you heard of Miles Davis?"

"I've got quite a few of his records—I love *Kind of Blue*. This summer I was working at the Verve during the jazz festival."

"So, you're a jazz-loving chef? Do you play any instruments?"

"No."

"Oh, that's a shame, that's a real shame. Come, come, I'll show you the kitchen."

"Is there anyone working in there?"

"Nah, no one. Out of the blue that son of a bitch walked out on me and I can't close down while I look for another chef so I've been doing everything myself."

"You mean you tend bar, take orders, and cook too?"

"I have to, who else otherwise? And it's not the first time, either. I've been doing this job forever. I was born into this life, customers, bars, restaurants. I was born into it."

The kitchen was a black hole, the likes of which I had never experienced before. To enter it, you went down three steps and then you were in a kind of windowless basement, with glaring neon lights. The first thing I saw was a filthy slicer clogged with bits of dried prosciutto fat and old cheese. There's nothing worse than sticky cheese for messing up the functionality of such a superb machine—the same kind that ransomed a piece of my thumb. At the Verve I would hover and fuss over the slicer as if it were a woman too beautiful to be left alone. It was always gleaming, wiped down after every use, taken apart and cleaned meticulously every blessed night, no matter how late we finished. The pasta boiler was switched off but still full of cloudy, yellowish water with dried starch residue sticking to the sides and the baskets. Of which there were only two, with the third missing. Next to the pasta cooker was a hot plate, blackened by the meat of ages, never touched by a scraper, and with the grease chute completely blocked.

While Arturo was talking, I opened the oven door and found the same grunge. The oven in itself was not half bad, a self-cleaning Rational that couldn't be more than three years old. Unbelievable that it was already in this woeful condition. I continued looking around, and the way the equipment was positioned was anything but typical: six cooktop burners in the center with a lopsided hood above — filthy — a pasta cooker, hot plate, and fryer along the wall. The pass — a steel trolley on wheels — over on the opposite side, near the steps leading out of the kitchen. So to hand dishes to the waitstaff, you were forced to go around the cookers and, on a really busy night, waste an awful lot of time zigging and zagging.

The floor was grimy, a minefield of leftover food scraps; and I spied a couple of mousetraps. The dishwashing area was separated by yet another step and contained two oversize dishwashers. I concluded that either this place used to be really busy or everything was bought at some liquidation auction. It transpired that the chef who preceded me was an alcoholic psychopath with manic depression, a compulsive masturbator, as well as a thief and a lowlife.

Apparently Arturo was drowning in a sea of shit at the moment. He didn't give a damn about my CV, he was just happy to find himself face-to-face with a wholesome-looking young guy who might turn out to be a stroke of good luck. He was already listing his grand designs, the potential of the place, the dishes that did really well and for which masses of hungry customers would happily wait in line. The more he talked — and I listened — the more he convinced himself I was the chosen one capable of turning this dire situation around. He apologized for the mess. Shit, even he was disgusted by the state of the kitchen, but that bastard had left him in the lurch, without warning, a real douche bag; he took his money, though. That he made sure he got, and the minute there was the smallest glitch, he took off without a moment's hesitation. But Arturo's tough. He refused to give in. He'd created this place from scratch. The best dishes were his own creations, and he'd been doing it all by himself for nearly two weeks. I can understand that; shit, after working fifteen hours straight, doing everything yourself, the last thing you feel like doing is cleaning. And if this place interested me, we could grow together, work out a plan, and he was willing to share the rewards as well as the workload. Plus we were only a stone's throw from Piazza Navona—so customers simply stumbled into the place—and he made a meat loaf that was the stuff of legends.

"But you don't even have a kitchen hand?"

"Believe it or not, that heathen took the dishwasher along with him. He found a job in another restaurant, and besides lifting my money and my knife kit, he took the dishwasher and the waitress with him. They all ditched me."

In reality, all I needed was a place without too many hassles to bide my time until the opening of Déjà-vu, and if he thought he could trust me, he was making a big mistake. Then again, I certainly didn't trust him either.

"What were you thinking in the way of wages?"

"You must be used to chef's wages in grander places than this. Here you'll have to roll up your sleeves and grow with me."

"Yeah, sure, so do you have a figure in mind, a contract?"

"For the time being, no contract. Let's say we start with a month's trial, how about that? We don't really know each other, do we? I can give you twelve hundred euros a month, six days a week, dinner only, from five p.m. onward. How about it?"

"It's not a great wage. Plus, there's a lot of work to do in the first few days...Can I have a look at the menu? That'll give me an idea."

He handed me a menu, all crumpled up and coffee stained. No removable pages; it's definitely been around for a helluva long time. No seasonal dishes. I gave it a cursory glance, with a quick look at the prices—not high but not dirt cheap—and mentally priced the ingredients and judged the difficulty of the dishes. There was no coherence in terms of culinary philosophy or any consideration for the work that needed to go into prepping and serving the dishes. Each dish stood alone, entirely disconnected from the next. The famous meat loaf—which I discovered was a recipe of Arturo's mother's, God rest her soul—was written in a larger font, indicating its status as the highlight of the restaurant. I looked at the desserts.

"Arturo, here's the deal. I'll accept the amount you're offering, but you'll pay me every night. I will do dinner service for the trial period, and when I finish, every night, you'll give me my fifty euros. Then maybe we can talk about a contract."

"Can you start tonight? I have a table for five booked, and this way you can start giving me a hand and getting a feel for the place..."

And so, here I was.

No chef's whites, just a clean T-shirt, a cap on my head, and a sauce-stained apron tied around my waist, while the range hood whirred, making an infernal, rattling metal noise.

But all things considered, tonight I'd be getting my hands on €50—better than a poke in the eye with a sharp stick.

Arturo was one very strange character. When I arrived he was at the bar, and when I left he was still there, often rambling on in his own peculiar way, without any pauses, to some unsavory-looking characters. But I didn't give a flying fuck; that was his business.

After a week, I asked him for a kitchen hand and he gave me the green light to find one. A few days later a waiter joined the staff, a young guy who rode a Honda 600. We talked about bikes and found common ground, and things started to look up. Even though the kitchen was a god-awful sauna, I wore my blacks and felt very professional. Arturo liked it and was always asking me to go into the restaurant and explain dishes to the diners; he was thrilled to show off his new chef.

The restaurant was staying afloat. I don't know how or why, but we always managed to get between twenty and thirty covers a night. Arturo's forehead sported permanent beads of sweat and this worried me. I kept on working and waiting for Déjà-vu, content to fuss over the stove and chat with the waiter. Arturo didn't mind us having the odd drink, and I was never entirely sure whether or not he was drunk.

One evening the kitchen door opened, and a cute girl with a pixie haircut and huge dark eyes appeared, asking if she could have a word with the chef. I told her I was the chef. She was genuinely taken aback. She'd had a really great meal and never imagined that the chef would be so young. What time do you get off? she asked. Soon, I replied, and she said she'd wait for me outside and we could go for a drink. She'd known Arturo for ages and had left his place many times the worse for wear. Her name was Samba.

Her name made me laugh. We called the kitchen hand at the Verve Mambo, and now all I needed was to meet Polka. But I didn't tell her that.

She had a fantastic bicycle with an aluminum and carbon fiber frame and disc brakes. It probably cost as much as my motorbike, I mused. She was self-assured and a little taller than me. She loved to eat well and said that it was true, the chef before me was indeed a stuck-up piece of shit, my cooking was much better. Even the meat loaf was better. Time flew, and we found ourselves in front of her apartment building. We'd had quite a lot to drink, and she said, Why don't you come up, and so I went through a cavernous and untidy kitchen where she told me her mother was sleeping, and to not worry about anything. Her father was from Algeria but he wasn't around anymore—that's all she said, he wasn't around anymore. There were photos of her with long hair, and I sensed something awful in her life, but I didn't believe it had anything to do with her father.

As she spoke, I wondered where the hell the logic was in my stupidity. I was twenty-six, I had had a sore back all day, my temples were throbbing because of the booze, but I was happy to be a chef because I was about to screw a customer. She obviously craved human contact, and the nearest human to her right now was me. Her home was a dusty attic near Piazza Navona, with stacks of books all over the place, crumbling stucco in a state of disrepair. The apartment had once belonged to rich folk but had fallen into the hands of people who couldn't afford its upkeep. But it was still beautiful, maybe even more so than originally. Even Samba was beautiful just the way she was, with that thin veil of despair, the only thing covering her naked body but not diminishing her dignity.

Life is strange, all right, and I was grateful that Déjà-vu hadn't opened yet, because I needed a night like this, with Samba reminding me of when I used to use food to pick up girls at the university. I watched her breasts moving in sync with every beat of her heart. I couldn't hear it—her heart, I mean—but I could see it. I think cooking has taught me to know people more deeply than studying anthropology ever could.

I've learned to expect the unexpected behind my pots and pans; all that matters are the details, and I scoff at those who worry themselves sick over possessions and having their needs fulfilled. I'm the one who fulfils their needs, when they're hungry or they want to celebrate something. Like stoned drug addicts, they fall into my lap, and I try to not disappoint them. From time to time, I'm the one who's stoned and falls. I'm not interested in sous-vide cooking and I don't need a de Manicor range cooker to get my fix of satisfaction. Whereupon, I fell asleep and had a beautifully vivid dream. I dreamed that I wasn't me.

24.

The owners of Déjà-vu finally called me with news that the project was off the ground at long last and they were about to open for real. They didn't know I was working for Arturo. In fact, hardly anyone knew. I had no idea how to break it to Arturo that I was about to fly the coop—what else was he supposed to expect? Maybe I could leave the kitchen in the hands of the dishwasher, because that's often how a cook's life begins. Someone gets into trouble, or gets lucky, or has some terrible mess to clean up, and you suddenly find yourself in charge of a kitchen. If it suits you, from that moment onward you embark on your journey. If you like it a lot, after some years a cook can even become a decent chef. Saving someone's ass lends dignity to your profession.

There wasn't a lot going on. As I glanced toward the bar, a man entered the restaurant and sat with his back to me, followed by another man in his fifties, solidly built, who turned around, saw me, and looked me straight in the eye. The man sitting down had a shaved, square-shaped head. Arturo left the bar and went over to them, not casting a glance at the handful of diners in the room. An argument appeared to ensue. From the kitchen I could see Arturo sweating profusely. His gestures piled up like dirty clothes in a laundry hamper; his feet shuffled nervously, and from his movements he seemed to be pleading for a break. I opened the door a crack and hissed to the waiter to come and get a couple of dishes. The two stood up and left. Arturo returned to his spot and poured himself a whiskey. I went back to the stove.

When I arrived the following day, the roller shutters at the front of the restaurant were half closed. Strange. I ducked to give Arturo a shout from under the shutters, and he answered from the darkness inside, telling me to come in, without pulling them up. Inside was a disaster zone. The bar was a shambles: the mirror in shards, shelves and chairs broken, bottles all over the floor, tables upturned, even the beer taps seemed to have taken a beating. Only then did I look at Arturo, who was busily trying to clean up, and I realized that he too had been knocked around: a black eye, his hand bandaged, and limping.

"What the fuck's happened, Arturo?"

"Er, last night. After you guys left, two troublemakers came in, a couple of junkies maybe, I dunno, they wanted money. Got it? These two came in and wanted my fucking money, but I told them I didn't have any and they started smashing the place up. What a hellhole this city's become. It was much better when the Magliana Gang was around. Now it's a wilderness out there, you're not even safe in your own restaurant."

"Shit...But what do we do about tonight?"

"We open, what else can we do? They even stole coins out of the cash register. We can't give in to them, we have to stand tall, we can't let them get the better of us, we'll clean up a little in here, thank God they didn't touch the kitchen. Ask the dishwasher to come in a bit earlier and give us a hand. Why isn't he here with you?"

"Today's his day off. I'll call him now."

Shortly afterward, the waiter arrived, made a few comments, and started to clean up, seeming to take Arturo's explanation in stride. After a few hours we'd swept up, straightened the taps, taken out all the broken chairs and tables, covered the mirror with a tablecloth, recovered all the bottles that were intact and replaced the broken ones with what we found in the storeroom. At seven o'clock we raised the shutters, Arturo behind the bar as usual, sporting a swollen eye and an air about him that said, *What, me? Oh, it was nothing*, while the rest of us went about our business in the kitchen. As for customers—luckily, I thought—no sign of them.

"Junkies, my ass, Leo..." said the waiter.

"What do you mean?"

"Last night as I was leaving I saw those two, just outside. You know, the guy with the square head and his sidekick, the two who were talking to Arturo. One of them had a bat. They went in and closed the shutters behind them. I hung around for a minute but didn't hear any yelling. Just Arturo saying, 'What the hell are you doing?' and moaning a bit, then stuff being smashed. It must have gone on for about five minutes at the very most. I hightailed it out of there as soon as all the noise died down."

"What do you mean, you left? You didn't even check to see if he was all right? And see what the fuck those two had done?"

"Leo, this is dangerous shit, protection money, loan sharks. Are you joking? If those two thugs had seen me, I'd have gotten my ass beat too. And then what? This is his shit. Next week I'm outta here."

The waiter returned to the dining room without a second glance at Arturo, because failure is contagious, even if you only look at it. I was sorry it had to go this way, but that same evening I told Arturo that the dishwasher wanted to move on, but he had a friend who was willing to take his place, and that I had been offered a position I simply couldn't turn down and I was sorry. When I left, *Kind of Blue* was playing. At least they didn't smash the stereo. And Arturo was saying the exact same words he'd said to me a month earlier to the now former dishwasher, who had just been promoted.

25.

The pace was feverish, as openings always are. You take it on knowing you'll eventually be rewarded, that the momentum you create during those first grueling months will carry over and everything will flow smoothly. But more than that, predictions aside, I really needed to fill up my days with this job. All I wanted was a pass full of outstanding bite-size morsels, a different selection every day, designed for minimum waste but thought through well enough to be replaced effortlessly in case food runs out and intelligently recycled if any's left over.

The grand opening kicked off in high gear, attracting throngs of curious people. None of my hors d'oeuvres were ever left over. Déjà-vu was an ambitious project and the owners' basic premise wasn't a bad one. In fact, the concept couldn't have been simpler: a ritzy place in Rome offering world-class cocktails and superb finger food, served with flair. In other words, your typical Milanese place. The owners were a recently married couple from the boonies, one aluminum step up from trailer trash and with a basically rudderless existence. They'd latched on to some gay fashionistas, and after many nights rubbing shoulders in Rome's nightspots, where they'd learned how to dress and act real cool, they decided to turn their dream into reality.

The entrance to Déjà-vu gave onto a long room. On the left, the bar was a resin counter that rose seamlessly from the floor. On the right, some steel cages, and under the cages, a counter with white barstools. At the back of the room was a marble staircase leading to the cellar for the wine tastings, and a cast-iron spiral staircase led up to the DJ's box in the gallery.

As far as staffing was concerned, the wife sat at the cash register, there was a barman and a barmaid (with extra staff on weekends), a waitress, and myself on the ground floor, the sommelier in the basement, and the DJ in the gallery on Fridays and Saturdays. The husband managed the place, and he and his hideous white shoes were constantly hovering. Closing time? Never.

My workstation was the continuation of the bar counter, the size of a cockpit, and as jam-packed as it was functional. Behind was the oven where I cooked everything from cannelloni to rice pilaf and canapés. I also managed to rustle up a variety of mini bread rolls—with olive oil, sun-dried tomatoes, sesame seeds, and walnuts—using an old fridge that was beyond repair as a proofer; wedged between the functioning fridges, it maintained a constant temperature of 86°, which was perfect. It was brunches and dinners on weekends and finger food and canapés on weekdays. All in all, I could happily feed up to sixty customers.

I was constantly under the gun, but I so desperately wanted to distance myself from the bleak emptiness of the previous months that I said yes to everything and took on more responsibilities by the day. I'd get up at eight in the morning, gulp down a quick coffee, grab the enormous army surplus backpack I'd bought at the backstreet flea market in Via Sannio, jump on my bike, and head for the big outdoor food stalls of the Esquilino market. By now, everyone there knew me. Often I'd send though a preliminary order by SMS the day before. Then I'd get whatever spices I needed. Green pods containing incredibly perfumed cardamom seeds, fresh coriander (sometimes called Asian parsley in Italy, even though the taste is far from the same). Thai ginger, caraway seeds (from the same family as coriander but with elongated seeds and an intense sweetish flavor not unlike that of cumin). Grains of paradise, crunchy pods that come from flowers similar to orchids, also known as Guinea pepper (but this type originating in Ghana); mace, the yellowish netlike sheath covering the nutmeg seed, whose aromatic notes are more fragrant than the fruit itself; Sarawak white peppercorns, resembling the more common Muntok pepper but far superior, obtained by removing the black outer hull and thus less pungent than traditional pepper (piperine—what makes pepper peppery—is found mainly in the hull); pimento or allspice; and herbs including savory, thyme, fenugreek, and marjoram. Advice was always welcome as I checked out unusual herbs and aromas. I was forever sniffing the creases in my palms, where all the essential oils get trapped. My fingers finally started acquiring the unmistakable calluses that are a badge of honor in the kitchen, which I had always envied in real chefs.

I tried to be economical. I shopped at discount stores, using my wits and scraping by, as I always had. I stockpiled all the semiprocessed products I could lay my hands on, which I'd never be able to make myself in that claustrophobic cranny.

Déjà-vu had absolutely no space for storing food, so I had to shop daily. I even enlisted the help of my grandmother, flying in the face of food service regulations by serving her fantastic home-made sardines cured in vinegar on crostini with fennel and orange segments.

At around ten I would arrive in Trastevere, park my bike, shed my backpack bursting with supplies, greet my coworkers, who had been on the job since breakfast, drink my cappuccino, get changed in the small locker room downstairs, and by ten thirty I'd be prepping.

By midday my pass was all lined up and ready to go. I'd continue cooking and adding the finishing touches, which I did with a theatrical flourish, because by this stage I was ready to start my one-man show. Customers would begin to trickle in. There was one guy who came in nearly every day. He dished out compliments and obviously recognized a lot of what I was making. He was an architect whose office was on the same street as ours, and he always wore arty, loose-fitting jackets. One evening, after receiving his usual plate of nibbles to accompany his martini, he handed me a small box.

"What's that?"

"It's a little something for you, Chef. Go on, open it."

Inside was a flattish, oval-shaped metal object with beveled edges.

"I'm sorry, but I don't know what it is. It's beautiful, all shiny..."

"It's a stainless steel soap bar. It will remove the odor of fish or whatever else you handle from your hands. It's called chef soap. And it never wears out."

I was nearly moved to tears. It was the first time a client had ever given me a gift. A gift that would last forever! All my hard work was paying off. That was all I needed to make up for the fact that this was only the end of our second month, there was still no sign of a contract, and our wages were ten days late. Already some of the staff were complaining, and I was one of them. There was nothing unusual about my working side by side with people who, the day before, had been in a completely different line of work and, in all likelihood, would move to something completely different again a few days from now. A small bunch of good-for-nothings who tired easily, had smiles painted on their faces, and submitted meekly to whoever they recognized as the alpha male. All in their first "real" job, and all claiming outstanding if not flawless skills. A mixed bag of bastards of the worst kind. No one cared in the least about anything but their own tiny domain.

As long as they saw my position as being the most secure, with decision-making power and direct access to the owners, they showed me a certain amount of respect, an attitude that I smugly used to my advantage. But when the organizational side of things started to show a few cracks, with wages in arrears and initial signs of my caving in, they started to gang up on me. The only one I had some faith in was Mattia, the head barman. He didn't waste time gossiping and didn't wallow in self-pity. This place is getting risky, he'd say. And the boss should stop wearing those appallingly ugly shoes and doing blow from morning to night, he would also say.

The husband-and-wife team wore worried looks that didn't bode well for the future. You could tell they were teetering on the brink. We could see it and so could the clients. I'd started less than two months ago, but I was there from ten in the morning until almost midnight, without a break. Always cheek by jowl with the two owners. I sincerely tried to find rational solutions to the problems facing the place. To name just one: No more than thirty diners could fit into the venue at once. Our prices naturally had to match what other places were charging, but every day there were five staff members on hand to serve a maximum of sixty covers. It doesn't take a genius, just someone who can count. I tried to avoid the boss as much as possible, with his horrendous shoes and his shyster ways. But I couldn't always dodge him.

"Leo, we were thinking that maybe we should start charging for the nibbles we're serving with the cocktails. And that you should be plating the dishes instead of letting clients serve themselves."

"But...I do plate most things and I only let people serve themselves the easy stuff like the crostini and the finger food. Don't you think it's a bad idea to start changing so soon after our grand opening?"

"That's the point. The clients haven't gotten used to doing things a certain way yet, so we can say it was only an introductory offer...I mean, if you knew you could get free food, only a stone's throw from home, for the price of a drink, wouldn't you be there all the time? We've made it onto the local scene, now we have to make it worth our while. Otherwise the costs will blow out. You understand that, Leo, don't you?"

If the costs were about to blow out after just two months in business, then we were on red alert, we'd sprung a leak, the airlock was out of action, and we were definitely sinking.

"With what I buy, I spend forty euros a day on average. With forty euros I can feed roughly forty people, and adding rice, bread, or cannelloni, I can make it to sixty. In this sort of business, you can't base everything on the two or three freeloaders you're always going to get. The profit is all in the drinks, not the food. At most, we could offer just one plate of free finger food per beverage, so they get food and a drink for eight euros and maybe that way they'll order two."

"No, Leo, this is way beyond a joke. We have to pay the bank massive monthly interest on our loan. I've taken time off work to set up the business, and now it's my only source of income. In the first month we didn't even break even; we actually lost money. If you were my banker, and I owed you more than two hundred thousand euros, and you knew I was giving food away for free, what would you do? Would you be happy about it?"

These were the words I was dreading, the words no employee should ever have to hear. These two had gone into business without a cent to spare. No fucking buffer. And they were already up to their necks in debt. No wiggle room for fixing even the smallest errors. They'd already reached that paranoid stage where they viewed diners as usurpers occupying their space and robbing them of all their hard work. We were well and truly screwed.

"Sure, whatever you say, this is your place. Why don't we go with a choice of two plates of food, one for three and one for five euros?"

"We were thinking more along the lines of five and eight euros, but maybe we can meet in the middle."

We can meet in the middle? Do you hear those bells? Do you know for whom those bells are tolling? This spells the end of your business, is what I wanted to say. I felt kind of sorry for Arturo, getting himself beaten up by his creditors; at least here I hadn't got my hopes up only to come crashing back down to earth.

I shook the boss's flabby hand and screwed my face into a tight smile that masked my true feelings. These are just growing pains, I tried to persuade myself. It's always like this, tough at the beginning, but then things fall into place and it all works out in the end.

One morning the wife was in a gloomier mood than usual. Her husband had gone to try to cancel a check, but it was unlikely he'd succeed, because it was made out to the wine and spirits supplier. Failing to pay so soon after opening would create huge problems for us, I knew this for a fact, and if they demanded immediate payment, then we were up shit creek with no paddle. I knew this for a fact, too: When suppliers are no longer prepared to accept payment at thirty or sixty days, you might as well shut up shop and wave goodbye. Suppliers are quick to recognize when a business is going belly-up, and it's always well before the owners do.

"How much money do you need to cover the check?" I asked.

"Five thousand euros, Leo."

There were two possibilities: If a business doesn't have even that much ready cash, then all you can do is dive into the deep blue sea and swim as fast as you can to avoid being sucked under and swept away by the current. Or else—somehow—scrape together the money and try to survive.

"Have you got any money coming in, Sara?"

"Yeah, Leo, yeah... In a week's time we should be getting our hands on a new loan we've applied for, thirty thousand euros, so we can pay the suppliers, and with the month's takings, we should be able to pay the next installment on our first loan."

"Okay, then I can come up with the five thousand euros. If someone can cover for me in the kitchen, I'll go to the bank, get the cash, and be back here with it in a couple of hours."

What I was aiming to do was not help them as such, but win their trust and gratitude. Save their asses. If the time came for lifeboats, my name was going to be on one of them, and if any-one was going to get the boot, it wouldn't be me. I didn't feel like throwing myself overboard yet, I was not a good swimmer and I wouldn't know where to go anyway. I withdrew the cash and took it to them.

It was the middle of May, I was making €1,500 a month, and none of us had anything even remotely resembling a contract. This week's changes had nothing to do with last week's and did nothing but dishearten the staff, who were already deeply dispirited. The name, Déjà-vu, now seemed heartlessly ironic. By evening, Mattia and I were always buzzed, if not completely hammered. Every damn night. He said we deserved to be. All I knew was that it was getting harder and harder to get up in the morning, and one day I was really running late. Instead of shopping at the outdoor market, I went directly to the discount store. I grabbed an armful of ready-made sauces, breads, and lasagna from the freezer section, and with my backpack starting to drip, I arrived at Déjà-vu just in time for service. In less than half an hour I was ready. I'd had a brilliant idea: a dunking line. Chunks of soft fresh bread for dipping in small bowls of sauce. The best part of a meal is when you mop up all the sauce at the end, right? I'd be offering it at the beginning: carbonara, amatriciana, pesto, and arrabbiata sauces. Some of the discount store sauces were halfway decent, while others, like the pesto, were merely disgusting.

I'd just tied on my apron, tucked a clean side towel over my hip, and placed the last plate on the pass when I saw the architect stroll in, the guy who had given me the gift. Fuck, today of all days! I was about to blurt out that this was a bad day, there had been some problems and... and... I froze. I just couldn't do it. Then the boss lady arrived and started carrying on like she always did.

The architect draped his baggy jacket over a chair and wandered over to say hello. I started filling a plate for him without even asking if he wanted one, which one he wanted, or if he'd even paid for it. I carefully avoided giving him the pesto sauce. He asked me how come there were all these colored bowls and chunks of bread, what brainwave had I come up with today? I told him about the dunking concept, and his face positively lit up.

"Why aren't I getting that one? I love mopping up pesto sauce with bread!"

"Sure, sure thing, here," I said, without batting an eye.

He went and sat down at the counter and I went back to doing what I was doing. After a short while he came back over with his hand outstretched.

"Chef, you have outdone yourself. That pesto sauce is absolutely delicious, you can taste the fresh basil, the pine nuts, and that note of sharpness from the pecorino cheese. I might perhaps have added a touch of garlic, which as you have pointed out to me, is a natural antibiotic. But it's excellent just the way it is, congratulations, superb."

And then he left. Taking with him my last shred of pride and every illusion I'd ever had. I was furious.

My phone rang, the dialing code was 055, Florence. I went out through the glass doors.

"Hello, am I speaking with Leonardo?"

"Yes. Who is this?"

"My name's Orlando, Orlando Fusilli. You don't know me, but my brother, Patrizio, gave me your number. You guys worked together at the Verve. Let me get straight to the point. Are you employed at the moment?"

"Yes, I am. In fact I'm at work right now."

"Would you like me to call back later?"

"No, it's fine, we're quiet at the moment. Tell me, what can I do for you?"

"Look, if you're working, then there's probably nothing much for me to say. I'm a chef in a restaurant just outside Florence. The owners are loaded. The location's fantastic, near Lake Bilancino, with beautiful scenery, mushrooms, fruit trees, everything. If you feel like taking a break from Rome, then it's the perfect spot."

"How long before you need an answer?"

"Probably by tonight, it opens at the beginning of June."

"Damn, I can't make the beginning of June. Even if I wanted to leave, I'd still have to give a month's notice..."

"That's fine, don't worry. If you change your mind, call back this number and ask for me."

End of conversation. And end of the day as far as I was concerned. The place was empty, and even outside there didn't seem to be a lot of people about. Although it was still early, I decided to clean up and close my station. I'll be back at six, I told the boss lady, I need a siesta.

My pay was late and they still had to pony up 1,000 of the €5,000 they owed me. The wife was forever tittering and flapping about, the husband snorted coke all day long and bossed everyone around, and yes, I was pissed off big time. I'd be a good chef only when I learned that a measure of your character is when you manage to steer clear of bad opportunities. And when, a couple of days later, I went out for a drink—actually, quite a few drinks, with two really cute girls who happened to be customers—I started venting. The more I drank, the more I vented.

Next morning I was barely inside the joint when the boss asked me to come downstairs with him, the usual bags under his eyes and as stony-faced as ever. Mightily unhappy, too, it seemed. He didn't mince words and didn't let me get a word in edgewise. He got right to the point: Leonardo, last night you went too far, you poured a bucket load of shit over this place, the place that employs you, and you did it in front of two of our clients.

I tried to reply, but all I could think of was the switch in my brain that had been on stupid for a whole year, leaving no room for a single rational move. He blabbed on, and all that registered was that one of the girls from last night went to school with his wife.

"From this moment onward, you are no longer part of the Déjà-Vu team, Leo. Gather your stuff and get the hell outta here."

I didn't have much to collect, my jacket was in my backpack and my smelly plastic clogs could stay where they were, in the closet. I got up and left.

And that's how it ended.

I walked up the stairs, said so long to Mattia, gave a brief goodbye to the others and an even briefer goodbye to the wife. No mention of my money, my fucking money. I was in the right, but it stung like crazy. I'd wanted to split but didn't know how to without being unfair, and here I was, out. Outside, in fact, just a few steps from the entrance. I checked the calls I'd received and found the only one with the 055 area code. Yes, Orlando still needed me, plus another chef. "I know a guy," I told him, "his name's Michele."

As soon as I got home, I began packing for my job interview in Tuscany. I tried on a shirt, changed my mind, and put on the T-shirt that Valeria had brought me back from Brazil, the one that said NO STRESS, and hoped that the message was clear.

26.

Michel Foucault said that people may know what they do; frequently they know why they do what they do. However, what they don't know is what what they do does. The larvae of certain cicadas live underground for seventeen years before reaching adulthood. Then they die within the space of a single summer. What we recognize as a cicada is only the last, fleeting phase of a very different life. The seeds of many plants remain dormant for even longer periods of time until the right conditions arrive for them to germinate. Trees continue to bear fruit years and years after the people who planted them are six feet under.

A while ago I was reading that you can still pick pears from a tree in Massachusetts that was planted in 1630 by a Puritan. When Henry David Thoreau's books were published, no one read them. At home he had shelves full of his unsold books. Then an Indian lawyer went to work in South Africa, his name was Mohandas Karamchand Gandhi. He discovered Thoreau and read his essays on civil disobedience and became Mahatma Gandhi. Later on, Martin Luther King Jr.'s battles were influenced by both Thoreau and Gandhi, while a young Nelson Mandela was inspired by Thoreau, Gandhi, and King in his struggle against apartheid.

Often, cause and effect are separated by long stretches of time.

Orlando was six foot two and had a mop of wavy hair. Big hands, powerful shoulders and arms, and a sparkle in his eye when he talked. And he talked a lot.

There was nothing in the least unusual about his rise through the culinary ranks. He'd run away from his parents' home in Perugia, attended a cheerless culinary course in Florence at a community college run by the city council, where he made his first contacts in the business, worked his ass off, and ended up in the finest fish restaurant around. He'd gone on to work in catering all over Europe and moved to London, spending six months on a culinary intership with Gianfranco Vissani, where he slept on the floor next to sacks of potatoes between shifts. Now he'd just finished a two-year stint at Boccanegra, a Florentine institution. They'd invited him to become the head chef at this new restaurant attached to an enormous club, newly built, in San Pietro di Sieve, not far from the Barberino di Mugello exit on the Florence–Bologna highway.

When his brother told him, "Leo's good, give him a ring," Orlando called me. He was keen for a change, wanted to earn more money, make a name for himself, and quickly set up a kitchen brigade that was ready to go. He dreamed of opening his own restaurant sooner or later. Long-term project. I signed up because I needed to get away from the kicks in the teeth that Rome had been dishing out to me, and earn some money at least until the end of summer. Short-term project.

With me was Longo Longo. I'd never quite understood what plans he had. Heightwise, I was dwarfed by both Michele and Orlando. I'd never even heard of San Piero a Sieve, a speck on the map, and I knew where Barberino was only because they're always talking about this section of the highway on the radio: It carries more than twice the traffic it was designed for and has one of the highest accident rates in Italy.

The interview was over in a flash. The managing director introduced himself as Giustini, and was always referred to only by his surname. Short and stocky, he was sixty years old and wore a white shirt with the buttons open to his chest, under a leather vest. His eyes were two slits, and he sported a skinny ponytail, his hair slicked back with gel. It transpired that he had managed a number of successful clubs in locations between Florence and Livorno. That was an area I wasn't familiar with, and I'd never been to a club in my entire life. But according to Orlando, there was loads of money floating around. Money is the magic word for short-term plans, long-term plans, and any plans in between.

"Orlando, whaddaya want me to say? I've never even set foot in a kitchen, you're the one who's gotta decide who you want to work with," Giustini had said.

And Orlando had decided. All that remained was to talk to Giustini about the terms and conditions of his hiring us. Once again, no one asked to see a résumé and I was happy to not have to proffer mine, which was hardly worth writing home about. Upshot, an open-ended contract, an official wage of €750 plus €1,050 under the table, for a grand total of €1,800 a month. The business was just starting up. The club could hold up to three thousand people; there was an oversize bar at the entrance (plus two more inside the club) and a restaurant that could seat more than two hundred people. We shook hands. We'd have two weeks to move into lodgings rented for us and paid for by the owners.

We entered the kitchen at San Piero a Sieve on June 3, 2004. I turned on the convection oven of the station I had chosen for myself, the one where the main courses would be prepared.

"First things first, we'll clean some meat and use the bones to make a fond brun," Orlando said.

I nodded obediently, even though I'd never made brown stock from scratch; I'd always used the ready-made version. I did know how to make it, at least in theory.

Orlando started deboning while we cleaned and trimmed. Then he put the bones in the oven at over 460°. When it was time to get the bones out—well browned before going into the stockpot—I looked around, utterly bewildered. I stood on the tips of my toes, searching above, beside, and below the oven, went into the storeroom and rummaged around among some dish towels. I didn't want to have to ask—I am a fucking chef, after all, I can work things out for myself. But I was stumped, so I approached Orlando.

"Excuse me, but where are the oven mitts?"

"The what?" he asked, with a deliberately puzzled expression on his face.

"The oven mitts, to get the trays out of the oven, I can't find them…"

"Excuse me, but what exactly do you have hanging from your apron?"

"What, you mean this cloth?"

"First of all, it's called a torchon, Leo, or maybe a side towel, and second, I have never heard of a chef looking for oven mitts in a kitchen, ever. I swear, this is the first time."

He removed his side towel, folded it in two, and used it to take the tray out of the oven. I looked at Michele, and then at the hot tray on the stainless steel counter. Well, this was the first clear sign that Longo Longo and I were two first-rate dickheads. And that I had no place acting like a smart-ass.

Luckily, we had Pietro at the stove with us. Besides being a dickhead himself, he was a hypochondriac and way too old to be starting a career as a chef. He had to be, give or take a year, at least fifteen years older than me. A native of Rome, he looked lost and his hands shook. He was forty, which was a heavy burden to be carrying at this stage of his new calling as a chef. He painstakingly, albeit sometimes argumentatively, followed every little rule, was overly cautious, kindhearted, and entirely ineffectual. Michele was the same as he had been at the Verve—wordlessly going about his business, weary in his own distinctive way, biologically out of sync. My strange and sensitive buddy, my kitchen- and roommate, and the only person I could share secrets with. At the sink, washing dishes, was an Albanian grunt. The cleaners were two Russian girls with eyes the color of Lake Bilancino. Both extremely young, but they had lived far beyond their years and had a child each. The maître d', also around forty, had the face of someone who had gone a few rounds with Lady Luck and come out the worse for wear. He was Calabrian and had mentioned a wife and son in Argentina. It was clear that he and Orlando didn't get along. Maybe it had to do with their age and the pressure to be top dog. Orlando spoke down to him, and the maître d' didn't like it.

The big bar at the entrance had a manager, and so did the bars in the club, with an assortment of girls working shifts and a crowd of other staff I never had time to talk to.

It was just me, my knives, and my blacks—which Orlando found objectionable—facing a mountain of meat I had absolutely no idea how to handle. I had never seen anything remotely like it: entire quarters of cows, dozens of rabbits, fresh truffles, crates of porcini mushrooms, exotic fruit, bags and bags of different flours, and all sorts of dairy products. At the Verve I was in charge of the broiler, a big one, but the steaks came already butchered and the skewers already assembled and needing only to be defrosted. I realized that my notion of a "skilled" and "capable" chef was a far cry from what it meant in the real world, and that all I knew were the basics. I wondered whether Orlando, the pompous chef, might be a little to blame for my incompetence suddenly becoming so evident. His condescension was seasoned with a large pinch of disdain.

The best times were when Michele and I got home at night. Our apartment was a stone's throw from the off-ramp of the highway. On the same floor as us lived a Romanian hooker working in Italy to pay for her daughter's schooling back home, where she had left her with the grandparents. And also to buy a home and a little store in Romania. "Life isn't so bad," she said, "and I don't have anyone making decisions for me. I'm happy." She actually seemed happier than we were.

Michele didn't mind us getting chewed out in the kitchen, it didn't bother him the way it did me. Yes, he was tired of it, but he didn't feel like he had his back to the wall. He said Orlando reminded him of his father, and he was used to that kind of crap.

"All we have to do is memorize the menu, Leo."

"It's not a question of memory, it's all about technique."

Maybe Michele was just better than me, or maybe his short-lived and menial role in a serious restaurant with its high-class menu was standing him in good stead and highlighting the gap between our two careers. My résumé listed only five places, two of which were to be avoided at all costs, and one that in all likelihood had shut down. Either his approach to this place was wide of the mark, or he had some aces up his sleeve that I was unaware of, but I was embarrassingly inadequate. Can you think of anything more pathetic than a guy who's always comparing himself to his coworkers to gauge his own worth, and gets a kick out of knowing there is at least one person sorrier than he is? No, neither can I. Luckily there was Pietro; otherwise I would have quit on my fourth day.

So far no one had called my bluff, and I had always blatantly bluffed. I arrived like a big shot joining a team of rookies. But here was this twenty-six-year-old with major balls, who's handed me half a cow and wants me to turn it into Bistecca alla Fiorentina — Steak Florentine — cooked to perfection. This was putting your cards on the table, and you needed a winning hand. No bluffing. Not only had I never butchered a cow, I'd never cooked a "Bistecca" in my entire life. I'd never even eaten one. In the kitchens I'd worked in, you grabbed trays from the oven with oven mitts, because that's what you did at home. And logic would suggest that in a bigger kitchen, you would just use bigger mitts. Here, either you knew how to do things or you didn't. And when it became painfully obvious that I didn't, Orlando put me under the gun. No damn bluffing.

While I was sweating bullets, up to my armpits in poultry and boar, Michele was daintily designing patterns on plates with sauces. When it was my turn to decorate the dishes, my red and yellow reductions looked like a snail trail, and I was scared. Scared I wasn't up to the task. Scared shitless. Even my hands started to shake like Pietro's when it came to plating, especially under Orlando's icy stare. Shuddering, it felt like I was the only one Orlando was bawling out, ignoring Pietro because he was useless and Michele because he was smart. He kept saying we were bone fucking lazy, and that the real work was yet to start, but in the meantime we were serving thirty, forty people, nearly all of whom were friends, or friends of friends, of the owners, with everyone ordering different dishes with different cooking times, wanting to put the kitchen to the test, and deliberately making life difficult for us.

"C'mon, Leo, isn't it ready yet?!" That damn scream of Orlando's amplified my lack of ability at every service. Without pausing to breathe, my answer was invariably, "Right, Chef, three minutes and it's on the pass." And that was inevitably three minutes too late, because Orlando would rush over, rearrange the orders on the pass, grab the tongs out of my hands, turn the meat, turn up the gas under a pan, tweak the sauce, and plate.

27.

Something gets me thinking about the kitchen and its occupants, and how it's just not possible that all of a sudden I've become the only misfit. It's not an altogether unfamiliar sensation, though. When I started working at Sessanta, my first restaurant, I genuinely believed that I needed the job only to pay for a shrink. The paranoia eventually tapered off, and those first paychecks went toward the rent and books instead. Hard work was my medicine. Nothing new there. My grandma used to say that during the war, people were too hungry to be depressed. But this time hard work wasn't doing it for me, and I needed some new wonder drug to allay my obsessions.

Through the wall I shared with the apartment next door, I could hear the groans of the latest in a steady flow of truck drivers. This one was Speedy Gonzales. I used to have fun calculating how long the johns would last with the Romanian hooker: It was rarely more than ten minutes. Then they'd go and catch some shut-eye in their cabs parked below.

I was on my own because Michele had gone back to Rome and I'd needed to stay this week. The arrangement with Giustini was that we'd be open from Wednesday through Sunday, with two whole days off a week. Piece of cake, if you think about it. So I was all alone, trying to unscramble causes and effects, and the myriad experiences that had led me to this room. I was the Cincinnati Kid facing off Lancey Howard's queen-high straight flush. With a bad beat of three aces. A smart gambler never changes his bets and never leaves the table on a losing streak. If he loses everything, it just means he's not as smart as he thought he was. Of course, the temptation to hightail it to

Rome and hole up somewhere was powerful. But I had to keep going. There was no other option, friends couldn't help, I just had to become better, and not simply by memorizing the menu. I wouldn't go down without a fight.

"Do you mind if I spend the next couple of days sorting a few things out in the kitchen while we're closed?" I mulled over the question before texting it to Orlando, then I hit Send and turned off the light. As I was about to fall asleep, my cell pinged.

"Okay, whatever. I'll let you in. But only tomorrow. I'm away Tuesday, and the day after all hell breaks loose."

Monday morning I made sure I was standing at the back door that led directly to the kitchen. Orlando arrived right on time, said hello, and went into the office to write up the weekly orders.

So far the restaurant hadn't been under too much pressure (although to me it felt like a grueling obstacle course), but the club was opening now and the celebrations included dinner for a bunch of special guests. It was time to rock and roll. You could tell that Orlando was fretting. He'd quarreled with just about everyone, starting with the maître d' and his beaten-up face. Stupid squabbles that could easily have been avoided, about the salad for staff meals using the end slices of the tomatoes, the sequence that the orders arrived in, what to do with leftover unfinished bottles of mineral water, and which wine to use for cooking.

Even the head chef had started showing some chinks in his armor, flaring up more often than usual over minor hiccups. He must be a tad paranoid too. And Pietro kept firing off questions and getting in the way. Michele was the only one who remained as cool as a cucumber. Way too cool, in fact, which left me wondering how long he'd get away with being so aloof. Maybe he didn't realize it, I thought, or maybe he felt that he was all set.

Admittedly, his freshly made pasta, his ricotta gnudi, his stylishly smeared sauces were in a league of their own, leaving us eating his dust. A commercial kitchen, like any finely tuned machine, can function only when all of its cogs move in unison, and when one cog starts going it alone, and in slow motion, to boot, it is a bad, bad thing. You can't work in isolation. Michele could no longer be my go-to person, not the way he'd been at the Verve.

I tied my apron around my waist, grabbed a clean side towel and folded it over the string at my hip, and got down to work. Starting with the mise en place.

Orlando had been on my back for days, moving my things around and bellowing when anything was out of place at my station. I could do the mise en place with my eyes closed; it was an extension of my nervous system. I had it down pat, or so I thought, because by the end of every service I was a filthy, disorganized mess, rummaging through the fridges, groping for stuff, like a blind man without a guide dog or a white stick, in need of a familiar landmark or a helping hand.

Deep breath. I cleared everything away and picked up the menu. First I wrote a list of ingredients — the ones I needed and the ones I might need. A few kitchen tools, knives, cloths, a lighter, a scourer, and some containers for scraps and food. I glanced at Orlando's station. When he was on duty it looked like an operating room. Nothing out of place, it was his temple, his religion. And don't even think of touching anything. Number one, because it's unnecessary, and number two, because you touch something at another chef's station — especially the head chef's — only if you've been repeatedly asked to do so.

So here we go: fine and coarse sea salt, Maldon crystal salt for the steaks, guesstimating the amount I'll need for service, plus a little extra. Whole black and green peppercorns, pink pepper berries, ground pepper. A large container for salt and pepper mixed together in the exact ratio. Butter cut into cubes, all the same size and placed in a gastronorm, ready for prepping and softened by the time service starts. Enough big sheets of absorbent paper under the fryer. Curls of tomato skin for frying as garnishes. Lava rock char broiler all set up. Day-old bread sliced thinly on the slicing machine for pressing into muffin tins and turning into crunchy bread cups. Layers of grated Parmesan cheese on Silpat baking mats to be melted in the microwave and laid over wafer-thin broiled beef "rags." Preparations stashed in the fridge in the correct order: first, containers of chopped parsley; followed by leafy aromatics prepared daily and immersed in iced water; tomato sauce, plain and seasoned; caramelized apples; shallots braised in butter; peeled garlic cloves; baby sage leaves on layers of damp kitchen towels; and roasted garlic pureed with oil in the food processor. Everything I'd need, and every spare cranny filled with empty containers to fill as required. Sauces, precooked brunoise-cut vegetables, bases. Clean cloths stacked in a neat pile for my sole use during service, kept in what I decide will be their secret hiding place because clean cloths are a precious resource. I open the sliding doors of the cupboard above my head and arrange its contents from left to right. First the coarse breadcrumbs, then the fine, the olive oil delivered straight from the press for the carpaccio; an oil and red wine vinegar mixture; white wine behind the red; juniper berries; apple cider vinegar; dried capers; ruby paprika for decoration; brandy, balsamic, and Lambrusco reductions; dried habanero chilies; a sheaf of white paper for orders and prep lists; a caddy full of pens that all write; and an empty tin for my tobacco and papers.

On the workbench I sort out my favorite ladles and lay them out beside the long grilling tongs and the spaghetti tongs. Two small copper pans for sauces (copper is a better conductor of heat than any other metal, and it heats everything more quickly and evenly). Small stainless steel trays for resting grilled meat in the oven and locking in the juices. Spoons of two different lengths, a meat fork, stainless steel spatulas for the grill, and a cleaning brush. A thick-bottomed stainless steel braising pot to keep at my station, and an assortment of aluminum pans (aluminum being almost as good as copper for conducting heat).

From the pot cupboard I select a cast-iron casserole pan and place it on the shelf under my grill. From now on that will be its home. The casserole pan, unlike other cook pots and pans, has to be made of a material that is a low conductor of heat, to maintain a barrier between the exterior—in an oven or on a cooktop—and the interior at approximately 212° Fahrenheit, the temperature at which water slowly comes to the boil. There are two in the kitchen. I take the one with the heavier lid for myself; it will stay perfectly sealed during cooking.

Then I enter the walk-in where the meat is hanging. I trim the cuts, removing only the darkest bits, and arrange the fillets from the oldest to the freshest, wrapping them in a clean cloth—carefully choosing only the ones that don't smell of fabric softener (there's nothing worse than meat that smells of Marseille soap)—and wiping them thoroughly.

Leaving the walk-in, I sharpen my knives one at a time. A dull blade is the biggest humiliation for a chef.

Does an orderly kitchen make for an orderly life? Yes, it certainly does, both while you're cooking and when you knock off at the end of service. I shut my eyes and feel where everything is, and move a few containers around, making it easier for me to reach the ones at the back. Then I do it again, and again, until every piece is within easy reach. In my defense, I don't want to waste time thinking or looking for things. I'm fanatical about my mise en place, which is strictly off-limits to everyone, including Orlando.

Then I roll myself a joint and go outside to smoke it in the garden behind the kitchen. Back inside, I take out my cell phone, set up the stopwatch, and grab a chicken from the walk-in. I start the timer on the phone and insert my knife into the flesh, running the blade between muscle, ligament, cartilage, and bone. I try to visualize the bird's anatomy so as to prise it open without tearing the meat, damaging the skin, or leaving any good bits on the bones. At the end, staring back at me, is a chicken that seems to have been mauled by a hungry half-crazed lion, and a time of eighteen minutes, twenty-seven seconds, and forty-three hundredths of a second.

I wrap the mangled bird carefully in cling film and start on the second one. Then the third. At this point Orlando comes in to tell me it's time to go and I'd better clear up the kitchen. His gaze turns to the knife smeared in chicken fat and the bird splayed out on the cutting board.

"What the fuck are you doing?"

"I'm getting ahead with my work, I'm preparing the chickens for Wednesday..."

"Have you lost your mind? First of all, the chickens are for Thursday, and second, do you know what happens to chicken meat if you debone it now?"

"But...I'm putting it straight in the fridge, it's all sealed..."

"Sealed, my ass, Leo. After you take meat off the bone, it gets exposed to air, at room temperature, and the heat from your hands, and in the meantime bacteria start multiplying. By the time Thursday swings around, all you'll have left is a fucking old chicken. I told you yesterday: Only remove the giblets. Otherwise I would have got you to stay on and clean them all. I'm not afraid to, you know. There are three of you in here working full time and doing half the work of a very middling chef. I'd have no qualms at all about telling you to stay behind to do more. If I didn't, it's simply because it's a bad idea. Put that poor thing away this minute, you dickhead. You told me you wanted to set things up, not start prepping!"

I head back to the apartment overlooking the exit ramp on foot. Maybe I need a Moleskine notebook to write down all the things I still don't know. Just as I enter a stationer's, I get a text message, which I expected would be from Orlando, but it wasn't.

"Howzit goin', Leo?"

Shit. It's Matteo.

"Real tough, only going to get worse."

"Women?"

"Nope. You?"

"Maddalena might move into our place. With me. What do you think?"

"Better chained to a kitchen than a chick. Cheers."

28.

I lost track of time as the days flew by. From time to time we'd chill out and fool around, of course. We listened to music from a whacked-out radio that had seen better days. Orlando let me wear my black uniform; at least he stopped giving me a hard time over that. I gradually got my mojo back and felt more in control.

My orders were getting picked up and taken to the dining room quickly; now the one lagging behind was Michele. I did not help him. I'd put my dishes on the pass and complain loudly when his weren't ready—there was no way my Steak Tagliata was going to dry out while the fucking pasta was still being tossed around in the pan! I was ready and didn't mind everyone knowing it. Later on I'd realize how wrong I was. That for a machine to run smoothly, the cogs have to mesh together perfectly, and if one is running slower, then the faster one is going to have problems too.

Pietro chatted nervously as he went about his business, dripping with sweat, his hands always shaking, and when he plated I had to wipe beads of perspiration from the edges with a clean cloth.

I laid a chicken on its side, tossed the carcass into the food scrap bucket, and pressed the timer on my cell phone with my greasy hands: eight minutes, six seconds, and seventy-four hundredths of a second.

Now I could bring my CD player into the kitchen and listen to Amália Rodrigues, while Orlando preferred the Italian singer-songwriter Fabrizio De André. Our respective roles became more sharply defined, day after day, hour after hour.

Michele was still trailing behind. As I gained ground, he lost it. Longo was happy to be the straight man, the sidekick, the unwitting tension breaker. I was the jester, the king-size fool. Orlando was the chief, the brains and the hands of the operation, whereas Pietro was meek, mild, and modest in every way, yet he managed to keep Michele and me on an even keel, easing tensions before I lashed out against my old head chef.

In an average life, extraordinary events, positive or negative, are rare and usually involve extraordinary people. We who are not extraordinary tend to believe that any old garbage that happens to us is extraordinary. And if people aren't interested in our fantastic stories, we feel cheated, which makes us competitive and mean. Orlando's rivalry was catching. Day after day I soaked up his arrogance, along with his speed and stubbornness.

I watched his every move, and even though it pissed me off, I had to admit that, yes, he really was extraordinary, but while he didn't need to be so aggressive, I did. And I became more and more of a bully. Especially toward Pietro. His relentless blabbering drove me nuts, his clumsiness, his miserable outlook on life, his guileless expression, and his foul-smelling armpits. We were both losers learning a trade we had fallen into more by chance than by choice. Only he was a forty-year-old loser.

"I'm free, Leo, can I give you a hand?"

I was juggling ten orders including a roast still in the oven that was taking longer than usual, and Pietro kept bugging me, asking if he could help. Not just once, at least a dozen times.

"Leo, I'm here if you need me, just tell me what I can do for you..."

He couldn't do anything for me. Nothing at all. I was in the trenches returning fire, engaging the enemy, shot after shot.

Mentally ticking off cooking times actually fired me up, pumped blood to my brain. I was in my element.

"Leo, do you want me to keep an eye on the meat? I think it's time to turn it..."

Do not touch that damn meat. I know when it's time to turn it. If he so much as touches that meat, I swear, he'll end up with a knife between his shoulder blades.

"Leo, c'mon, don't be afraid to ask, if there's anything I can do for you, anything at all..."

I stopped in my tracks and looked at him, his uniform sticking to his damp skin, burns all over his hands, two gigantic stains on his apron, three different cloths hanging from his belt, a tray in one hand and a pot in the other. I turned on a great big smile.

"Hey, Pietro, you know, my balls have been itching for the last ten minutes but I can't scratch them 'cause my hands are full. If you want, you could give my nuts a real going over, it'd be such a relief."

Pietro's eyeballs nearly popped out of his head. I turned around to place orders on the pass and call the maître d'—"Go with number 5! One minute for 14 and I'll get it out!"—to find Orlando shrieking with laughter, and not even Michele could keep the grin off his face, however hard he tried.

"No, I won't put up with that. Not that. Not from a fucking twenty-year-old, no, that's just too much."

I heard some grumbling but didn't pay him any attention. Service came to an end and I dumped the last plate on the pass, then I drew a black line through the last order slip. That's it. I'm done. I spiked it on the docket spindle and stretched my neck and back until I felt them cracking. Once the kitchen was cleaned up, I realized that Pietro had already left. He'd scrubbed down the dessert station and disappeared without a word. His letter of resignation arrived in the mail, and we never saw hide nor hair of him again.

July was nearly over in San Piero a Sieve, the girls stripped down to sunbathe on the pebbly lakefront beach, sometimes to their bikini bottoms. The weather was warm, the dining room fairly full...and something snapped. If you leave meat in the fridge too long it will eventually rot, and so will relationships if you don't nurture them. Precarious at the best of times, the delicate balance between Michele and me disintegrated. I was an asshole, therefore I was becoming a better chef.

Michele was struggling to endure life in this godforsaken village. The more Orlando and I mingled with the coke dealers in the club, ending every damn night drinking booze and playing poker in the empty bar, the more withdrawn and melancholy he became. We started playing cards into the early morning hours, with the exception of Saturdays and Sundays. On weekends the club stayed open until dawn, with thousands of kids inside, and us, the staff, reigning supreme. No part of the venue was off-limits to any of the staff: The cooks could go into the private club room just off the dance floor, and behind the bar, and the bartenders could come into the kitchen for snacks or to heat up coke in the microwave. We'd all end up in the huge cocktail bar, which was closed on weekends, to catch our breath before throwing ourselves back into the club mix. But not Michele, who was generally asleep by the time we came clattering and crashing back home at seven in the morning.

I continued timing how long it took me to debone a rabbit, and I was getting faster; there was dried blood under my nails and bits of meat stuck to the cuticles. I discovered that calves have the same dislocated shoulder joints as rabbits and that a boar's ligaments are damned tough. By now I could debone a chicken with my eyes closed. Beef carcasses still posed a few problems, but I was learning how to deal with them too.

My personal best for skinning a whole rabbit was four minutes and forty-seven seconds, without so much as a tear in the back skin. If you don't know what I'm talking about and you don't understand how difficult it is, just try deboning a rabbit yourself. It's extremely tricky—the skin is thin and with very little fat.

When I started out I didn't even know how to grill a tagliata properly. Now I was placing and checking orders to suppliers together with Orlando, putting the screws on Michele during service so our dishes came out together, and taking care of tour bus menus. Eventually I left Michele behind. Worse than that, I'd thrown him off a moving train, as if there wasn't room for the two of us and that was reason enough to demolish him. After a month and a half, there was no fucking doubt: I was the chef supremo, the smartest, slickest, sharpest chef there had ever been, and I had Michele in the crosshairs.

The best medicine to treat a bad case of exhaustion and paranoia is egotism. I snorted coke until I was blue in the face, smoked more and more pot, and wrecked my four-cylinder Suzuki when I swerved off the road halfway between the restaurant and home. Three weeks after buying it secondhand for €2,000, but I didn't give a shit. I took it to a repair shop in San Piero a Sieve. "Fix it," I told the mechanic without another word. I was earning more than I could spend and hadn't hurt myself, although I'd lost a shoe down the escarpment. Leaving the club, I'd taken the second curve way too fast, lost control, smashed into a tree, then rolled fifteen, twenty feet down the slope, hitting the only boulder for miles around. I was so pissed off and so stoned that I turned the ignition back on and dragged the bike up to the road, pushing the handlebars as I put it into first gear, minus one shoe and with prickly twigs sticking to my sock. Exactly one week later, right where it happened, construction started on an outlet mall—Europe's biggest, according to Orlando—and they cut down the tree and removed the boulder, leaving in their place a mound of soft, upturned soil. For some reason, the irony of it all put me in a good mood.

29.

My approach to food began to change, the forces of randomness no longer dictated whether my dishes were a hit or a miss, and I liberated my food from the shackles of recipes.

It's like when you move to a new city and you progress from having to check the street directory all the time, to learning a few familiar routes, to having the whole city mapped out in your head and coming up with clever shortcuts or choosing scenic routes. I learned from what was happening at my station and from Orlando's unrelenting stream of explanations. Food's mysteries unfolded before my eyes like coils of collagen molecules in the connective tissue of muscle that heating at a constant temperature transforms from a tough, stringy mass into soft, pliable gelatin. Leftovers? Not scraps, but rather interesting elements to repurpose and recombine, combinations to tease apart and reunite; I learned all manner of devilry for transmuting random bits and pieces into dishes of unimaginable perfection.

Techniques, temperatures, and the most effective ratios between fat and protein were all entered meticulously into my Moleskine notebook. Unexpectedly, a bond began forming between Orlando and me. But not between Orlando and Michele. It was Michele's turn to be the dickhead. And Orlando decided that the maître d' was the bad guy.

Before long cracks began to appear. Not in terms of numbers but in terms of quality. Orlando's creative streak was at odds with the reality of this place: We were filling the bellies of a pack of kids whose only interest was to ogle the asses of the pole dancers, drink themselves into oblivion, and boast about whom they'd screwed. Every now and again I'd get to work late. Summer was nearly over and I was a cocky Mohammed Ali dancing around George Foreman before knocking him out, hammerfists low and smelling blood.

The maître d' and Orlando had declared open war on each other, and it all seemed so utterly pointless that I'd often stop for a chat with the maître d' and listen to yarns about his adventurous past, and sympathize when he let off steam. I was vying with Orlando to be the top dog, not openly, but it was pretty obvious. I took certain liberties without asking and dissed him in front of the others.

It's nine o'clock on the dot. I should be in the kitchen, but Veronica has just drawn a towel across her breasts and seems fairly willing to remove it, together with everything else, if we retire to a room somewhere. The sound of waves gently rippling over the lake and the warmth of the pebbly beach are far more tempting than a room, let alone a kitchen. But I leave her my cell phone number, hop on my bike, and get to the restaurant at ten past nine. Michele's in the locker room getting changed, and Orlando is at my workstation peeling apples for the sauce to go with the pork.

When you get to work and find the head chef at your workstation, the message is crystal clear. No one responds to my hello. I get changed. Fuck it, I say to myself—my line is all in order, in two hours tops I'll have everything ready. As I open the cold room, I start telling Orlando about Veronica. In my mind I'm dancing around in my boxing boots, delivering swift, low jabs—I'm invulnerable.

"It's a quarter past nine. Do this one more time and I'll have you sent a warning letter. Three strikes you're out, and you'll be going back to Rome."

"What the fuck are you talking about? We don't have any bookings for tonight, it's Thursday. We're nearly ready for the group coming in tomorrow, you know everything will be ready for service, as usual..."

"I don't give a shit. And I have already told you that I don't like that black uniform. You're the only one dressed in black; what's that supposed to mean anyway?"

"But...you told me I could wear it, why the hell are you bringing it up now?"

"Follow the rules and you can wear the uniform. The first rule is be on time."

I get hustling and make up for lost time to be ready for service ahead of schedule and prove to the prick that his dressing-downs are a waste of time. Hop, hippity hop, I'm dancing around, raising my guard a little, really dancing. But it's useless, because there he is, breathing down my neck at every turn, worse than before, crossing every *t* and dotting every *i*, grabbing things out of my hands, making it difficult for me on purpose. I hate his arrogance, his ingratitude, his stupidity. I wish I could gouge his eyes out and piss in his skull because I have earned this sliver of freedom. I am his backbone in here, his fingers, his nails, and even his eyes, I'm the only one who can see what's going on between the kitchen and the dining room. How the fuck dare he treat me like that?

As he reaches over for a pan at my workstation, I lunge and grasp it before he does, then I throw it against the wall and glare at him menacingly. A solid high guard. I'm just waiting for him to react, and then I'll really thrash him. I am going to take him down. His face turns crimson, then he blanches, and just as he inhales deeply, the maître d' comes in with the first order.

"A house antipasto for two, followed by one ricotta ravioli and one tagliatelle, then a Steak Florentine to share."

Static's swirling through the air and he stares at us, expecting the kitchen to blow up and shatter Orlando's hubris. If he had a bag of popcorn, he'd be sitting back enjoying the show. A couple of seconds pass, maybe three, and he ups and leaves, otherwise people will catch on.

Orlando stops in his tracks, and so do I. Service has started. You can't argue during service, not ever, no matter what. That's a given.

Lunch is strange today. It seems that every truck driver on the highway has decided to stop here and order my steak. Wordlessly, I cut the meat, toss it on the grill, raise and lower the flame, then slide it into the oven, slice, garnish, plate, and call for the waiter.

Every now and again I shout, "Yes, Chef," "It's on the pass, Chef," "One more minute, Chef," "I'm doing the next four, Chef." Chef, that's what I call him. To put some distance between us. It's also a position that, no matter what, I do not question.

Then Orlando goes to the pass, puts down a Crema Catalana with strawberries, removes a pen from his sleeve pocket, draws a diagonal line across the docket, and says, "Last table, service over, kitchen closed." Then he turns toward me. I place my knife on the red cutting board, parallel to the short side, and take off my apron.

"Shall we step outside?"

We take long strides to get as far away as possible from the building, in silence, to the far end of the garden.

"What the fuck do you think you're doing? Are you challenging me?"

"You're the one who's picking on me for no reason at all."

"The fuck I am. You've been getting my goat. Every single day. The way you clown around and give lip all the time. Do you think learning how to butcher a cow and debone a quail gives you the right to do as you fucking well please? We are working here, not playing around. I can put up with pretty much anything, but I won't tolerate you jerking around."

"Who? Me? Jerking around? But my mise is always perfect."

"You think your mise is perfect because I let you get away with it like that. Do you know how many things I let you get away with every day? How many things you should be doing better? Do you think you have the right to roll in late just because there's less work? I don't give a shit if you are a junkie, a pervert, a whore, a psycho, a drunken thug, or a social misfit. Just never lie to me. I need to be able to trust you. Are you prepared to begin service on time? Not a minute before or a minute after, or when you've had a rest, or when you're feeling better, or because there isn't much happening today. On time. Every day. Can I rest assured that tomorrow you'll be here on time and you won't leave me screwed six ways to Sunday? If you can, then we can make beautiful food together. But you slip one more time, and I'll kick your teeth in and send you away. We have to be unassailable in the kitchen, it's the only way to command respect."

"But you're on my back all the fucking time—explain that."

"Why do I give you a harder time than Michele? Because kitchen staff fall into three categories. The self-styled artists, who want people to call them 'Maestro' and do all that molecular shit, the mad scientists who charge millions and get away with murder. That's not us. And then the poor schmucks who end up in the kitchen because they don't know what else to do. They learn to cook because they have to, otherwise they'll fall to pieces. It's what they do to escape from some failure or another. Like Pietro, who couldn't hack it here and won't hack it anywhere else either. Or Michele, who doesn't have the cojones to run a poker game let alone a dog and pony show like this, and crashed before the first month was up. I'd never hire him again. Then you have the mercenaries, the loners who only do it for the money but are on top of their game. Bright, fast learners, able to think on their feet. They've got a gift for cooking and manage to have other interests on the side as well. The only reason they hang out in a place like this is that they're well paid. That's you. And it's me too. But if you lose face, you're a worthless piece of shit. So you can do as you please, take photos, shoot up, screw around, but do not lie to me and do not try to fuck me over. I'd rather have a keen worker bee with no talent than a fucking artist with no backbone. You're either born with guts or you're not—nobody can teach you. This is not a post office, it's a kitchen. It is a privilege to work in one. If a waiter doesn't turn up for work, we can still get by, but if there's no chef, the restaurant might as well close down."

I back down. I get it. Orlando wants me to be like him, he wants me to put the kitchen first while we are both working in it, the way he does. There is no other way. It's either black or white, you are either in or out, right or wrong. No room for interpretation. When we both stopped talking, it was out of respect for the service, and in that precise moment we were speaking the same language, following the same rules, playing the same game. Interrupting the argument because the first order coming through means that work and success are our top priorities. "Respect" is the magic word. Total commitment entitles us to do as we please, but not a minute before closing time. Simple. It's all about doing the right thing.

I start turning up for work a quarter of an hour early so I don't have to rush and I can be in my black jacket with a knife in my hand and the cutting board on the pass five minutes before service. I tell Orlando of my comings and goings, without fail. He knows when I'm back in Rome, when I sleep over at Thiene, if there's a girl with me or if I'm by myself.

I used to admire Orlando, but now I am his faithful follower. I cling to my chef, my knives, and everything else in this cramped, sweltering space like the acrobat clings to the trapeze in Kafka's short story.

30.

I was sitting on the stainless steel counter of the pass, in darkness, the only light coming from the emergency exit sign. I was wearing my low-rise Levi's, NO STRESS T-shirt, and Adidas sports shoes. Orlando was with me, and he was still pissed off at the maître d' over their latest ludicrous spat. I told him that toning it down a bit might be a good idea, especially for himself. He was leaning against the door leading into the dining room. From the club came the muffled thump of the bass beat and the strains of the summer hit "San Salvador": "hear the voices ringing, people singing. San Salvador, now the festival is just beginning." We were knocking back mojitos and waiting for Gabriel to wander over from the bar with a couple lines of coke. Yesterday we gave him our share of the money — he was the kitchen staff's official dealer.

Gabriel was tall and black, and he cracked jokes in a thick Florentine accent. He had two small children and a very patient wife. The previous week he'd wrecked his Beemer. Said that someone cut him off and then sped away. Saturdays he would head off to Florence completely tanked, and only a line of blow would sober him up long enough to drive back home. He probably came to with the air bag in his face and no idea what the fuck had happened.

He boasted about the women he picked up and the blow jobs he scored in the private club room. He was a good-looking guy, to say the least, and he was a masterful juggler of bottles and shakers behind the bar. Women liked that sort of thing. They liked the ones who strutted center stage and stole the spotlight.

His real name was Gabriele, but everyone called him Gabriel, without the final *e*, and he was fine with that.

"It's good shit. A bit scant, but good," Orlando said.

We moseyed down to the club. It was packed but not to the rafters. There should have been a much larger turnout according to the estimates of the three hotshot owners. "They spent a cool million," Orlando told us. But the bar was swamped. I didn't like the crush, so I ducked behind the counter. Orlando followed and started mixing cocktails next to Monica. I took four swigs of ice-cold beer and felt reborn.

"Why aren't you guys dancing?" Monica asked. So we did. Orlando climbed onto the bar. "Saaaan Salvador!" And I climbed up too. Off came my T-shirt. I'd lost some weight and looked damn hot. "Saaaaaan Salvador!" No one told us to get off—we were the lords and masters of the venue. The restaurant manager was Orlando, and the bar manager was our dealer.

I felt someone tugging at my belt. It was Gabriel mouthing something and pointing upstairs. I bent down and put my ear to his lips.

"Fill in for me at the bar for five minutes, will you? I have to go upstairs, Giustini wants me in his office!"

I scrambled down from the bar, put my sweaty T-shirt back on, and started haphazardly mixing cocktails. Gabriel supplied everyone in here with drugs, from the dishwasher to the managing director. Two jobs and twice the benefits, more money and a rock-solid day job.

The dance floor was packed and slutty hostesses worked the room. People were thronging to the bar, waving money around, Orlando was still dancing at the far end of the counter, the boys looking at us with a mixture of scorn and admiration, the girls with curiosity.

I felt my jaw clench and broke out in a sweat. The expressions on the dancers' faces were scary. You'd find more sanity in a mental hospital or a mortuary. Except that here the strobe lights messed with your head. Some of the girls, however, were luscious.

"What the fuck do you mean by luscious, Leo?"

"Great tits and world-class booty!"

"You are such a lowbrow!"

"Well, I'll leave all the highbrow ones to you."

The crowd was jiving and the music was crap. I felt a notch above them all. I weaved my way over to Orlando, and he bent down and roared, "Don't you feel a notch above them, Leo? Above them all!"

I left the bar with another mojito—the alcohol seemed to be winning against the coke, and my head was spinning. Kids were roaming around like the morons they were, coming here to spend money while the only reason I was here was that I worked here. I was earning a living in this place, and I could shit all over those clowns. Someone came up behind me and covered my eyes with soft, small hands that smelled of soap and beer.

It was Anna. Last week she'd hung out at our place to work off a hangover and do a couple of lines with some friends of hers. Strangers hanging out with other strangers, doing things nobody found at all strange. The others had left and she'd stayed behind with me.

"How about going back to your place?" she asked.

"Not just yet, there's something I have to do with Orlando first."

"Can I do it too? With both of you?"

"No, it's not what you think, tonight we two boys are behaving."

"But have you seen yourself in the mirror?"

She kissed me on the mouth and left with her girlfriend, who'd been waiting nearby. I surveyed the room and saw all these people I had nothing in common with. Orlando took me by the arm and we returned to the kitchen with Gabriel. Orlando picked up a dessert platter, one of the big flat ones.

"Who's gonna do it?"

I got my driver's license and a credit card out of my pocket. "I'll take care of this," I said. In the meantime Gabriel put the plate in the microwave to dry the coke properly.

"I think we should be careful," I said.

"About what?"

"Those kids. The ones who were over at our place the other night and just came out and called us cokeheads."

"What are you saying? They paid me two hundred euros for a teener!"

"Yeah, but you know what it's like, don't you? It's a small town, people gossip..."

"Leo's right. We need to play it safe," Orlando said. "I mean, we work here after all."

"Hey, guys, snap out of it! Even if word gets out that people are doing drugs here, it sure ain't nothing new. Show me a club where that doesn't happen..."

"What about restaurants?" Orlando retorted.

I enjoy learning to do new things, starting to feel at home in new places, knowing my way around kitchens. And there's nothing I like more than chopping three perfectly straight rails in a matter of seconds.

"You know what's funny?"

"What, Leo?"

"That one of the reasons I took this job was that I wanted to chill out somewhere quiet, in the country. You know, close to nature, the lake, and all that. I actually thought that with all this peace and tranquility I'd be able to start writing my dissertation."

"Sure, that's why you decided to work in a club. Great choice. Let's go back in and dance some more."

We staggered out of the place at dawn. In four hours we had to be back in the kitchen. The three of us were wasted, but it had definitely been a night to remember.

It was pouring rain but it wasn't cold. There had to be an umbrella somewhere, but I couldn't find it. I headed home on foot. Walking in the rain, it occurred to me that what I needed was a nice sensible girl and an undemanding relationship. Maybe a farmer's daughter, living with her family near our place, who'd definitely be into long flowing skirts. I'd want nothing more than to be with her in a dry, sweet-smelling bed, under clean scented sheets.

"Hey, Matte."

"Yo."

"Have you still got that girl hanging out at our place?"

"Nope, you were right. I'm not cut out for commitment and living with a girl."

"I guess I'll come back to Rome, then."

"What happened?"

"Dunno. It's like there's something missing."

"What on earth do you mean?"

"Nah, it's nothing, I just miss things. I'm coming home."

"D'you miss your days as a rookie here in Rome? Or is it more than that?"

"It's like I miss the person I could maybe become. It's kind of like if I stay here, the person I was is never going to be the one I might be..."

"Gimme a break, Leo. Stop overthinking everything."

"My pay is a month late."

"Ah, right, then you'd better come back. I'll be waiting."

31.

I got up from my chair and shut my laptop on the round table in the living room and rolled and lit a cigarette, having almost given up pot because it made me paranoid. The radio was playing "La guerra è finita" by Baustelle. If I had a decent connection, I'd download it. Instead, this crap heap of a laptop was barely good enough for me to write my dissertation on. I felt as emotionally unstable as the girl in the song, who cries and doesn't want to be caught shoplifting in supermarkets. I'd been caught red-handed robbing from destiny, and even though I wasn't crying, it felt pretty damn awful.

I'd done it yet again—found myself wallowing in abject misery. I let my thoughts flow like ripples lapping the shore, on the off chance a few rivulets might trickle into the questions that lay buried in my mind and wash up the answers. I sat down again, turned the laptop on, and begged my mind to get its act together. No luck: The tide was out. Nothing but a wasteland. Asking myself questions didn't do me much good anyway. When I just lumbered on without asking too many questions or waiting for answers, things generally turned out for the better.

Which they did in 2005, amid stacks of assignments, loads of anxiety, some good times, and a few fleeting moments in the kitchen, even though I had promised myself to stay away from work until I'd graduated. The panic attacks had started in Tuscany, and I had no idea why. It wasn't the cocaine or the fact that my wages were always late. So it had to be because I'd allowed myself to drift through life without a rudder. Because I had something to prove. It was time to start something from scratch, and succeed because I wanted to, not because fate had blindly thrown some good luck my way.

Matteo's reaction to my musings had been: graduate. I thought it might work. I checked my bank balance and calculated that €12,000 would just see me through the year. Twelve months to take my final exams and write my dissertation.

But in July a friend told me someone with a yacht was looking for a private chef. I'd never been on a yacht, and €1,600 a month under the table would come in handy. What about the license that all working seafarers had to have? The Standards of Training and Certification of Watchkeeping is a bit like a résumé—no one ever asks you for it. The name of the yacht was *Miles*, and the old owner had apparently been a jazz enthusiast. I don't think the new owner even knew how to spell "jazz." He was a sleazy property developer from Rome, allergic to anything remotely resembling refinement or good taste, a mouth-breathing knuckle dragger with money. Funny, in some ways he reminded me of Arturo.

We moored the seventy-two-foot Comar in various locations between Sardinia's jet-set hot spot of Porto Cervo and other stunning nearby inlets, sharing the crystal-clear waters of the Costa Smeralda with Silvio Berlusconi's three-masted super-yacht and the pleasure craft owned by the pop singer Lucio Dalla. My duties were to cook for the captain, prepare salads with no dressings for the brute of a diet-obsessed owner, whip up pasta dishes at midnight (or two or three in the morning) for his eighteen-year-old firstborn and buddies, heat up and process baby food for the twins from his second marriage, and throw something together for the two nannies. I had to do the food shopping for the nannies separately, at the only discount store, which was located on the outskirts of Porto Rotondo. I had no idea when and where his young Dominican wife and her two surgically enhanced boobs went to eat. The whole setup couldn't have oozed more stereotypes if I'd made it up.

I actually liked life at sea: getting a tan while I washed down the walls of the boat, going to do the shopping in the chase boat, learning how to tie knots and nonchalantly toss off nautical terms, and gazing from a suitable distance at seriously blinged wannabe fashionistas shelling out €60 for a pair of plastic flip-flops. I had a camera with me that I'd bought just before leaving, my first digital SLR.

"Hey, Leo, nice camera, does it take good pictures? What is it?"

"Yeah, nice. It's a Nikon."

"Gimme a look."

I showed him the LCD screen and the latest shots I'd taken. At the third picture he punched in a number on his cell phone.

"Hello? Hey, Frank, can you hear me? Look, I want you to go buy me a camera. Yeah. Yeah, that's right. Today, yeah. It's a Nikon. A Nikon..." He turned to me. "What model is it?"

"A D70 —" I said.

"D70," he repeated into the phone.

"S," I added.

"S," he echoed. "S for shithead. Right. Great. Okay. Okay, Yeah, yeah, see ya tomorrow, at the airport."

S for shithead. But that wasn't the only reason I jumped ship. I left because of the time he clapped his hands to call me while I was putting together his shitty salad with no fucking dressing.

I stood in the stairwell leading up to the deck and told him, "No, no way, no clapping. Clapping, N-O."

I don't think it hurt my pride as much as the realization that I couldn't afford to mess around with college. Kitchen jobs come and go, something always turns up, often when you least expect it, but a degree is one of those things that if you miss the train, you'll never catch it again.

I saw the *Miles* again the night I returned to the jetty at Fiumicino where it was moored, with Michele and a backpack containing a two-pound packet of sugar. Michele was back in Rome fresh from his last and final squabble with Orlando. It's easier for two out-of-work cooks to hatch a devious plan than two busy chefs with full-time jobs.

All you have to do is find a €700,000 yacht, I'd told him over the phone. You locate the fuel tank and there's a hatch lid, you give it a half turn, the way the captain taught you in case someone gets left outside, you yank it open and pour in two pounds of sugar. About half an hour into sailing the engine seizes.

Sugar in his fucking yacht would throttle that jackass and his salads and diets and whims. Except the hatch was bolted shut from the inside and we ended up sitting on the jetty, smoking and planning our future dream jobs, with two pounds of sugar lying idly next to us.

"There's a good chance our old crew of the summer of 2003 is getting back together again," he said.

"What, the Verve?"

"Yep. It's reopening in January. Lucrezia, the owner, called. She wants to manage it herself, and she asked about you too."

"And when did we ever see this Lucrezia person?"

"I bumped into her a couple of times; she'd drop in for a quick drink and then disappear. Our bosses reported to her. This time, we'd be reporting to her directly."

When December rolled around, and with it the oral exam during which I'd be defending my dissertation, it had been exactly one year since my last shift at San Piero a Sieve. The day I graduated was one of the happiest in living memory. We partied all night long with Emiliano, Orlando, Michele, Ciccio, Patrizio, and lots of other people.

So what's the number-one reason I work in a kitchen? Money. Number two? Money. Three? Four? Five? The first ten reasons why I work as a cook, hanging in there and relentlessly signing up for any job in any way connected to food, is money. If I hadn't earned enough money to let me take a year off, I'd never have graduated. If I hadn't earned enough money to buy a camera and pay for the darkroom photography course, I wouldn't be taking photos. I owe who I am to the kitchen. Therefore, the eleventh reason is gratitude.

32.

Michele and I put our heads together and came up with an awesome menu. We'd give people what they wanted: the illusion of a well-earned reward. Most people can't cook, haven't a clue where to start, and don't even know what good food is. All they have is a hazy recollection of wonderful Sunday lunches at Grandma's (bearing in mind that not all grandmas know how to cook), and a palate accustomed to the assembly line flavors of ready-made food and restaurant fare.

We, on the other side of the swinging door, know how to rustle up reassuring dishes that are beyond the capabilities of people who do not work in a commercial kitchen. Or maybe they can, but only with humongous effort, and the results are seldom consistent. We, instead, have some pretty amazing kitchen tools to help us: six-burner gas cookers, a convection oven that's always on, a blast chiller, and—most important—razor-sharp knives. Even if you had a set of knives like ours in your own kitchen, you probably wouldn't know how to use them. It's all in the handles, someone used to say. No, I say, it's all in the blades.

Immediately after our meeting with Lucrezia in January, I decided I deserved a present and bought myself a small set of Global Vanadium chef's knives: pricey but not extravagant, Japanese made, lightweight, well-balanced and, of course, visually stunning. There are better—and worse—knives, but at the end of the day the only thing that matters is that they're easy to sharpen. I get a kick out of watching an ultrasharp blade cut cleanly through a tomato, trim away cartilage without mangling the meat, or slice the tough skin of an eggplant. My knives are an extension of my thoughts; when they cut through ingredients and food, they are an extension of my fingertips. A good knife accounts for at least 40 percent of the skills that amateurs admire in professional chefs.

I'd liked them all, but I bought just the basic set of four to add to the twelve-inch Steinbach carving knife I'd used every day at the Verve, three years earlier. It was part of the utensils and smallwares Mauro had purchased for the season, and it had the longest blade, which is why I'd chosen it. I used that knife for everything, even peeling grapes. When the 2003 season finished, I took it away with me. It had become just as much mine as the scars it had made on my left thumb and knuckles. I sharpened it every time I used it and it could shave a hair on a hair. Now I had a proper chef's knife with a beautiful eight-inch curved blade that I used to cut cheese and vegetables and to fan fruit for decorating desserts. Not meat or fish, though; that would be mistreating it.

You use a fillet knife for fish. It has a long, flexible blade to separate the skin from the soft flesh and enough bend to keep the edge close to the bone or table with the lightest of pressure. You can tell if someone's any good at filleting fish and meat by the amount of waste they produce. In fact, that distinction applies across the board: You can tell a real chef from an amateur by the amount of waste produced.

I have a good boning knife, which sometimes gets called a boner (surprise!). It has a short tapered blade, a little thicker than a fillet knife but stiffer and heavier because it has to work harder. Tendons, ligaments, and connective tissue require more strength than fish, and they too require a sharp knife. You're much more likely to cut yourself with a dull blade that slips when you least expect it than with a scalpel that meekly follows the slightest tilt of the wrist or pressure from the hand.

My fourth knife, which is just as essential as the others, is the paring knife. Everyone has a favorite: the bird's beak, with an inwardly curved blade; the miniature chef's knife, with a triangular blade; and others in different lengths and thicknesses. Mine is a simple serrated stainless steel number, perfect for tough skins like tomatoes and bell peppers in particular, but also for bread, celery, or just about anything else. Knives with serrated blades have the advantage of superior edge retention. They don't cost an arm and a leg, and when they lose their edge (it takes a lot for that to happen!), you just throw them away and buy another one.

A chef's personal knives are seldom used by anyone else in the kitchen. If you need someone's knife, you ask for it politely and expect the answer to be no. If you want me to stop treating you nicely, then use one of my knives on a ceramic plate. If you want me to kick you out of the kitchen, use it on the stainless steel pass.

Two years ago, neither Michele nor I had our own personal knives, and now I couldn't do a half-decent job without them. But the knives and our awesome menu were not the only things that had changed over the last three years. Other than the two of us, there was no one from the old brigade, and the hiring process resembled a virus that spreads through direct contact.

Staff was taken on day by day, following the simple rules of nepotism and chemistry. Among the first to arrive were Luana, who had shared an apartment with Giusy for a year, and Mario, who was Patrizio's second cousin. Then all the others followed. I got into the act as well, bringing in Nicolò, an old friend still studying at the Academy of Dramatic Arts, to work front of house, and Angelo, a guy I knew from school—we'd spent many nights at his place printing photographs. For desserts, I'd pulled in Sara, the weird and wonderful pusher from our rave party days, who had just Xanaxed herself out of severe depression and earned a diploma from the A Tavola con lo Chef culinary school in Rome (she'd be making straightforward dishes, nothing overly elaborate). Another Gabriele (this one known as Gaby Baby, a buddy of Matteo's from university with a passion for Foucault and a latecomer to the world of cooking) was also sweet-talked into joining us with the promise of running the appetizer station once he'd cut his teeth as a dishwasher. Gaby Baby was the weakest link in our kitchen chain gang.

Mauro was right about the difference between Italian and non-Italian kitchen hands. It didn't take Gaby Baby long to flounder. He ranted and raved and swore like a trooper. He treated an extra spoon in the sink like a dagger between his shoulder blades. He'd throw regular tantrums and, all in all, behaved egregiously during service. I helped out whenever I could, washing pots and pans, especially early in the week when it was quieter, and very occasionally let him prepare the main course. I wanted to keep my word, but my power was, in all fairness, quite limited. A line cook makes at least €1,500 a month, while he, as dishwasher, made €1,000. And I didn't have anyone else to take his place at the sink. Another young guy in the kitchen was Sampath, from Sri Lanka, who knew Michele. He was thorough and meticulous, quick to learn, and unobtrusive, with an uncanny knack for stepping in a second before being asked to. Sampath coped unfailingly and uncomplainingly with heavy-duty everyday drudgery, going about his business as service got into full swing and giving Michele and me the space and calm we needed to put the finishing touches on dishes and keep the wheels turning. Gaby Baby was champing at the bit to stop washing and start cooking, but he still had a long way to go. Other than dumping his frustrations on everyone during service, the rest of the day he managed to be quite pleasant and i became fond of his defiant outlook on life and his distinctive habit of analyzing things deeply, one syllable at a time.

"Hey, Gaby Baby, do you believe in eternal life?"

"Yeah."

"Why?"

"Because."

"Then you believe in God?"

"Nope."

"But that doesn't make sense."

"The only completely consistent people are the dead."

One Friday he texted me he was sick and would not be coming in, which I expected would happen sooner or later. I phoned him back immediately, but his cell was switched off.

In a flash, I remembered Joseph. I'd met him a few weeks earlier at a gas station on Via Tuscolana. My bike had refused to start and it was the middle of the night. He'd helped me push it more than half a mile along the deserted road, until the damn machine finally sputtered to life. I offered him a kebab and a glass of wine (he was a Christian Indian, the first I'd ever met; I'd taken it for granted he was a Pakistani Muslim, big mistake!), and listened, engrossed, to his life story as we ate together, before giving him a ride home. He had been working for a year at the Esso gas station, he was an illegal immigrant, spoke no Italian at all and just enough English to get by. His wage was made up entirely of tips. He worked there Saturday afternoons and all day Sunday, always during lunch breaks, and often all night. He never sat down because his boss didn't want him to even though he was not paying him a cent. He slept a few hours in the morning, and every day around three he would pass by home to say good night to his eleven-year-old son and eight-year-old daughter. This he did like all immigrants: Seated on a plastic stool in front of an ancient computer on a table made of chipboard in a room shared with five other people, he would sign into Skype, draw his face nearer to the monitor and wait. The connection was slow, the voices choppy, and the image of the two children often froze, but since the arrival of Skype, everything seemed easier and closer. Before that there had been only letters, a few photographs, and the weekly remittances. So I remembered Joseph as being a cheerful guy, his speech interspersed not with expletives but "Thank God."

I told Michele I thought I'd found a solution and to wait for me. Still in my blacks, I grabbed my helmet and asked the barman, who had just arrived on his motorbike, to lend me his. I headed toward Via Tuscolana, praying I'd find Joseph there. When I got to the gas station, there he was, wearing his hat and a checked shirt over a white undershirt. As soon as he saw me, he broke out into a big grin and came over to give me a hug. I talked to him without even taking my helmet off.

Five minutes later he was awkwardly climbing onto the back of the bike and grabbing me for dear life, his ribs pressing into my back.

"Joseph... not so tightly please, I can't breathe..."

We arrived at the restaurant, I introduced Joseph to Michele and the others, tossed him a plastic apron, showed him more or less where things were and where to put the plates, flatware, and pans, and then I gave him a pat on the back and marched up the stairs to Lucrezia's office. I explained that we had a new kitchen hand as of today because Sara could no longer manage the desserts by herself; what with prep, service, and the business starting to take off, we really needed another person in the kitchen. The best solution was to shift Gabriele over to Sara's station, which he would agree to do for the same pay, and find a new dishwasher. For the time being we could try out this Indian guy. I hoped the prospect of saving money by not getting a new cook to help Sara would make Lucrezia ignore the fact that I was actually asking her to spend more on staff. I waited for an answer, then realized that her eyes had a faraway glazed-over look. I reached across her desk and gave her a gentle prod. Lucrezia suffered from narcolepsy. She shuddered and picked up the conversation as if nothing had happened.

"What were you saying? A new dishwasher?"

"Yeah, Gabriele on desserts and appetizers with Sara, and a new dishwasher...did you get all that?"

"Yes, of course. I'm not deaf, you know. Well, okay, if that's what you want and what's needed. But does this Indian guy have all his papers in order?"

"Of course he does. It's the first thing I asked him."

"Fine. Bring him upstairs and I'll add him to the paperwork."

"Are you thinking of giving him a contract?"

"I'll put him on the payroll along with everyone else as soon as our license comes through from the council."

"Yeah, well. Do you know when that'll be? May has come and gone."

"Look, you know how important this place is to me. You've got to give me a hand, Leo, the others look up to you. Have a word with them. And don't worry."

I left the office thinking she was nothing but a spoiled forty-something fucking bimbo with overly indulgent über-rich parents backing her. Getting a manager in to run the restaurant hadn't caused enough grief—and debts—so she'd decided to manage the place herself and lose more money even faster.

The business about the license had come out early on because both Michele and I had been convinced she owned the property. Instead, it turned out that the local city council owned it and had rented it under a ninety-year lease to a private investor who—according to Lucrezia—was soon to take possession and sublet it to her. Since we were occupying the premises and working here, we should, in theory, be entitled to take over the license. It was not at all clear to me how the council could possibly license an establishment like this with none of the staff holding a legally binding work contract. Wasn't this in total breach of labor laws? Was being in cahoots with a couple of local councilors enough to get away with fucking murder? What actually constitutes employment? I was unfamiliar with the ins and outs of these machinations, and up to a certain point, I didn't give a shit. All I needed was a kitchen to run and my pay packet at the end of the month: how I got it, I didn't care. It was the slapdash way money was splurged on concerts that we couldn't afford that caused me the greatest concern. The new artistic director was learning the ropes at Lucrezia's expense, a bit like everyone else, for sure, but he was throwing bucket loads of cash to pay for bigger-name artists—as well as to tart up his résumé. Performers of the caliber of Ferruccio Spinetti and Petra Magoni, Avion Travel and Kocani Orkestar had already soaked up rivers of cash. Going back downstairs to the kitchen, it occurred to me that my job was taking care of the kitchen and keeping my team together. My job was to balance the restaurant's books. The artistic director would have to deal with Lucrezia, and Lucrezia would have to deal with the council, and that was their business.

"Hi, Gaby Baby, don't worry, get well soon. New dishwasher hired, you promoted to appetizers. Same pay as before. Hope this news makes you feel better. See you tomorrow."

I pressed Send, put my phone back in my pocket, adjusted my cap, and passed the joint I'd just lit to one of the sound guys heading over to the mixer. "Here, you finish it."

Joseph turned on the dishwasher and beamed at me. Michele told me to get a move on, we're running late with prep. In one fell swoop I had a kitchen hand delighted to do his job and a line cook delighted to do appetizers and grateful for his sort-of promotion. I was a genius. All I had to do now was wing it when it came to Joseph's imaginary papers.

33.

During service, and especially afterward, I urged Gaby Baby, Sara, Sampath, and all the servers to keep up the pace, because the only way the boss was going to stay out of our hair was if we never let our guard down and never laid bare any weaknesses. It became my own personal crusade, just as it had been Orlando's in San Piero a Sieve. It takes a common enemy to rally the troops, and I found one in the shape of that fuckwit of an artistic director. The kitchen brigade's pact of loyalty had been signed only a few days before, the night the fuckwit sent Luana into the kitchen to ask for a beef fillet with myrtle sauce at one o'clock in the morning, after everything had been switched off, the workstations buffed to a lustrous sheen, and only the floors to mop and the last pans to be put away. I took it upon myself to walk over to where he was sitting, in front of the stage, and personally explain to him, ever so politely, that the kitchen was closed for the night, but if he wanted, we could grill him a steak. Upon which he decided to pull rank and demand the freaking fillet with the freaking sauce, calling Lucrezia on his mobile to complain that the cook refused to feed him even though he had been slaving away all day, working his ass off to keep the place humming. His idea of slaving away was most likely monkeying around on the computer and scoffing up beer between Marlboros, when he wasn't munching on sandwiches ordered from the bar.

Smiling, I told him it was no problem and that there had been a misunderstanding. Mine was simply a suggestion that at this late hour it might be a good idea to keep things light and his dish would be ready in a few minutes. I returned to the kitchen, opened the meat fridge, cut a nice ten-ounce slice from the middle of the fillet—the best part—massaged it lovingly, added a pinch of green pepper and a dusting of flour, heated and greased the pan, and seared it over a high flame. After turning it, I retrieved the bottle of myrtle liqueur and got a knob of butter that had been in the fridge for only a short time, so it was still soft. I poured the liqueur into the pan and tilted it to set it alight and shook the pan so the juices and liqueur would combine, then tossed in the butter with a good pinch of salt, moving the pan continuously in a circular motion to emulsify the melted butter with the sugars in the myrtle liqueur without burning it. When the sauce reached the right consistency, I picked up the fillet with a pair of tongs and placed it in the middle of the plate. I then poked my head out the kitchen door and called in all the waitstaff. I called in the girl at the cash register too. Michele, Gaby Baby, Sampath, and Sara were already there. Then all I said was, "This is the fillet for our artistic director, will you help me put the finishing touches on the sauce?" and then I hawked and spat a whopping big glob of phlegm right in the center of the pan. First Sampath, then Gabriele and, one by one, all the others, did the same. Even Luana managed to produce a tiny fleck of spittle, apologizing for not doing a better job. "I've never spat before in my entire life" she said. I put the sauce back on the flame, added a little more butter and stirred using the beech wood spoon (the best for sauces, and to hell with the health authorities). Then I poured it over the fillet with a flourish.

Never cross a chef. He always has the upper hand. There's no way you can win against the person who has the power to decide what you put in your mouth.

That's what I was thinking as I turned on my heels after graciously serving the fuckwit his freaking fillet.

34.

The days flew by and I was still winging it. I told Lucrezia that Joseph had given me a copy of his residence permit, it was downstairs and I'd bring it to her tomorrow. Meanwhile, she shouldn't worry, it was in the kitchen with all the other important paperwork, and Joseph knew he had to sneak out the back door in the unhappy event of an inspection.

And as time went by, there was still no sign of a contract. Some of the staff were starting to grumble. One of the waitresses, after a particularly grueling dinner service, suggested we all go on strike. Michele worked himself up into a lather and went all union rep on us. I was against striking. I felt that the place was mine. I needed it as much as someone in love clings to a dream. But above all, the days were whizzing by and I was determined to keep my job, at least until September.

The general sense of disquiet was so evident that Lucrezia called a meeting with all the staff. We found ourselves sitting in a circle, with her in the middle urging us to be patient a little while longer, the contracts were on the way. While the others muttered, rolled their eyes, or pretended to send text messages, I was all ears. In a nutshell, she said, this venue was her home, but it was ours too, and we wouldn't have a roof over our heads without her. She didn't explain how or when she'd be getting the famous permits from the Rome City Council and legally taking over the venue. Nor did she enlighten us with any well-thought-out strategies for balancing the books and finally posting a profit, starting with the overdue bills for the concerts. All she talked about was her dream, which if we pulled together and worked as a team, with drive and determination, we could share. In the end, she put on a fairly creditable performance, transfiguring her self-indulgent palaver into something she believed to be substance. It was hard to tell if she knew how vacuous she sounded and that she had no chance whatsoever of putting any concrete plans into action or getting anyone to back them, and was relying on her own egocentricity and our understanding. A master of mendacity without a shred of embarrassment.

She was a seasoned politician in full campaign mode, a fine example of faith in the magic of words, the abracadabra, and the *hey, presto!* of our times. Lucrezia talked to her staff the way incumbents talk to constituents, acknowledging their needs and offering reassurances that their problems would be addressed and resolved because that was the right thing to do, there was no other option, right? Everyone would get a contract. Because the council would give us the venue. They would give it to us because we were working together as a team. Like many other restaurant owners, she made out that the business's success depended entirely on the staff's perseverance, and the contracts and everything else would follow as a matter of course.

It was just like Santa Claus when you're a kid. You don't need to meet him or talk to him to believe in Santa. They tell you a fat man in a red suit with a long white beard brings you presents. Therefore, if there are presents under the tree, then there has to be a fat man in a red suit with a long white beard who slides down the chimney on Christmas Eve with a big bag of toys. If there's work, then there must be a business. And we were working, all right, working our asses off.

After she'd finished and even shed a few tears for good measure, we all got up and returned to our stations. She was right, after all.

Politicians can fool voters, and bosses can fool staff, but only up to a certain point. If they overdo it, voters tire of getting screwed by one politician and elect someone new to screw them. Michele was incensed and invited his uncle, the lawyer, to dinner. He arrived and said hello, without a word about how he had saved my ass three years earlier. No one believed that the contracts would ever materialize, and our wages, all under the table, were still overdue.

To keep the waiters and sous chefs happy, I gave up my own wages so they could be paid. Michele did the same. But after a couple of months, everyone's wages were overdue, with Michele and me owed nearly €5,000 each. The term "labor dispute" started floating around. I didn't like it. People talked about industrial action, and all it added up to for me was having coworkers I couldn't count on when the going got tough. It meant having to go the extra mile to keep the wheels turning while I hatched my own plan to jump ship without drowning in the process. More like jumping from the frying pan into the fire, as usual, but I wanted at least to finish the season in peace.

Trying to put together a plan to get out with money in my pocket and a clear conscience made me nervous and taciturn. Michele, who already scored pretty low on the chattiness scale, virtually gave up talking altogether. As soon as service ended, he'd clean up his station quickly and then disappear. Most times I was the only one left to order supplies and close up, and the only other one who might stay back with me occasionally was Nicolò. This particular evening, I actually had to wait for him, keys in hand.

"Hey, Nicolò, get a move on, I wanna go home!" I yelled at the dining room door. He rushed in, still buttoning his shirt, and laying his backpack on the floor. Hearing the dull clink of glass on glass, I asked him to open the backpack. He asked why. I asked again. He opened it, and inside were three bottles of wine, including a bottle of Barolo Chinato.

"They're not paying me, and they're not giving me a contract, so I'm paying myself!" he said, not quite defiantly. I could tell he was uncomfortable.

"So I guess after you've taken the wine, you're going to stop wanting to be paid, right?" I sighed. "And you think taking three bottles of wine will fix everything? Go put them back where you found them. Do it one more time, and I'll send you packing."

"What the fuck do you mean, Leo? Aren't we friends? And you're breaking my balls over three bottles of wine, when we're not getting paid and God knows if they'll ever actually hire us. People who live in glass houses and all that crap..."

"You want to know if I've ever swiped anything? Maybe I have. The problem isn't that you've swiped something, Nicolò, but that you've stolen it from *me*. I do the food shopping, Michele and I are in charge of food costs. But the worst thing of all is that you got yourself caught red-handed. So either you're a wise guy and you think that because you're my friend I'll let you get away with whatever the fuck you want, or you're a dickhead. Two types of people I dislike working with."

Nicolò put down the bottles and turned to go, mightily pissed off. "Whatever. See ya around, Chef," he murmured as he walked away.

I couldn't have felt more disappointed. I was losing control and I couldn't afford to; I wasn't ready to give up. What did it matter that Nicolò was the best waiter we had? If he didn't respect his work, then he'd never respect me. And I would never be able to really, truly trust him. Friendship doesn't come into the equation. I needed people I could trust.

The following day I told Lucrezia that I was letting Nicolò go, that I'd let him stay until Saturday but I wouldn't be calling him back. She didn't even ask me why and said it was fine.

Nicolò deleted my name from his contacts before leaving. Which I knew because he shoved his phone under my nose while I was checking the meat orders.

That night Michele informed me that he was leaving. His uncle was suing, and when I asked him why he wasn't going to the union instead, he replied that that was what he wanted and that he was heading off to England to work.

William was waiting for me in front of the gate in the courtyard. He'd come and go, like grown-up kids who stop by every now and again to visit their elderly parents, telling them jack shit about their lives. I scratched him under the chin and he purred back. His fur was wiry and wild: He'd become one very big, badass cat. I felt ridiculously proud of him. We went up the stairs together.

"Hey."

"Yo."

"It's happened again, Matte, I'm up shit creek. Wages overdue, people pissing me off, and the usual house of cards that's come tumbling down."

"So you must be used to it by now."

"Yeah, but it's just not normal."

"What's not normal?"

"That the same thing keeps happening over and over again."

"I dunno. Sometimes it's a matter of timing."

"What...?"

"You say, 'I want to quit the rat race,' so you do, but then wham bam, you land in an even bigger rat race."

"And so?"

"So it's all normal."

"You're saying I should quit?"

"Sure, what else?"

35.

Lucrezia's brother shook my hand and promised things would get better. I'd be the first to receive my overdue wages, but even the cockroaches hiding in the walls of the farmhouse that had been converted to a concert venue knew that things could only get worse.

I told him it was fine, we'd keep the restaurant going through winter, but I wanted all my money right now. That would prove his goodwill, then we could wipe the slate clean. In reality, I had already found a chef to replace Michele. His name was Vincenzo. We were good friends and, in the name of friendship, he had agreed to work as a chef de partie, one step down for someone of his caliber. So I told him he was hired. Lucrezia's brother told me to pass by his sister's office the following week, she'd be paying me all my arrears.

Michele sent me an e-mail telling me all about his new life in London. He'd shaved his head like me, and had an American girlfriend who was mixed race, with green eyes. The restaurant he was working in as a line cook had a good chance of earning its first Michelin star next year.

"Here you are, Leo, as agreed, here's your back pay, exactly six thousand euros. It's all in the envelope."

I stretched out my hand and put the envelope in my pocket without opening it, then I looked Lucrezia square in the eye and took a deep breath.

"Thanks. I'm finishing up today. I'm sorry, but I'm leaving."

"What? What do you mean? You said that you'd stay, we had an agreement..."

"If I hadn't said that, you would never have paid me. Michele is suing you, the others have left with money owing, and who knows if and when they'll ever get it. It's been nine months now that you've been promising us contracts. I'm sorry, but I'm sick and tired of working for nothing. Vincenzo is a good guy, he'll keep the kitchen running smoothly, no need to worry. I'm not leaving you short staffed. I think that's all I owe you."

She muttered something and remained immobile with her vacuous thoughts, as useless as an ear trumpet for a deaf man. She shook her head and I could practically hear her brain bouncing around in her skull. We both knew there was nothing else to say. As I exited the office, I thought about Sessanta and how I had agreed with Sandro to start working there three days from now. I'd be returning, with my name embroidered in burgundy on my black uniform, to the place I had left wearing the white T-shirt of a dishwasher—cum–salad guy. I should be happy, and I was, I suppose, and as I walked away my heels made a pleasing tapping noise. I stopped and closed my eyes, letting the sun warm my eyelids, and felt my last paranoid thoughts plop to the ground like ripe peaches.

In the weeks that followed, I spoke to Ciccio and he told me things were going a whole lot better at the Verve. He'd changed the menu, though he wasn't thrilled with the waitstaff. Everyone adored him, he said. Michele wrote to say he couldn't take England anymore and was returning to Italy. They'd offered him a chef's position at Il Quadraro. Sampath and Gaby Baby would be joining him there.

Dirty tricks, corrupt politicians, and cocaine made the headlines in 2006. The news on TV droned on endlessly about the left-wing coalition captained by Romano Prodi winning the elections by a handful of votes, and the arrest of the Sicilian

Mafia boss Bernardo Provenzano. A book by a twenty-seven-year-old journalist lifted the lid on the Italian crime syndicate La Camorra, which no one had ever done before. I read it and admired the author (as much as I envied him) for his skill and daring. The word "Camorra" towered over everything else because it seemed that the young author had received death threats. I envied him a little less after that.

Sandro loved Southern Italian cooking, running kitchens by the seat of his pants, and men. The realization that he was gay hit him almost overnight. Giovanna fleeing back to Paris into the arms of the sales assistant now made sense. I believe that some things happen like that, out of the blue. All your life you've driven a sport bike and then one day you wake up and discover that all you ever wanted was a Harley, so you go out and buy a Hog. You've always lived and thrived in the homophobic environment of a restaurant kitchen and you've joked about tits and asses with your work buddies and cheated on your girlfriend with the waitresses, and then one fine day you discover you like men. It doesn't solve any problems, nor does it create any new ones, life just goes on as it did before, period.

The buzzwords in restaurant circles were "fusion" and "molecular cuisine" and Sandro didn't like either, just as he did not like flouncing queens. Obsessively plating every dish with the same swoosh of sauce and decorative droplets of balsamic reduction made him puke (as it did me). His tastes were not that far removed from mine, except for his disgusting mint panna cotta and his penchant for men. I still preferred women, but there's no saying where curiosity will lead you.

Sandro wanted a chef who would liven the place up and let him take care of the admin side of the business. But he got really antsy whenever he saw a gastronorm out of place. He said he preferred to be in the front of the house and look after the guests, but when the restaurant filled up, he'd make a panic-stricken dive for the cookers and mess up my work flow, creating more problems. Sandro took pandemonium in stride, and despite claiming that he wanted to revolutionize everything, it was clear that the pandemonium calmed him down. Because he knew his way around it.

I returned to Sessanta because I needed to get away from the Verve before it went belly up and because returning to the place where I had started out as a dishwasher was an irresistible temptation. But I truly believed I could leave my mark there. Eventually realizing that all this was just talk and that I'd fallen for it—yet again—during my first few weeks there angered and disappointed me. For me the kitchen is a place for experimentation, but experimentation with ironclad rules. It's where you keep everything under control but never forget to have a good time, where you never let customers get the better of you. Where you scrap a little food every night to guarantee impeccable service and nothing but the freshest ingredients. I hate throwing things together at the last minute, and I hate dashing to the supermarket only when the restaurant is fully booked, keeping leftover prep to save food, and the thoughtless management of meat and fish. A few years had passed and I'd changed, but Sandro was still the same. At the first opportunity, I emptied the fridge and got the place set up my way. Pointless to even discuss it. Far better to present Sandro with a fait accompli and let him draw his own conclusions.

"What do you know about the restaurant business, Leo?"

He was forty-two years old and had spent twenty-two of them cooking. For me, life as a chef was what I had experienced at San Piero a Sieve, the stories Orlando had told me, the stuff

I'd read about in food magazines like *Gambero Rosso*, and what I had learned firsthand bouncing around from one place to another. It was the condescending way you talked to people, as if the fact that they had less than no idea how to prepare a demi-glace sauce meant that they had less than no idea about life in general. Sandro had left Matera at the age of eighteen without a cent to his name and had become a half-decent cook, but an apprenticeship with Paul Bocuse had hoisted him into the rarefied world of real chefs. He'd run a number of restaurants into the ground but had managed to save enough money to take over Sessanta from the same owners who had once kicked him out. Perhaps more out of revenge than any real desire to have a restaurant of his own. He'd managed places for years, but I was convinced that his success derived exclusively from a flair for making commonsense, snap decisions, a flair that I had too, only in spades.

"I know everything I need to know," I said to him.

"But you've never lasted more than a year in the same place," he countered.

"So what?"

Sandro looked at me the way a loving granddad looks at his favorite grandson, alternating affectionate hugs with the odd sharp rebuke, when required. He placed a hand on my shoulder and whispered, ever so sweetly, "If only you weren't so full of shit, you could become a great chef."

36.

My second time around at Sessanta started out a little shakily. I reorganized some of the prep work, which got Sandro screaming that it wasn't the right way to cook his recipes. I put my own spin on the mise en place and ticket flow so that the dishes were picked up and the tables were managed my way, which he tried hard to undo and keep his way. Some things I'd pre-fry, and some I'd blanch, claiming that all the best restaurants did it, and his answer was that he couldn't bear food that wasn't freshly prepared every time, listing all the organoleptic proper-ties of healthy, traditional, made-to-order food.

Every so often I'd roll in late, as was my usual, and he rapped me over the knuckles for disregarding the rules. Moral of the story: I got used to cooking everything to order but managed to sneak in some simple tricks of the trade that didn't give away what I had precooked, and tried to follow Sandro's recipes to the letter. He got used to my coming in late occasionally and to a few other displays of what he regarded as my sloppiness, and the day he walked into a totally overhauled kitchen, he wasn't too fazed. He even seemed to genuinely like many of my own dishes and added them to the menu. We learned to respect each other, on top of the real affection we felt, mainly because both of us had started working at a young age to earn a living and nei-ther believed the world owed us anything.

Soon our agreements reflected how things were actually being run and were according to our personal, rather than pro-fessional, expectations: I worked five nights a week and took two days off, whichever two I wanted. When I was off, he ran the kitchen; that way he didn't feel left out and I could catch up on things that needed attending to. If Sandro wanted to take a few days off, he knew that the restaurant was in good hands and I covered for him whenever he was away. Finally, I had the security of a permanent job that wasn't at odds with living a normal life. And I really liked it that the food at Sessanta was honest and somehow respected for what it was. This was where Sandro and I found ourselves on common ground. No contrived presentations (like ring molds or other such things), but unpretentious, well-put-together dishes; no pointless concoctions involving herbs or oils infused and pigmented with parsley or bell peppers, and no tricks to plump up food. The garnishes were basic and always edible, and the food had an appeal all its own even without them. Everything was straightforward without being austere.

And the sore points? Until I started moving things around, the menu had not changed in six years, and the kitchen was neither spotless nor well organized. I craved working in a pristine uniform, without any pressure, whipping up risottos, emulsifying sauces, coating vegetables in batter for a massive mixed vegetarian platter, following my three, four, five orders all at the same time with smoothly mechanical movements, quickly tasting sauces and perfecting flavors and getting the dishes out in the correct sequence and with perfect timing. None of this was achievable in Sandro's kitchen. Every time he stepped in, he'd leave a trail of scraps, pots and pans used and discarded for no reason, cutting boards stacked one on top of the other, and prep ingredients cluttering up the pass. I got used to it and tried to stop food bombs from exploding all over the kitchen, at least on the nights he wasn't around. Adriano was a great help. He was a young guy from Sicily who was working with us to pay his way through university to become a chiropractor. He also kept an eye on me, to stop me nibbling on leftovers. Adriano alternated with Sandro's nephew as commis chef.

Italy won the soccer World Cup in 2006, the Italian politician Luca Coscioni and champion of freedom for scientific research died of ALS, and Piergiorgio Welby chose assisted suicide—both dying with the dignity they demanded and deserved. Marches were held to protest overaggressive medical treatments. At last I started living the life I wanted—or at least that's what it seemed—without undue aggravation.

In January 2007 I traveled to India and spent forty days there. In December I headed off to Puerto Rico for a month. Every morning I went for a run with my cousin, I swam twice a week, and I hit the gym every other day. Payday was Saturday, my wages coming directly out of the night's takings. As far as Italy was concerned, I was an unemployment statistic, and that didn't worry me a bit. No bank would lend me money to buy an apartment, but I still managed to squirrel away a sizable amount of money. In 2008, after working at Sandro's for nearly two years, I smashed my personal best for duration of employment in the same restaurant, and things had never been better.

It was nearly three in the morning. I was riding my bike home, still buzzing from the adrenaline high and the hits of coke we did every weekend at Sessanta. From outside I could see the living room lights on, so Matteo must still be awake. I climbed the stairs, opened the door, and took off my shoes.

"Hey!"

"Hi, Leo. How's it going?"

"Good. Tonight we served up garbage. Literally."

"What?"

"Well, the restaurant was packed, Sandro was off his head as usual, and I ran out of spelt penne, so I put a stop on orders for the oven-baked stuffed eggplant. But it was too late and there was still one more order for a table that had been waiting for ages."

"So you used a different type of pasta."

"Nope. I saw the waitress throwing out a portion of spelt penne with sauce that some kid hadn't finished that had just come back to the kitchen."

"Who, Jessica? That girl you brought back home the other night?"

"Yeah, her."

"So?"

"Well, it was a split-second decision. I grabbed the penne, picked out the chewed bits, got Adriano to rinse them, and I added the eggplant sauce and provolone, filled the hollow eggplant halves, and tossed them into the oven, with heaps of grated pecorino cheese on top. And *buon appetito!*"

"That's the worst thing you have ever told me. Absolutely revolting."

"I know. And it makes me feel good. It's nice to know I'll never stoop this low again in a professional kitchen."

But as it happened I went on to stoop even lower, but that's another story. In any case, life was good at Sessanta. I was happy, Adriano was happy, and Sandro's nephew was happy, although he had absolutely no interests, no passions, no girlfriends. His life revolved around Sessanta, the small apartment he rented sixty-five feet away from the restaurant's front door, and cocaine. He was a cokehead. Adriano and I had a passing appreciation for it, and Sandro joined in from time to time. There was a bunch of guys from the Basilicata region who hung around the restaurant and could get you anything. No one had a bad word to say about working at Sessanta, we all had our own personal expectations and balanced our existences inside and outside the restaurant. Even the waitresses were happy. There were two of them, and both had slept, at least once, at my place. When they left, another one arrived, a new girl I liked a lot. She'd slept at my place too, but in Matteo's room. I thought it was someone else (I didn't even know Matteo had met her), so I called out another girl's name from behind the closed door, and when she poked her head out, I must have looked like an idiot. Adriano left Sessanta and became a personal trainer in a gym and made quite a name for himself.

I had no real reason to leave, but then one of those days came along when you're drinking your coffee, and it's no different from any other coffee you've ever drunk, but that day it tastes wrong. And you can't get that taste out of your mouth. From then on the slow-moving pace of the restaurant and Sandro's hissy fits started to bug me. The bad taste would not go away, and I became unbearable to be around. So when Sandro overreacted to some piddling little thing like someone taking the cooked clams he wanted to do something with, I just lost it and hurled a pan against the wall. Enraged, I strode outside to smoke a cigarette, gripping my cell phone tightly. By the time I went back inside, I'd made an appointment to meet the following day with the owners of the restaurant Michele was working in, and I set a new record: quitting one job and finding a new one in three minutes. Sandro didn't put up a fight. I'd always known that one of our problems was that he wanted to take over his kitchen again, and I was the obstacle between the idea and the courage to do it.

37.

Being back with Michele, Sampath, and Gaby Baby had a familiar feel about it, like that distinctive hint of vanilla in the bouquet of a Brunello di Montalcino, or the blackcurrant nose in a Valpolicella Amarone. The arrangement was that I would work the same hours as at Sessanta. The money was the same too, and as usual there was no sign of a contract. In Italy some things never change: It was just another restaurant with a few added responsibilities in exchange for a few different privileges, but everything else remained the same.

Michele hoped that my presence in his kitchen would make him look good, and all I wanted to do was mind my own fucking business and grab some of the spotlight by making up for his shortcomings.

I was not the head chef, but I behaved like one.

A new guy arrived and introduced himself as Perewa. He was forty-eight and said he'd been a financial consultant and lived like a prince surrounded by Porsches and fancy restaurants, which he left behind to follow an irrepressible urge to keep it real. The only thing that wasn't real, that I could make out, were the stories he told. It sounded like yet another clumsy attempt to camouflage defeat as a courageous choice by someone who's suddenly changed his life. As if you change your life for any other reason than being forced to. I can't stand people who go around calling themselves by their nickname, let alone a nickname like that. From day one I called him Whatshisname. I hadn't singled out an enemy at Quadraro until he came along, on a silver platter.

Whatshisname had three main qualities. One: Nothing excited him. He saw the kitchen only as a source of suffering and fatigue. His behavior in the kitchen was that of an unwilling robot, always ready to abuse any foolhardy waiter who asked him to serve the last three diners one minute after the official closing time, even on a really quiet night. Two: He turned the simplest concepts into really complicated ones. If new apprentices turned up in the kitchen, he'd never teach them or just leave them alone to peel potatoes. No way. He would continually berate them for their lack of a detailed existential project, because it's not the technical errors that must be corrected, but the strategic ones. Three: He spewed out a never-ending flow of verbal diarrhea, no matter what he was doing. Especially if he had to explain something to you, which he did all the time. Humor and brevity annoyed him; all that mattered were productivity, numbers, and sweat. Cheffy flair didn't impress him. But serving two hundred covers with a ton of meat flung on the grill with meticulous skill and repetitiveness did.

Whatshisname's life was peppered with bizarre concepts such as "the philosophical kitchen," "a percentage approach to the production of food," and "the geometry of the pantry."

He discoursed relentlessly and at length about the proxemics of the spatial separation between cookware and chefs, and the chemical reactions between different foods and the alkalinity of the environment. Anything out of place threw him into a tizzy. He wanted all the jellied fruits to be weighed. One by one. Otherwise he got frazzled. Of himself, he said he was the superhero of tidiness and just like Superman he had his kryptonite: talent—a concept he associated with disorder, shamelessly denying its importance. In his opinion, Maradona's big mistake in the controversial match against England in '86 was to hog the ball and dribble it along way too randomly. The only monument worthy of worship was technique—the futile and idiotic technique he'd read about in some book and learned in a six-month course that cost as much as my whole year's wages. He got a real kick out of repeating "I was right" and "I told you so."

Whatshisname transferred to the kitchen values and ways of doing things that belonged to another world and had nothing to do with the reality, sensuousness, and extravagance needed to survive in a professional kitchen. In short, he was a bigmouth, know-it-all, boring old fart. This would have been a bearable and normal part of the absurd interaction that exists between cooks, except...he didn't understand a fucking thing about cooking, and if you didn't keep a watchful eye over him, he'd screw things up. So I decided he had to go. Whatshisname fawned over Michele, and the two hit it off immediately. One day I asked him to prepare the head cheese. He asked me how far up he had to fill the glass jars. I told him more or less up to here, and placed my index finger just under the top. He stiffened and told me that he needed to know the exact amount, otherwise the job wouldn't be done correctly. I stopped what I was doing, picked up a glass jar, filled it with the head cheese nearly to the top, weighed it, and told him that it was two point five ounces. I waited until he had filled about fifty jars, then I approached him and started weighing the jars. This one is two point four ounces, I said, and poured the contents into a gastronorm. This one is not quite two point three ounces, and I emptied another. I continued until I had emptied a dozen or so jars. Then I told him to empty all the jars, because not a single jar was exactly two point five ounces. He grumbled and muttered something to Michele, who didn't say a word but gave me a dirty look, and started emptying all the jars. Being nasty is a great way to calm your nerves. When you're not too secure in your job, you take it out on those who are even less secure than you. When you take it out on someone, you don't think about his problems, or about the consequences. Thinking about other people's problems doesn't calm your nerves. Mine was a solitary battle that I relished one day at a time.

38.

In January 2009 Michele married the green-eyed American girl. She had a twinkle in her eye that didn't bode well. Everyone thought it but no one said it out loud. I tried, without much conviction, and as expected I failed to convince him. Angelo, an old friend of mine, in the meantime had got his degree in anthropology and left for Brazil to work on a project for international cooperation. I was tired of the same old routine, and in February I decided to visit him. I talked about it with Michele and the owners. I'd be away for more than a month, but I wouldn't leave until everything was sorted out in the kitchen. Both Michele and the owners said that it wouldn't be a problem. Perewa couldn't cover my station on his own, so he would be flanked by Fabrizio, a young guy and a massive heavy-metal fan, who had dropped off his résumé a few weeks earlier.

From: Leonardo Lucarelli
To: Michele Savio
Date: March 6, 2009, 12:28 a.m.
Subject: irmão

Hello, my wonderful chef friend!! What can I say? I'm happy, happy, happy.

Everything fills me with joy: the weather, the people, even the Italians I've met here working on the project, the carnival, the women, smooching like a kid, the samba, the food, these incredible mornings, my Italiany Spanish that's turning into Italiany Portuguese and seems to be working out just fine.

And I've met a beautiful mixed-race girl, Aymara. Even her name is beautiful. A vivacious, silky-soft 22-year-old with hair that's a mass of tight curls.

But you don't need to worry, you really don't. I'm drunk on happiness, but luckily I haven't forgotten that even back in Rome I used to say I was happy, which eases that nagging fear of coming back that's already creeping into my mind.

Yesterday I went to a favela and cooked for the whole neighborhood, and I even managed to bake some great bread thanks to the Italians who'd brought the starter over with them on the plane. Here everyone eats just one dish, and it's taken me a while to make them understand the concept of appetizer, main, side dish, and dessert. It's like...you know, when you can't quite decide if what you're feeling is joy or pain, maybe both. Anyhow, try to imagine a whole community made up of 150 families living next to a dump, with no running water, no bathrooms, no fridges (and mind, we're at the equator), no social dignity (many don't have documents and don't know how to read or write). These people have absolutely nothing and yet they have these huge smiles, and you know your camera is worth 5 years' income for a family of 10 people...

So how about you?

All cooking, love, marriage? How about the Testaccio, any new chefs? What's happening? And the waiters?

Oh, and do you miss me in the kitchen? Just a bit?? Are my text messages getting to you?? You never answer them, you dog...

See you soon, buddy. Let me know what's going on in my beautiful home town and get everything spick and span for when I get back.

Seu irmão,

Leo

From: Michele Savio
To: Leonardo Lucarelli
Date: March 6, 2009, 1:16 p.m.
Subject: irmão

Thanks for your great e-mail—I got a real kick out of it!

Sorry it's taken me so long to get back to you. It wasn't to make you think we're so busy I don't have the time. It's just that we really are, busy that is, but I'm happy just the same. We're doing well, things are moving along, and the atmosphere is relaxed and peaceable, at least as far as the chefs are concerned. Francesca, the new waitress, kicked off with the usual "...nooo...yeees...I know you said those dishes were for table 10 but I took them to table 5...because, well, because they ordered them first...but, but..." In here we need people who aren't just willing and able, but won't mess up the restaurant or, more important, me.

No one can be a prima donna in here, especially a newcomer, and when the going gets tough, we all have to get our act together. There are certain displays of respect that make me truly admire people. Take Sampath: Sri Lankan rice is one example of his strength of character. When asked, "Who cooked this rice?" he proudly answers, "All of us," which is partly true, and partly it's an answer that looks ahead to a place we are all aiming to reach. I mean, what's more important than Sampath becoming famous for his rice or whatever is that we all recognize and reproduce the same excellent food. And it would be a major step forward if everyone could genuinely comprehend the secrets behind the great dishes that someone puts out before they become famous for being so talented. You asked about the others? Well, Fabrizio (the chef who's replacing you) has an incredible gift for remembering orders, he's without equal. Perewa still believes in precision and attention to detail—which I deeply appreciate (unlike you). Mamun manages to wash mountains of dirty dishes and pots and pans all by himself, and yesterday he celebrated his eighth wedding anniversary by phoning his wife who had just finished saying her prayers at 5 in the morning. Even though he's exhausted, he always gives me a smile when he hands me a cup of tea. And I'm sincerely grateful to him.

When you get back, we'll have to talk, because Fabrizio and Perewa have actually managed to make themselves useful without carrying on like prima donnas. There ain't no such thing as a free lunch, Leo. I'm learning this now, and it was partly you who taught me. I imagine (and hope) you can read between the lines.

I'm glad to hear you're so happy.

Ciao!!!

Mic

I was wearing shorts and black-and-yellow Havaianas, a backpack sat next to my chair, and the whole of Brazil was at my doorstep. I reread Michele's e-mail because I wasn't sure I'd understood it properly. My head was throbbing and not because of the humidity. Michele had just screwed me over, among the winks and nudges and exclamation points, this was what I gleaned: I'd been let go from a contract I didn't have. If only I weren't so full of shit, I could become a great chef. Sandro had been right all along.

Michele was an asshole and a coward who didn't have the guts to tell me to my face during those last few months, and waited until I had left to send me this shitty e-mail. That was my first thought. My second was: Maybe I'm just not good enough. Which anyone with the slightest sense of reality sooner or later ends up muttering to himself in a crisis situation. Sooner or later you have to face up to the possibility that your ambition might outweigh your talent.

Shit. I'd return to Italy without knowing what to do next. On the other hand, all this made perfect sense. Usually most people's greatest achievement is to feel adequate — big dreams are just crap. My worst sin, since moving to Tuscany, had been to make Michele feel nothing but inadequate. How long did I think he'd put up with feeling that way? When you play Russian roulette, the problem isn't whether the shot will fire or not, it's when.

In the end, the one who had to go was me, because it doesn't matter what you think you've learned. What matters is who the chef is, and that's life.

39.

Going out for a run the next morning helped to soothe my troubles and fears. Michele's wasn't the only e-mail to reach me in Brazil. I also received a message from a Neapolitan chef I had met years before. He was considering taking up an interesting offer and wanted to leave the restaurant he was currently working in, a pretentious little place with seating for thirty, situated at the end of Via Veneto. He asked if I'd like to replace him, but I hadn't answered yet. I'd also received a half-baked proposal to open a new restaurant in Costa Rica.

The Neapolitan's offer didn't strike me as much of an opportunity; in fact, it told me I had dug myself into a fucking hole that was entirely of my own making. The idea of being the chef in a new restaurant in Rome terrified me. Working at Sessanta or in Michele's kitchen had felt reassuringly temporary, there was nothing tying me down, the sky's the limit.

According to Mendel, genes have a plan for us; for Darwin, it's the environment; for Karl Marx, it is history. My grandma is convinced that only Almighty God has a plan for us. My plan is to travel through life without being weighed down.

When it comes to important decisions, I stall and dream of the most outrageous situations in the kitchen. Sometimes, I remembered those dreams, other times I didn't, but I knew I had them because I'd wake up with my heart in tatters. Going for a run can help, which is why so many people are out there pounding the pavements every morning.

"Yo."

"Oh, hi, Matt."

"So what about the Via Veneto gig?"

"Nice place."

"Are you going or not?"

"Don't know. It's my life we're talking about."

"What life?"

"A life where I'm free to travel, to move around, okay?"

"Ah. So that's your life? I had no idea. I thought it was being a chef. Who knew?"

"Okay, I got it. But I need more time to decide."

"You always give yourself plenty of time, that's why you're always late."

"You're right."

"So, are you going or not?"

"Well, yeah, I'm going."

The restaurant was called Castore e Polluce. It was built on the ruins of a Roman temple, and the floor in the dining room was glass so you could make out the remains of the old walls below. Red curtains, fancy silverware, porcelain plates, Doric columns — just walking in made me blush. The owners were a couple of laid-back twins, in suits and white shirts, who wasted no time getting straight to the point. They asked me to prepare a trial dinner by myself for them, their two other brothers, and their parents. If they hired me, I'd have a yearly contract paying €700 per month, plus another €1,600 under the table. Fourteen months of pay, with the cash payments to include bonuses and holiday pay. The restaurant was open for lunch and dinner and closed on Sundays. I would work every dinner service and do lunches only when needed. The kitchen staff included Aref, a Moroccan cook who was fast and very experienced, but sloppy, and Tommaso, a thirty-year-old with some high-class experience as a commis chef and very little self-confidence. Aref took care of the appetizers and mains, Tommaso was responsible for the entrées and desserts. I could carve out my role in the kitchen as I pleased. The twins didn't care if I got behind the burners or not, all they wanted was good food and for everything to run smoothly.

40.

Badrinat, also known as Nat, was fifty-two, wore thick-lensed glasses, and had been busted on a murder rap, forcing him to flee Bangladesh, where he risked a death sentence.

He got up every morning at seven in the house he shared with ten other fellow Bengalis in the rough neighborhood of Centocelle. He waited his turn to use the bathroom, got dressed, and took bus number 105 to Termini station and from there hopped on metro line A to Piazza Barberini. Then he walked the rest of the way. At nine he punched in, and his day began by snaking out the drain in the ladies' restroom that got blocked on a regular basis. Then he mopped the dining room floor and polished the silverware. At nine thirty, Aref and Tommaso arrived. They started prepping for lunch, and Nat began washing the pots and pans. If the restaurant was busy, he'd be chained to the dishwasher; if it was quiet, he would go into the kitchen to give a hand with prep. During the afternoon break, Nat sometimes managed to go home, but on public transport it was a long, drawn-out procedure, so he usually stayed at the restaurant to rest and clean out the fridges. At five o'clock, the second shift started, I arrived at six, and we closed the kitchen at around midnight. Nat hardly ever made it in time to catch the last metro, so he'd walk to the station and wait there for the number 50 night owl bus that passed every forty-five minutes. If you missed it, you were screwed. One evening I gave him a ride as far as Termini station on the back of my bicycle, but the bus had just left so I hung around with him until the next one came.

"I left because big problem at home. No money, *big* problem. Everything possible overseas. Much work, much money. God willing, life better overseas."

Nat's journey to Via Veneto was predicated on the belief that Overseas was a country in itself, whence all good things came: money, canned meat, Colgate toothpaste. In his country, the houses made out of brick and stone were built with money from Overseas. He and his family lived in a wooden shack. Nat was part of that multitude of money and mankind that ceaselessly crisscrossed the globe, a flow every bit as complex and ever-changing as the climate. He had no contract, and at the end of the month he pocketed €650 in cash. They couldn't give him a contract because he didn't have a residence permit, and he couldn't get a residence permit because he didn't have a job. On Fridays and Saturdays, the two nights we stayed open later, I would leave my bicycle at home and take my motorbike so that I could give Nat a ride home. Occasionally I would go up to his place for some rice with chicken and cardamom and listen to his incredible adventures while the others slept.

I didn't get on so well with Aref, although we managed to respect each other. The problem was that he was forty-two, married, and had two kids, and he was working alongside a chef ten years younger than him who did half the number of hours and earned twice as much as he did. Those kinds of thoughts tend to ruin your day and generate conflict. The owners were two nice enough guys from a very wealthy family, a fact that set everyone's mind at ease. Before long, Tommaso became like a brother, Aref turned into a chef I could count on, and Nat was a good friend.

Working at Castore e Polluce, I realized that there was plenty of stuff I didn't know I didn't know. The owners shared my ignorance and appreciated my experiments. The difference between Tommaso and Aref was that Tommaso wanted to be a chef because he loved the profession and believed in passion, while Aref had to send money back home to Morocco every month and hadn't yet found a simpler way of doing it. I cooked to stay clean and out of trouble, earn money, and have fun. I still believed that food was my alibi and not my destiny, even though Matteo continued to tell me the opposite. When I cooked, I neither feared nor needed to avoid dark alleyways on my way home. And anyway, I didn't cook to hang stars on my résumé but to blend into the background. The difference between me and Tommaso was that he, sooner or later, would make it to the top, whereas my cooking would never create the kind of buzz that attracted the attention of so many bombastic foodies.

Without me around, Tommaso would have become more and more withdrawn, and without him, my menus would be a stale version of the Verve's, or San Piero a Sieve's, or Sessanta's. Tommaso was one of those people who never aspire to a better life, who get along with everyone because they fit in wherever they go, and have nothing even remotely to do with the drug addicts, weirdos, megalomaniacs, and unfulfilled bastards I'd become used to working with over the years. He was a reliable, honest guy, in love with Rome and good food. I couldn't wrangle a wage increase for him, but I did treat him like my de facto sous chef, and he, in exchange, spared me the hassle of double checking whether this or that problem had been solved. This or that problem was regularly solved. In the kitchen, we listened to the Roman crooner Franco Califano.

Late one night, I checked my online bank balance and found more money than I'd ever had in my entire life. I remembered the job in Costa Rica and wondered how I could ever have taken the offer seriously. I bought a new motorbike, another black Japanese number with the same inline four-cylinder engine, but with more grunt. Nat said the old bike was more comfortable and he sat bolt upright behind me, clinging on for dear life.

In 2009, America inaugurated its first black president, and Italy gave undocumented immigrants a chance to become regularized on the back of an amnesty for illegal foreign house-maids and carers. What actually transpired was the latest in a long line of tactics for the government to make and move money with no respect for the reality or needs of illegal workers. I heard about the amnesty on the news, and Nat explained it to me. First of all, the amnesty was directed at a specific category of workers—dishwashers, waiters, pizza makers, brick-layers; therefore, a huge proportion of foreigners who had been working in Italy for years were not included. Second, the paper-work could be submitted only by employers willing to pay a €500 lump sum as a penalty for failing to pay the social security contributions of their "employee."

The result was that a mammoth system of scams was set in motion, where the first in line were the Italians, closely followed by the Senegalese and the Egyptians. Nat asked our bosses to file an application in his name, passing him off as a cleaner at their luxury villa in Piazza di Spagna. Not possible, they already had three cleaners there who were on the books. So he asked to borrow €1,000, so he could pay someone else to regularize him. Not possible, they did not lend money to employees. Before talking to Nat, I made a few inquiries at the local employment bureau: I couldn't sponsor anyone myself because I was below the minimum income threshold and, apart from my motorbike, I owned no assets and lived in financial no-man's-land.

I wanted to help in some way so Nat would not have to pay for something he was entitled to and shell out €500 for social security contributions that his employers should have paid. Then it struck me that there was one thing and one thing only that I could do for him: Give him €1,000 to get a residence permit as per the new anticrisis legislation. I will give a Bronx cheer to the next person who tells me that foreigners are stealing our money and our jobs.

The kitchen was clean. Nat dipped the mop into the bucket I had filled with water from the boiler, and I went out so he could wash the floor. Aref had already left, Tommaso pulled on his crash helmet and said good night. I took my apron off and went down the three steps that led to the pantry and the back of the kitchen. I entered the change room and took off my black jacket, remaining in my undershirt. I laced my fingers together and stretched my arms above my head until my shoulder blades creaked and cracked. I put on my sweatshirt, grabbed a glass while the maître d' finished balancing the cash register, poured myself a beer, and went outside. I pressed my nose against the window and cupped my hands around my eyes to shade them from the reflection of the streetlamps. Inside, some of the diners were lingering over dessert or coffee or a liqueur while they enjoyed the warmth of the open fireplace and the soft lighting. In my mind I could hear the echoes of jaws chomping on food that had come out of my kitchen. Every table had its own story to tell, and I had been part of them all, at least in some small way, this evening.

Doing a job you love is a punishment. It prevents you from doing any of the other things you might like or might have felt drawn toward at least once in your life. It's that illness of mine that goes by the name of dignity and manifests itself in highs

and lows. I sipped my beer and looked at my burned and cal-
loused hands. One of the twins gave me a big friendly smile
from inside the restaurant while he was clearing a table, and I
acknowledged him by tipping my glass to him. As I was saying,
this job, my job, is all about crests and troughs, comings and
goings. It's not hard to work out when you're content with what
you're doing. You look at the people around you and sense that
you're holding them in the palm of your hand. Deep down you
know we are not all equal, because you can stand outside and
watch them, knowing that their satisfaction or disappointment
is all up to you.

41.

Mine was a simple life: the gym, my morning run, a swim, the restaurant. My new motorbike, the odd night out, heart-to-hearts with Matteo in the evening, a woman once in a while, riding my bicycle after dark past the Imperial Forums or along the old Appian Way and the feeling that this, in itself, makes me a very lucky guy indeed.

What I remember of that night is the birthday party I hadn't been invited to and a smiling girl from the Veneto region with a trace of D minor in the pitch of her voice that revealed a melancholy side that all the smiles in the world could not entirely conceal. I remember her words crushed between the walls of the venue and, later, in the darkness of the night. I don't remember what she was wearing, there was nothing special about her clothes, but those eyes were too beautiful for anything else to matter. She spoke to me about her work in the infectious diseases unit of a hospital in Rome, and about Africa. I told her that the birthday girl's tiramisù was shit. Then I went looking for her at the address she'd given me, but she wasn't there and I thought I'd never see her again.

Instead she found me. She came to dinner at the restaurant on Via Veneto with a girlfriend. Her sense of direction was non-existent (the name of the street she told me she lived on was wrong), but she had a good memory and plenty of initiative. She'd never been with a man she later despised, which in itself was a good enough reason to fall in love with her.

Her name was Giuliana. She had long shapely legs and the most beautiful breasts I had ever seen, and she was very shy. She said that statistically love did not exist, and I agreed with her. She said that spending €100 on a meal was insulting, and I did not agree with her. We continued to meet after I finished dinner service at the restaurant, and both of us regarded those nights as thumbing our noses at statistics. She made me listen to rapper Ascanio Celestini's "L'amore stupisce" (Love Surprises). Love hits you and you don't know why, loves pollutes like a Chinese multinational. Love isn't, no it isn't possible, the song goes, in the fragile world of flowers. I made her listen to "E statte zitta" (Just Shut Up) by the Roman singer-songwriter Alessandro Mannarino. Love, yeah right, the clothes will dry by themselves and this chill doesn't come from outside, it comes from inside of me.

Then she won a residency at a hospital in Bologna and I decided to follow her there. I left the restaurant on Via Veneto and filled my backpack. I had no control over the life and moods of this woman, so it didn't worry me that I didn't have any control over my own life either. Anyway, I landed a job pretty much as soon as I got there, and all was good with the world.

Nearly a year went by, and although Giuliana always wore black, she turned my life upside down with those eyes and the thoughts hidden behind them. When she took me to meet her mother in Thiene and then to dinner at a nearby restaurant, I ate one of the best pizzas I'd ever had and stopped to have a few words with the owner of the restaurant. He needed a chef. Giuliana's residency in Bologna was coming to an end and she was moving to Asiago. I looked at the map. Thiene was only twenty miles from Asiago, so I made an appointment for an interview and soon after started my new life in the Veneto region.

Learning to master yeast seemed like a good idea at the time.

42.

The restaurant in Thiene was called Fermento, and after thirteen years at the burners, it shall go down in history as my one and only abysmal failure. The only restaurant that features in my nightmares.

Anthony Bourdain wrote years ago that the back of a restaurant is a subculture whose military hierarchy and centuries-old practices based on rum, sodomy, and the lash create a blend of tough and solid order together with chaos, able to put the resolve of just about anyone to the test. It is still true. Beyond the door of a professional kitchen, you have to prove what you are worth, there is no other way. You have to earn the respect first of those above you, and then of those below you. There are only so many feathers you can ruffle, and only when it is necessary to clarify that you will take only so much before lashing out and that you expect to be shown some respect. And you can do that only when you are sure your work is beyond reproach, because the respect you demand is not for you, it is for the tangible results of your efforts. If you don't, you're a loser. If you do it at the wrong time, if you flare up when you've been caught out, you're a loser. And if you are known as a loser, then it's over, life in a commercial kitchen will be unendurable.

I started out at the sink, washing dishes, then when I became a chef, kitchen hands became my best sounding boards. Foreign in every way, always slightly offbeat, marching to a different drummer, watching from the sidelines, but with some of the best stories ever told, as is generally the case with people who come from faraway lands. Maybe this was why things came crashing down in Thiene. Because there, the outsider was me, but no one was interested in hearing my stories. The rest of the staff were local, from the Veneto region, with the sole exception of Sofia, the Nigerian dishwasher. She struggled with Italian, although she understood the local dialect. The chef-owner was a master baker and an expert at anything that involved leavening agents; he was a genius when it came to cakes and pastries. A fascinating character, much better educated and knowledgeable than the average cook, a wizard who could make magic with gluten and sourdough starters, and a trickster like so many others.

Dishonesty, shoddiness, crass ignorance, and systematic lying to cover up all manner of misdeeds, along with the heartless bullying of the most vulnerable staff members, were the distinctive features of this restaurant, which clung desperately to a false perception of its own success. Before wishing they would all die a long and painful death, like kittens mauled by a pack of wolves, I did manage to have some good times. My plan was to acquire the skills I had neglected to learn during my Roman years; it was possibly the perfect place to fill in the gaps in my culinary education. The kitchen was equipped with sous-vide machines, plenty of fridges, spectacular fresh produce, blast chiller cabinets, and ovens that were precise down to a tenth of a degree. The only problem was that my opinion of myself was a long stretch from their opinion of me, and it didn't take long to become mightily confused about who was right.

I had never plumbed the depths of cruelty that a kitchen brigade that doesn't want you will go to. The pastry chef told me harrowing tales of her rootless existence, her inability to stay in one place, and her craving to challenge herself in new directions. She had worked in Cittadella, Borso del Grappa, then a stint on Lake Garda, Malcesine, and even Madonna di Campiglio before landing here in Thiene. But she had never ventured farther than about ninety miles in any direction. She rattled on as I waited for the punch line, the part of the story that says: Okay, you can laugh now. It never came. She had the serious, self-satisfied air of someone dangerously unacquainted with irony. A fearless traveler in an unmoving and stagnant world. She must have read my mind because from that day onward she declared war on me, and I stopped pretending that I liked the place.

The head chef had a knack for selling his cuisine like a country you swear allegiance and devotion to. He knew the food that came out of his kitchen was blue-ribbon quality and expected nothing less than overt gratitude from his staff. Every chef wants to gain enough experience and expertise to open their own restaurant and demands loyalty and dedication from those still learning the trade. None of that interested me, but I had no alternative. I was on a part-time contract, officially working thirty hours a week for €900 a month, and unofficially slaving away another forty hours, for an additional €600 under the table. This highly desirable condition of legality and security would arrive after the usual two-month trial period, paid entirely cash in hand. Starting from the bottom of the ladder at thirty-four years of age and with twelve years of experience under my belt made me sick to my stomach.

"Do you know how to put together a lasagna?" the head chef asked me.

His were not merely recipes; they were a delicate balance of physics and the molecular compositions of the senses that called for considerable effort to recognize the essential elements of food—sugar, fat, protein, water—and from there to understand how they all interacted when cooked, emulsified, or frozen, even in the simplest of dishes. Mayonnaise is an emulsion of fat, water, acid, and protein. When you look at it like that, you can make "mayonnaise" out of just about anything and create some truly extraordinary food.

His lasagna with radicchio was like that, put together the way you'd normally create a dessert. A dessert treated like a chemistry lesson. Quantities precise to one-sixteenth of an ounce, cooking times calculated down to the second. For example: 180 minutes at 113°, no caramelization of the béchamel sauce on top, a flawless alternation of white layers with purple. The time and attention to detail required by this kind of approach is in no way comparable to what it takes to make a regular lasagna. Ladles are out, your tool of choice is the spatula. And the scales aren't just a platform, a spring, and a pointer, there's this hi-tech electronic gizmo that any pusher would be proud to call his own. You could use it to cut cocaine with mannitol, it's so precise, and some of them actually did.

"More or less," was my reply.

"Well, follow this recipe," he told me, handing me a sheet of paper. It was nearly two o'clock, the last lunch guests were leaving, and some of the cleaners were getting a head start. His recipes represented a wealth of knowledge that I respected deeply. So I stayed in the kitchen during the break and used the spatula, and weighed, adjusted, and double-checked everything, and waited the requisite three hours at 113°. Alvise was the sous chef, with the yellow-green eyes of a feral cat and nervous, twitchy hands. He approached the oven to look at the lasagna through the glass in the door as soon as the timer went off.

"That lasagna isn't done yet, leave it in," he said.

"Chef insisted I follow his recipe to the letter. I don't think it's done either, but..." I ventured.

"No buts, it's undercooked and that's that. Give it a blast at at least a hundred and forty-nine degrees for ten minutes, the béchamel has to cook."

"Are you sure?"

"Listen, leave that lasagna in the oven and set the timer."

Lasagna in the oven, 149°, ten minutes. I concentrated on tidying up the pass. When the oven timer rang again, I pulled the lasagna out and put it directly into the blast chiller. Temperature set to 3°, just to chill. Once it's been portioned, then it can be frozen. (Does anyone still believe in fresh food made to order? No. No, they don't.) The head chef returned to the kitchen and opened the blast chiller. Behind the puff of freezer vapor, the lasagna made its appearance. Slightly tinted around the edges, not crunchy, but the fats in the cheese and the béchamel sauce had turned pale gold. In here, the effect known as caramelization.

"What temperature did you cook it at?" he growled.

Speechless and confused, I looked over at Alvise.

"When I came in, he was getting it out of the oven. I have no idea how long it was in there," Alvise declared primly.

Random thoughts were running through my head: What do I say? The truth? But what is the truth? Which version of the truth sounds truer?

"A hundred and thirteen degrees, just like you said, but maybe it was left in a touch longer, because I went to change my clothes and I didn't hear the timer," was the truth I decided to go for.

The head chef stormed out, ranting and raving about wasting time and work and food that'll have to be thrown out. The lasagna was sliced into portions, frozen, and then served for the rest of the month. Like any other well-made fucking lasagna.

I waited for the right moment, boiling over inside. Then I took Alvise aside.

"You know perfectly well why the lasagna was the color it was," I said to him.

With his face inches away from mine, he whispered, a little smugly, I thought, "It's your own fault. The guy you call Chef is an asshole. His recipes are all theory. I told you to leave the lasagna in a bit longer because in here I'm the only one who really knows how to cook and when you got it out the first time it was undercooked. But you're the one who burned it. You should have kept an eye on it when it was in the oven at a hundred and forty-nine degrees and not trusted the timer."

Flecks of spit sprayed all over my face and my pride. I slowly cleaned myself up and went into the cold room. He stayed at the rotating pizza oven putting the finishing touches on the pizzas, and in that split second it hit me that I would never fit in here, where they didn't follow any of the rules I knew.

In the cold room, I bumped into the head chef and told him that I had raised the temperature to 149° on my own initiative. End of story. But that rift could now only widen. Those bastards were waging a war of supremacy, and €1,500 a month, half of which was paid under the table, was simply not enough for me to engage in it. Defending your ideas to the death is not always a noble thing to do, and the sincerity of your faith is not necessarily a virtue. I started brazenly copying out every single recipe—desserts, appetizers, entrées, everything. It was only a matter of time before I quit, and I had to make the most of my time there.

In the absence of fellowship, people will always do what's in their best interest, and there's nothing wrong with that. It isn't a question of cynicism or cunning, just survival. It's what the others were doing, except they had more time.

The head chef was hardly ever in the kitchen. He would turn up only to make some implausible request or whip up some showstopping dough for a panettone, the Italian Christmas cake, or to try out different glazes. Alvise never moved from his station and had the last word on everything. The pastry chef shamelessly buttered up Alvise for more perks and the chance to bully the apprentices, the commis chefs, and all the newbies. She was probably planning to wait until Alvise hung up his apron and left and then take his place and revel in her newfound power. Alvise was there to learn how to manage all the different sections of the kitchen, and to make sure that the clients knew who was doing all the cooking so they would follow him when he eventually opened his own place. The head chef was angling to get on TV and maybe even earn a Michelin star. The others were only bit players using every cigarette break to let rip a stream of profanities but otherwise dutifully bowing and scraping.

The head chef didn't trust Alvise and trusted the pastry chef even less, though he knew he would be lost without them. He constantly quizzed me about what they were saying in the kitchen, calling me into his office as often as three times a day. They would nod their heads in agreement and follow his orders when he was present, only to describe him later with the same two words: useless asshole. Alvise had less than no respect for the head chef and expected me to follow his lead in the kitchen. I, however, had been employed by the head chef, not by Alvise, and I was still in my fucking never-ending trial period. In other words, I was still under special surveillance and couldn't let on that everything the chef said was bullshit. As well, I was an all too frequent visitor to his office, and in the eyes of the neglected bastard descendants of the kitchen, I was a spineless spy. Definitely not one of them.

Everything was going downhill. It was there that I made the mother of all mistakes, a gigantic fuckup: I blabbed to the chef that those two snakes in the grass called him an asshole behind his back, adding that he should watch whom he left in charge of the kitchen, because I, a relative newcomer, was starting to think he was indeed an asshole, and it's not at all good for a newly employed member of staff to think his employer, the head chef, was an asshole. It's not good for the company and it's not healthy.

Where I *really* fucked up was trusting him and snitching on the others before getting to know him well enough. I gave in to my childish ego and started whining about how bad they were and how good I was. I chose to side with management when I was still on the bottom rung, an act of high treason toward the entire profession. I identified him as the All-Powerful One and curled up at his feet, licking my wounds and yelping like an abandoned puppy. Only the chef wasn't as powerful as I thought, because no one in the kitchen looked up to him as the head chef—they saw him as a kind of necessary tyrant. I behaved like a real novice and confirmed all the brigade's suspicions. I never found out what was said and by whom. But from that point onward I was undeniably on a slippery slope.

The only person I could still talk to was Sofia. A disarming smile, perfect teeth, a short, thick neck, strong hands, and beautiful brown skin over a stocky body, she had arrived from Libya as an illegal immigrant together with her husband and son. She had regularized her legal status following the amnesty in 2009 for domestic workers and carers. In Nigeria she had earned a degree in economics; here in Thiene she cleaned the house of the chef's mother and washed the dishes in his restaurant.

Since then she had had two more children, who now spoke the Veneto dialect. The oldest was a parking attendant at the restaurant on weekends, and at 11 p.m. earned the right to eat a plate of pasta, with or without sauce. Store-bought pasta, not freshly made, the head chef had insisted. I would cook it for him. I was bitterly ashamed to be cooking bought pasta, while leftover handmade tortellini stuffed with culatello, Italy's most prized and expensive prosciutto, was getting thrown in the garbage.

The more I hung out with Sofia and her son, the more suspicious people became of me. It wasn't just the visits to the boss's office; now I was shooting the breeze in English with the dishwasher. Who knows what they thought we were saying to each other. Sofia was on an on-call contract, fifteen hours a month, but she ended up putting in more than two hundred. This wasn't a case of her paying her dues; there were no promotions in sight for her. Front of house had swarms of waitstaff, mostly students (all paid under the table or with on-call contracts) and three part-time professionals. All of them earned between €400 and €700 a month, cash in hand, and they'd laugh heartily at jokes told in the local dialect I pretended to understand. The insults and jokes tossed back and forth between the kitchen brigade and the waitstaff are what help you make it through the day. To be left out of the game stinks like rotten fish, and when the stench sticks to your clothes and hands, it doesn't wash away.

Christmas was approaching, and our working hours were getting longer and longer. My trial period had morphed into a four-month contract, and the only visible difference was that my first official wage was late. I was beginning to come undone. I had to keep reminding myself who I was, how I had ended up in this place, and what I wanted to achieve—not only first thing in the morning as soon as I woke up, but even when I was toasting the demi-glace in a pot that was taller than I was. Orlando, years before, used to say to me, "When my fingers ache from filleting the umpteenth frozen yellowtail, when I just can't take it any longer, I visualize my paycheck and the restaurant I'll open one day, and I keep on going." Even he was being paid cash in hand at that stage, but he could visualize €2,300 cash on top of the €700 in his pay packet. In the end it boiled down to the money, as usual. A mere €1,500 a month was barely enough to stop me setting fire to the place.

I liked the kind of kitchens I'd worked in before: noisy, debauched, bursting with testosterone, and with a clear moral compass. Ass lickers and hypocrites are bad for your health. I could see no way out, and there were no more recipes for me to copy. The office was in semidarkness as usual, and the head chef was in his immaculate uniform as always, but this time I'd gone in on my own initiative.

"Chef, I'll do the New Year's Eve dinner and work New Year's Day, and then I'm through. As of the second of January I won't be coming back and here's why: You are a slave driver and the way you run your restaurant is criminal. On top of that, you're relying on a bunch of lying, cheating wimps, and I don't know whether to blame you or them. It pains me because the food you produce here is sheer art and poetry, and you'll get your star, for sure, but the way you're getting it is unconscionable."

New Year's Eve we all busted our asses, and if I thought I would be feeling so much lighter for having put an end to my

Kafkaesque loneliness, then what was this nagging sense of anxiety? I was retreating from the battlefield, and who cared if I was in the right or in the wrong. No one would miss me, I felt utterly defeated. Maybe I could have stuck it out and become inducted into the merry band of people who would earn a star (because sooner or later they would), set out on a proper career path, and turn into a real asshole. Instead I was cutting and running.

The text message arrived late at night, when I was with Giuliana and a couple of friends of hers, in some crappy club, getting sloshed. "Our business relationship ends here, don't bother coming in to work tomorrow." A lousy text message to settle a lousy score. Checkmate.

For the rest of the night I couldn't shake off the disturbing suspicion that maybe I was the one at fault, for raising the white flag after only six months and without winning anyone's respect. With the exception, perhaps, of Sofia.

What now? I was leaving Thiene battered and bruised, with my tail between my legs. Decked and dazed. Maybe if they had paid me more or if I had told Alvise and the dessert bitch to piss off with a smile on my face, it would have been just another job like all the others. Daily battles with diners and waitstaff, cash-in-hand wages, a life not too far removed from the rest of the world's.

I had spent half of my life (the part that started in a restaurant in Rome) roaming from place to place, sometimes taking friends along for the ride, but life in a professional kitchen hadn't suited them. I had persevered and this had become my calling. That first of January when I should have gone to work but instead spent the day at home was painful beyond belief. Maybe I was just hungover from the shitty wine of the night before. When you're hungover you tend to mistake tiredness for unhappiness. That fucking restaurant had hung me out to dry. When I went in to collect the money they owed me (my last wage and severance pay), they told me the cash was a bit less because the severance pay had to be deducted.

After all, our agreement had been for €1,500 a month, and €1,500 was all I'd get. A few days went by and I sent them an e-mail with my membership number in CGIL, Italy's largest trade union federation.

They gave me the rest of my fucking money and treated me like a piece of shit. I didn't say a word because I had all but exhausted my reserves of belief in the usefulness of anger.

Moral of the story: Working for a chef who doesn't cook and with a brigade that doesn't want you is not a good idea.

43.

Is there such a thing as a philosophy of nutrition? Nietzsche asked himself that question. And every now and again so do I.

The city and I wake up at the same time. Or at least that's what I like to think—the aroma of coffee, the sounds of shops opening and cars starting. Because when a city awakens, not only do its inhabitants open their eyes and reconnect with the world, but its walls are bathed in a certain light and its streets surrender once more to being trodden on and driven over. Silence lingers for a while and then breaks. Bologna is that kind of city, where it feels like everyone does everything in unison, even breathing. You learn things like that about a city, and then you feel less of a stranger.

Giuliana's already been up for a while and the baby is playing on a rug in the lounge, having had his full share of milk and breast. When I see him like that, just before leaving the house, I start to think about the future as something that has already begun. His existence is a sign of rebellion against modernity and all its perversions, urgency, and the eternal futility of tomorrow. My baby boy has helped me discover that I like being where I am, in the moment. And it doesn't matter whether it's Asiago or Rome, Bologna or Florence or L'Aquila. It doesn't matter at all because in a short while I'll be grilling a fillet steak or looking at myself in a mirror and deciding that the past few sleepless nights are showing in my face. A few years back I would have described it as a deceleration of the centrifugal forces hurtling me toward a waiting world. Today the place I'm at is a family, and the present has never been such a fundamental part of my life.

My morning coffee tastes just as it should. I get dressed, pack my laptop, a book, and my neatly folded uniform into my backpack and sling it over my shoulder. I say goodbye to Giuliana, give the little man a hug, and leave the house musing that I am now the same age as my dad was in my last memories of him.

I have a twofold image of my father. In one I can see him the way I did back then—when I was a scared and ravenous teenager—and in the other it's through the eyes of a man the same age. The time in between feels pleasantly familiar now.

I walk to the tram stop, running slightly late as I usually am and always have been. The morning cacophony of cars honking, shop shutters clanking, footsteps on pebble stones builds to a crescendo. Under the tram shelter there are people on their way to work, older people (where do all these elderly folk go every day?), and kids sneaking a cigarette before school, a flowing and purposeful rhythm of which I too am a part. A beautiful day under a lukewarm sun, a brisk mid-October breeze, the tram running on time, one every three minutes. Everything satisfactory, set out in the only way possible. Then I spot Carlo Cracco staring at me from a poster on the opposite side of the tracks, his arms crossed, leaning next to a potato chip topped with a sadly out-of-place quail egg, and urging me to "be daring and use it"—the potato chip—"in your dishes." Of course he's selling out our entire profession. In the sense that that poster says it all. I'm screwing with you. I've always screwed you, we're an army of people who've been screwing you around for a very long time, because you have no idea what we've been up to, you don't know the meaning of soul and harmony, all you need to be is punctual and able to regurgitate hackneyed

clichés. Here's a shitty quail egg on top of a potato chip out of a
€1 packet, and everyone opens their mouths like trained mon-
keys and makes a beeline for their wallets. Take a closer look
at the poster: The tagline is, "Cooking takes guts," in quota-
tion marks, followed by the *MasterChef* judge's signature. Right
concept, wrong context.

When I was a teenager, I was convinced that pain and hard
work added an extra measure of dignity, so when I first began
working in a professional kitchen, I believed it would wash away
all my sins and turn them into grace and pride. And that scraps
of meat, once they've gone through the mincer, would turn into
good food. Now I know I was wrong. It's television that adds an
extra measure of dignity and washes away all sins.

I get word that the restaurant where I worked my knuckles
to the bone and busted my ass in Thiene has closed and the
owner-chef has become a regular on a food program on TV. He
pretends he's cooking, he's become a familiar face, he can pay
off his mortgage and no longer has to deal with labor disputes
initiated by pissed-off former employees. Can you blame him?
No, neither can I.

It's not about whether or not you become a big shot. I believe
it's simpler than that: It's about working less and earning more.

In the end, this is a dream shared by many, and not just
chefs; maybe it's a question of well-being. As far as I'm concerned, my little boy has a huge bearing on my current well-
being and many of the choices I make. After all, we all dream
of being the piece of the puzzle that fits perfectly into someone
else's dream. My son is the piece that joins me to Giuliana.
I'm not being schmaltzy, just consistent. Years have passed and
I'm still a chef, cooking in the same spirit as when I started:

as a stepping-stone to something else, something else that reappears in a different guise over time. And then there are coincidences.

A few years back I was on my way home on a train from Florence, and I bumped into a girl from Bologna I had met in Rome. She had perky breasts and a mountain of dreams that hadn't yet collapsed into a mudslide. Her name was Aurora. We sat together and chatted the whole time. She showed me photos of Antonio, a geologist friend of hers with a passion for motorbikes and travel. In the winter of 2006, I had gone to India and written to her, and she had replied to say that that friend of hers was in India too. He was near the Pakistani border, on his motorbike, and she gave me his e-mail address and told me to contact him. I was in Karnataka on an Enfield 350 I had rented and more than a thousand miles from where he was, so there wasn't much point getting in touch. But I wrote to him nonetheless, just a few lines to say hello. Then I put it completely out of my mind and a week later I decided to head inland, toward Hampi. Hampi is a village famous for its ruins of the ancient Vijayanagara Empire, and it's the only place in India I visited where it is compulsory to register your name and details with the local police. After finding a guesthouse, taking a shower, and having a rest, I went to an Internet point, where I found an e-mail from Antonio: He had just arrived in Hampi and read my name in the police register, just above his own. He was leaving the following day, and if I wanted, we could meet at the Virupaksha Temple. He'd be waiting for me there at around eight. We talked all evening and stayed in contact for years afterward. We wrote to each other when I was in Puerto Rico and he in South Sudan, and then when I was in Brazil and he in Darfur, without ever meeting in person again. Four years after that night, I met and fell in love with Giuliana, she found a position in Bologna, and we moved in together in an apartment that turned out to be five hundred yards from Antonio's place.

Coincidences are proof that we are in the right place at the right time. I've built my whole life and all of my stories around them. For Kafka, coincidences were a sign, from either the angels or the hit men of fate, representing an uncontrollable slice of life that terrified him. When on June 29, 1920, he was in Vienna to meet Milena Jesenská, he wrote to her from his hotel to say she should not startle him by approaching from the side or from behind.

In *Death in Venice*, Aschenbach is informed that his luggage has been sent ahead to Como by mistake, and he takes it as a sign he must remain in Venice and contemplate his beloved Tadzio; it is ultimately his death warrant. In Jungian psychology, coincidence is known as synchronicity and always has meaning. Then Twitter, Facebook, and iPhones arrived on the scene, and if coincidences still happen it's become harder to recognize them. In any case, they continue to play a role in my life.

I look around the tram: There must be about fifteen of us, and everyone (including me) is holding a smartphone. I start reading the day's news, jumping from Twitter to various news sites. Italy's prime minister, Matteo Renzi, has made a few announcements; Silvio Berlusconi is doing community service at a hospice in Cesano Boscone; unrest is again stirring in the Middle East; the Roma soccer club won its last match. As did Juventus. Damn. I'd call Matteo, but he is traveling solo around Vietnam. As I mess around with my phone, an e-mail arrives: It's from Matteo.

From: Matteo Angius
To: Leonardo Lucarelli
Date: October 18, 2013, 10:38 p.m.
Subject: From the East

Here I am.

I'm writing to you from a place you'd love: a food court with
about 30 kiosks. There's people cooking meat stews, fish,
seafood, soups, and sweets. It's just outside the center of Ho
Chi Minh City, and tomorrow I'll be celebrating my first month
in Vietnam—on a 12-hour overnight bus to Cambodia. Being
so far away and for so long tempts me to just vanish into thin
air. Morph into someone else, like we used to fantasize about
in Rome. Be totally different from the person I thought I'd
become all those years ago. But just writing these things tells
me I haven't changed at all.

Here, everything is both real and fake at the same time. It's
weird. In any case, the Vietnamese seem happy; I'd say they're
content with the way they live and this reminds me of you. And
there are all these women whose age is impossible to guess,
tiny women, barefoot, that remind me so much of your mother.

It's been at least a couple of days since I spoke to anyone,
and I'm ok with that. It's just that when you don't talk much,
your thoughts start going off on a tangent and intertwining
with each other in the strangest ways. Just a moment or so
ago, for instance, I was thinking about the theory that
laughter lifts your mood because apparently it releases
endorphins and stimulates the production of serotonin. Who
knows if it's true. It's been weeks now since I last had a
laugh—I mean a big belly laugh—and yet I feel great. And I

don't even go running in the morning. And no, no sex. I guess I laughed more when I was younger. And you always laughed more than me anyway.

All this solitude makes me feel old. Seeing me old makes me feel like a kid again. But writing all this to you, who's had a son in the meantime, makes me feel like an adolescent again. And realizing that I'm here, writing all this to you, makes me feel like an old man again. Go figure.

In 12 years I'll be 50. The thought is banging around so loudly in my head that I wonder if people can hear it. No, I don't think so. Fifty is a nice round number and, in some ways, I'd like to be that age right now. But the point is not the number, 50. The point is us. Our life story. The score we settle with the meaning of things. I'm simply astonished at the power of ideas like this: a thought is like the last card that makes a house of cards come tumbling down. I've never actually built a house of cards, but I suppose that's how it must be. You used to say: "When you do something really well, everything else falls into place." In actual fact you've fucked up more times than I can remember. You also used to say that working as a cook was what saved you, but every time you needed to pull out all the stops, I had to remind you of it.

The years are passing and both of us are changing, and our relationship and the things we say to each other are changing too. When I came to see you before leaving, I thought the baby was awesome, and you're a good dad in a way that's both just like you and surprising at the same time. So maybe this is what saves us. I don't know exactly what it is you are doing — it doesn't even matter — but I'm thinking about you now and I think you're fine just where you are. Me, I don't know. And if I say I'm 27, they believe me.

Ok, I'll sign off now, my fried banana is ready. See you soon, my dear friend Leo.

Matt

44.

It was the second time I'd worked in Bologna. The first was when Giuliana and I moved there. Three years later I started out in a one-star place. They just happened to be looking for a chef de partie for entrées, and along I came knocking at their door. The head chef knew Sandro. This fact emerged while I was listing the restaurants I had worked in during the interview. The guy must have contacted him, and it turned out that despite everything, Sandro still put in a good word for me, because they snapped me up immediately. An elegant place, just like all the others that earn their stars from the handful of select clients in the hushed dining room and make their money from the bustling bistro. The bistro is the equivalent of a clearance outlet: the same quality as its distinguished counterpart but not as formal and slightly more reasonably priced. Only the superstars of the restaurant business can do without a bistro. I don't believe El Bulli has one, for example. Massimo Bottura, with his three stars, has had to give in and recently opened his own bistro, whereas Heinz Beck is one of those who are still holding strong.

At the one-star restaurant, I was making €1,300 a month, half cash in hand, in exchange for an unspecified and disproportionately large number of hours. The bistro served moderately priced meals, and the owners expected to pay moderately priced wages too. Although to be fair, the definition of moderately priced needs qualifying: Their entrée of Pasta all'Amatriciana cost €40. Within a few weeks I had copied most of their signature recipes and realized that scaling the dizzying heights of a star-studded restaurant wasn't that hard. I remember zucchini molding in the cold pantry alongside the fruit, pelting the apprentice with hot potatoes, and realizing, with cast-iron certainty, that I lacked the wherewithal to start from the ground up all over again. Not because I was too old, but because I just couldn't stomach it anymore. On top of which, €35 for an entrée of spaghetti aglio e olio was an insult to common sense. Even if the pasta is handmade and it's smothered with a fondue of award-winning Castelmagno cheese.

So I looked around and without undue effort found myself in this shabby dump of a place with a half-decent reputation, located just outside the city walls. The owner was your usual maverick restaurateur with a shady past, a few fleeting moments of financial good fortune, a rap sheet that included a couple of months in the slammer, and a tidy sum that had survived along with him and that he had wisely decided to invest—imagine that!—in the gold-plated world of restaurants. Anything but reliable but, all things considered, manageable. The pay was reasonable: €90 a day, payable weekly so as not to be owed too much money in one shot, all of it cash in hand, and with the usual fictitious on-call contract. At the end of the month I'd receive a semblance of an official wage that I'd deduct from the following week's pay.

For the first few months in Bologna, doubts continued to gnaw at me, but although I was working lunches and dinners seven days a week in an outlandish place, I could cook up beef fillet with myrtle sauce, deboned guinea fowl with lemon, steak tartare with artisanal sauces, breaded and fried egg yolk, handmade spaghetti aglio e olio (the same as the star-rated restaurant, but it cost just €9 here), and grouper carpaccio with horseradish, among much else.

And this made a difference. Whenever I wondered where the hell I was and what the hell I was doing, I'd remember

Orlando's advice—close your eyes, take a deep breath, and visualize the nearly €3,000 a month you're earning—and the jitters would fade away. I managed to take myself seriously even amid neon lights, paper napkins, and blue plastic tables that matched the sky in the monstrously hideous painting that dominated the dining area.

Getting into that dump convinced me that if I had choices here, I'd have them just about anywhere, and this luxury meant I could continue regarding everyone else as assholes.

In the kitchen with me, but mornings only, was the owner's mom, a sprightly seventy-year-old who sneaked a smoke when her son wasn't looking, called him "that idiot" behind his back, and always made me laugh out loud. We'd have deep and meaningful conversations from time to time and really got to like each other. Thanks to her, I learned how to make tortellini. I had never been friends with anyone seventy years of age, and this meant something too.

The president of one of the biggest multistakeholder social cooperatives in the Emilia-Romagna region had his office only a street away and soon became a regular at the restaurant. When we first met, he told me about the various activities and professional development programs they conducted for "the disadvantaged" (his words), and I told him about my work as a chef and my degree in anthropology. The co-op also ran a "restaurant" and two cafés, he added. We immediately locked eyes with interest. He told me bluntly that he wanted the cooperative's slapdash eatery to become a fully fledged restaurant and not just a black hole that gobbled up nearly €60,000 of European structural funds and local taxpayer money every year.

There were several good reasons for wanting to work with him, but foremost was to have free rein and show off my talents which, according to the president, no one else in the cooperative seemed to have. I ticked off all the other reasons, but kept this one to myself. When two people meet for the first time and each thinks he stands to gain something from the other, what usually happens is that they give each other a big smile and an agreement is entered into, whether it's a job or a marriage. Ours would be only a theoretical agreement, however, until the local authorities signed the necessary permits et cetera, so for the time being we just smiled.

Meanwhile, Giuliana was offered the residency in Asiago, so I left Bologna and went to work at the restaurant in Thiene, and things went the way they went. In any event, it took me two weeks to find a job as chef de partie in a hotel on the Asiago plateau and to convince myself that, all in all, I could cope with living in a tiny mountain village. Leaving Rome helped me realize that being a chef was a prerogative that belonged to me alone and not to the skills I had acquired in the kitchens of the Eternal City.

I wasn't tied to any particular place to bring home the bacon, and I had more freedom and power than I could have imagined. But when Giuliana received a telegram informing her that she had won another competitive exam, this time at a hospital in L'Aquila, and was happy to move again, I had just been offered a chef's position at a hotel up north in the Trentino region and I was sick of relocating. For a while our paths diverged, and although the house we were renting in Asiago was still our home, we were just not living in it together. I thoroughly enjoyed that isolated winter, high up in the Alps, though sometimes I even felt the cold in my dreams. Giuliana and I caught up with each other three times: The first time I went south to see her in Abruzzo; the second time she came up north to Trentino; and the third time we met in the middle, in Rome. She was a month late, and just before I left, in the restroom of a coffee shop near Termini station, we discovered she was pregnant. While making my way back north on the train, trying to figure out what to do next, the president of the cooperative in Emilia-Romagna called me. All the permits had come through from the local council for the restaurant we had discussed, and he wanted to know if I was still interested, even though nearly two years had passed. I accepted the offer on the spot. Sometimes my mouth knows the answer long before my brain does.

In reality, this particular answer was an easy one. Giuliana would be off work during her pregnancy, and moving in together down in L'Aquila would mean my starting from scratch, looking for a job in the city that had been flattened by the 2009 earthquake. The prospect of grilling pork chops in some mom-and-pop joint was far less appealing than setting up a new restaurant that would welcome me with open arms in Bologna. It would be for only a limited time, and our life in Abruzzo would just go on the back burner. But then again, I'd never imagined settling down in one place forever, and even a baby on the way was no reason to start now. Plus we both loved the vibrant Emilia-Romagna region.

So here I was, part chef, part coach, part consultant, and part teacher. Writing menus, forming robust working relationships with suppliers, and arranging schedules. Teaching the members of the cooperative who had managed it for years with little success how to run a restaurant, and teaching people assigned to the cooperative by social services to learn a trade. Put like that it seems complicated, but it really wasn't.

I started my new job by organizing a month-long cooking course for a very motley crew: Beatriz, a former Cuban hooker;

Giorgio, autistic; Alessia, a platinum blonde with obsessive-compulsive disorder, permanently attached to her iPhone; Silvio, schizophrenic; Claudio, heart disease; Simone, deeply depressed after losing first his job and then his wife, Serena, who'd been bipolar; and finally Marco. Marco was allergic to questions and black pepper. He was ten years older than me, with an unfathomable gaze and the values of a Boy Scout. Sometimes his eyes were as clear as a mountain lake, other times they were burning embers. He gained confidence little by little. He was always spotlessly clean and pleasant smelling, tackled every task with dogged determination, and tended to fumble his way through problems. I told him it wasn't always good enough to just make do; you also needed technique, and lack of technique was a huge shortcoming. He looked at me blankly, but he was a fast learner. He never backed down from a challenge and exchanged sweet nothings with his wife on Face-book. He had the hide of a rhinoceros and the sensitivity of a child. And every night, when he finished, he would return to his prison cell.

My ragtag band stumbled and screwed up every now and again, but they forged ahead. There were some warmhearted moments, and nobody went off the deep end, which was the main thing. And by the end of the course, their bread, home-made pasta, roasts, and cookies were... not bad. Better than anyone expected. When you cook good food, you win a small battle with the world around you, and somehow the world knows it. When you feel satisfied with yourself, you tend to step up your game, and I believe that's powerful medicine.

Marco overcomplicated things and had a somewhat limited approach to cooking, but he was passionate. And he recognized good food. When you've got passion, mastering technique is relatively simple—all you need is time. The restaurant was small and stopped just short of hospitable. The big bare windows looked onto a parking lot and the fluorescent lights were harsh, but the carved wooden tables and chairs were quite splendid. The problem was the desserts.

The pastry chef's name was Denisa, and she did her best, which was not much. She knew how to make no-bake Chocolate Salami with broken biscuits, Tiramisù, and Torta Tenerina, a chocolate cake traditionally made in the city of Ferrara. Three desserts, all chocolate. Denisa had worked in the kitchen for a few years. Before that she'd only made sandwiches and salads, after fleeing her homeland of Romania and a violent husband, together with her three daughters. Her missing teeth embarrassed her, but not enough to stop her from smiling. She didn't bat an eye when asked to come in an hour early or leave an hour late, or to serve forty meals single-handed. She was convinced that just getting the job done meant the job was well done, but that's beside the point. She did not, however, dodge difficulties, and after swearing like a sailor and taking the Lord's name in vain a couple of times, managed to see the funny side of them. So Denisa deservedly joined the army of potential cooks and people I unconditionally admired.

Life never asks people like Denisa for their opinion before dumping stuff on them; therefore, she never felt obliged to say thank you. She didn't have a clue about pastry making and did not recognize good food. She was too busy trying to recognize good people, and everything else was a waste of time. She was as stubborn as a mule and uninterested in learning technique. Technique without taste is as good as the fish they throw to trained seals, and a restaurant without a decent assortment of desserts will never make anyone's wish list.

My first step was to recommend hiring Marco, taking advantage of the prisoner employment program, for a total cost to the company of a few hundred euros a month. My second was to turn Marco into a pastry chef.

I don't know whether the size of the dream is proportional to the happiness you feel when it comes true, or whether Ferran Adrià's emotions exceed those of Grom's employee of the month. If you've just begun working in a gelateria like Grom and they name you employee of the month, you probably feel on top of the world. If you've been a chef for the better part of fifteen years, and even thumbed your nose at a star-rated restaurant, and now, for the first time in your life, they've given you carte blanche to turn a restaurant around and teach people how to manage it, you might not be on top of the world, but you can say you're happy. Of course, you don't have a restaurant of your own, your face doesn't grace the pages of a fancy food magazine or anything like that. A wage of €1,360 a month wasn't a fortune, but they let me choose my own hours, I could do some of my work from home, and I showed up in the kitchen only when I needed to. Yep, it was just what I wanted. I felt fine and that's all that mattered. Anyhow, most people's pipe dreams are fast forgotten, and then they focus on realizing the dreams that are within their reach, and I am no exception.

Debora was the president's chief assistant. She hardly ever went out for a meal, and when she did, it was usually pizza. She was mostly vegetarian and uninterested in spending money on food. Before I arrived, she and Denisa, both embarrassingly naïve, pieced together the menus, picking up ideas from cheap magazines or trawling through Web sites for housewives. Does this remind you of students who, the day before their exams, put together cheat sheets, copying a few lines here and there

of the basic stuff they haven't studied? As if it's easy to understand the basics. The notion that you can build a menu by grabbing a few dishes here and there without the slightest attempt
at coherency—and without ever even having tried or tasted the
dishes—revealed an unscrupulous and contemptible perception of what it means to be a chef and, if I have to be honest, is
downright offensive. I'm not saying that inspired creativity or
an artistic streak or business acumen is essential in this profession. I am talking about the fundamental principle of cooking,
which is pleasure. You have to believe you are a genius. You
are an idiot if you think you can make it big as a chef without
delighting in the flavor of what you produce. I leaf through food
magazines too. But I've been there, done that, seen it being prepared, tasted it on various occasions, including every variation
in taste and consistency, and I distinctly remember what it felt
like when I came across the version I liked the best. In other
words, I know what good food tastes like. I was taught it. When
I read a recipe, even one by Benedetta Parodi, Italy's Rachael
Ray, instinct kicks in. There are different ways of remembering
things, and this is difficult to teach, but I believe it goes by the
name of experience. Debora enjoyed my cooking and the type of
restaurant I was setting up, but she insisted on having the final
say on the menus and phoned me constantly.

The president of the cooperative looked like a gray-haired
hippie, with his jeans, leather sandals, and velvet jackets. But
he was only the president of a cooperative, and had never really
understood how Debora put the menus together or how Denisa
cooked the dishes. When he came for lunch, I tried to teach
Denisa a few things, like how to take advantage of the situation.
If the owners are sitting at a table, serve them first and better
than everyone else. I know, when I was twenty-five I thought it

sucked too. But when you're just starting out, you've still got a lot to learn, and then you grow up and all you want to do is live a peaceful life.

I began seeing dishes come out of the kitchen with a decorative flourish that followed some sort of logic rather than a few ham-fisted squirts of balsamic reduction. Denisa was beginning to pick up some of the butcher's best-kept secrets, no longer attempting recipes destined to fail miserably, showed greater respect for food and its safe storage, and had stopped guesstimating cooking times and service times. All this put my conscience at ease and told me I was achieving my goals. I received huge smiles from the president every time he saw me in the kitchen. Not one of the ragtag crew we were assigned would ever be chefs, except perhaps Marco, but here at least they knew they were capable of doing an outstanding job, and that's all that matters.

45.

Some things never change in a professional kitchen: Marco, Denisa, and I drew closer, although each continued living in solitude.

We knew a lot about one another: the way we like our coffee, the days we are unapproachable, the cruel things that make us laugh and the ones we can't stand to hear, the minor details that piss us off, how much we love to cook pasta, the untidiness we need and the tidiness we like. Sports, cars, clothes, shoes, ingredients, mom, children, politics, films, singers, zodiac signs, Denisa's tits and teeth, her baby granddaughter, my receding hairline, Marco's wedding anniversary, and the cities we've lived in. We acknowledged one another's habits, likes and dislikes, shortcomings and good qualities. We learned when to shut up and when to raise our voices. But in actual fact we remained strangers. Strangers who knew each other really well, but strangers nonetheless. We were a real kitchen crew.

I loved my role and I liked the connection that was forming between Denisa and Marco. But I missed the life in the trenches that I was used to, where drugs, booze, immorality, and nihilism are the common ground on which we join forces to kick a stupid and hypocritical world in the ass with our talent.

In here I had to be a bit of a hypocrite, and sharing how I felt with someone else would be a real weight off my shoulders. Stockholm syndrome was the only explanation for my relationship with the kitchen. The abuse I had been subjected to, the endless toil, the need to have my wits about me to avoid getting steamrolled, the pervasive illegality of the employment scene—all this and I had fallen in love with my torturer, forged an alliance between me and my executioner, and now I missed those things like crazy. It was less fun even though my life was arguably more peaceful. We were a functioning restaurant with clients, and that's why I'd been hired, but it was actually social work. People with serious problems were part of the program and alcohol was forbidden. Showing off about one's depraved and dissolute past was frowned upon, and it was imperative to conduct oneself responsibly and respect the sensitivity of others. Sexual innuendo was out of the question. In all the other places I had worked I merely had to look like the boy next door with the owners and churn out dish after dish during peak times, but here I really needed to be alert and level-headed.

Debora and the president went to Mass every Sunday and had way too much faith in the benefit of meetings. With them I could let my guard down, but a boxer's preferred stance is with his fists raised at nose-eye level. After Floyd Patterson landed the most beautiful jab in the history of boxing, he ran to assist his opponent, who gave no signs of getting up. He said, "They said I was the fighter who got knocked down the most, but I also got up the most."

Sonny Liston was from Arkansas, born into a sharecropping family who farmed cotton, and ended up knocking out thirteen contenders for the heavyweight title. Patterson would have gladly avoided getting into the ring with that fighting machine, but the day always comes when a man has to face his fears. On September 25, 1962, Frank Sinatra and nearly nineteen thousand other boxing fans gathered to watch the fight that was over in the blink of an eye. After two minutes and ten seconds, the son of slaves had knocked out his opponent and the world had a new heavyweight champion. Patterson lost by a knockout but was still on his feet. Before that match Liston had said, "In the films the good guy always wins, but this is one bad guy who ain't gonna lose." When I put on my black cap and tie my apron around my waist, I think I'd like to be Sonny, though I wouldn't mind being Floyd. Neither Debora nor the president had ever watched a boxing match. They didn't want a boxer; they wanted lots of meetings to work out how to turn a bunch of screwed-up people into a proper restaurant brigade.

When Debora and the president told me about Marco, they spoke of a person who had made a mistake and was paying his debt to society. He needed help and support to slowly find his way back to a normal life. Then I met Marco in person, and he seemed savvier than those two could ever have imagined.

If it is true that evolution has given us a powerful instinct to survive and adjust to our environment, then Marco was its happy-go-lucky ambassador. All he actually needed was a temporary release permit allowing him to spend a few hours every day out of prison. For me he was the linchpin of the kitchen, and he was fully aware of it. Competent, fast, determined, smart, helpful, intelligent, and honest too. A good guy, compared to the many assholes I'd come across. Someone I could trust and a necessary presence in the kitchen. I gained his trust forever when I requested that he be allowed to stay out of prison twelve hours a day instead of the six that were initially granted. No change to his contract—the extra hours were considered volunteer work—but the important thing was that he was out of his cell. Now he arrived at nine in the morning and left at nine at night. I had my right-hand man and he had more time and freedom to move.

"Hey, Marco, my man, how about we try a few desserts?"

"Sure, Leo. Let me have a smoke and I'll be there. Do you want some coffee?"

"Yes, please. A double espresso in a big cup."

"Long and black, just the way you like it," he said, chuckling.

I've always been fond of cooking in silence; ingredients are like the dreams you have when you're half asleep, crammed with seemingly disparate fragments that come together into something abstract and illogical but nonetheless flow. I tried out new dishes and modified old ones, delighted in the touch of my super-sharp knives, rejoiced at the jam-packed fridges, and let the sizzling pans and browning steaks warm the cockles of my heart. Marco and I would go from meditating about ingredients and ruminating about recipes to actually making the dishes, usually putting our own personal twist on them. Gliding from the former to the latter came naturally. Everybody needs a friend, and from the get-go I had singled him out.

There was still one thing that I didn't know, a subject we'd never talked about, and I wasn't sure I was in any position to inquire. I was afraid to push too hard and find myself having to slam on the brakes when it was too late.

What can ruin a perfectly good dish, and what causes numerous road accidents every day, is not knowing when to hit the brakes. We all tend to ask too many questions, say too much, add too much, go too fast, run yellow lights and believe others will admire our zeal or stop at the red light. The clock in the corridor said half past three on the dot.

"Okay, Marco, here's what we'll do: I'll prepare the mixture for the tuiles and you make the pastry cream. Okay?"

"But the cream is already made, it's over there."

"Yeah, but that's Chantilly, you can taste the cream in it, and it's three days old. Just make me a simple pastry cream."

"Sure. Have you tasted the puff pastry?"

"I have and I don't like it. It doesn't have enough layers and it's all misshapen."

"Oh, okay, I made it myself by hand."

"You made it by hand and you used margarine instead of butter."

"But it comes better with margarine."

"Jesus Christ, did I just hear what I thought I heard? The pastry has to taste buttery, that's what's so good about it. But let's leave it at that, let's not lose our cool. What we need is an electric dough roller, otherwise you spend hours and hours on a product we sell for peanuts and it's not even as good. Let's continue using the frozen pastry sheets."

A tuile mixture is easy to make. All the quantities are the same. Same number of egg whites to the same amount of flour, butter, and confectioner's sugar is the basic recipe, then you can add vanilla, cocoa, almonds, or whatever. I prepared the basic mixture. Melted the butter until it softened to a spreadable consistency, then whisked it together with the sugar and slowly added the egg whites. Then I added the sifted flour with a spatula. You must mix the ingredients until just combined; if you overdo it, the gluten develops and ruins everything. The oven was already heated to 390°. I poured three spoonfuls of batter separately onto the silicone baking sheet. I spread the batter so it formed thin rounds and placed the tray in the oven. As soon as the edges started turning golden brown, I took the discs out and placed them immediately onto overturned cups, gently pressing them into the shape I wanted in the few seconds that they were still hot and malleable.

"See how beautiful they are?"

"Beautiful. So beautiful they look fake. What do you want to fill them with?"

"I don't know. Maybe pastry cream and fruit or some kind of mousse. How 'bout that?"

"How about leaving them flat and making a mille-feuille, layered with something like ricotta and chocolate?"

"Yep, I like the sound of that. Where's the pastry cream?"

"I still have to cook it."

He put the pot on the stove, lit the gas, and started whisking like crazy.

"Whoa, Marco, slow down, you're whisking too hard. If it develops too much gluten, you'll end up with glue."

Marco's eyes narrowed, and it didn't take much imagination to sense that if he chose to, he could easily turn feral.

"Hey, Leo, gimme a break. Let's see how it turns out first, and then you can say what you want..."

"Okay, okay... be my guest and see what happens. But it also depends on the recipe you're following."

I waited till he finished, highly skeptical of the outcome. When the custard cream was cooked, he put it on the pass next to the stove. I came closer and pressed some cling film over the surface—that way it doesn't form a skin, I told him. He nodded. If he didn't reply, it meant he was taking note of what I said. I knew him by now. We went outside to smoke a cigarette.

We returned to the kitchen, I lifted off the cling film, making sure no drops of condensation fell onto the cream, then dipped my finger into the beautiful pale yellow mixture. I didn't like the consistency—too thick and not silky enough. When I licked my finger, the sugary sweetness hit me like a slap in the face.

"Marco, I have to be honest here, this pastry cream is shit, it's absolutely disgusting."

"What do you mean disgusting? I've been making it like this forever."

"Well, you've been making it wrong forever. It's like putty, you can taste the flour, and it's far too sweet. Pastry cream has to be smooth but not slimy, the sweetness shouldn't overpower the other flavors, and the flour has to be cooked thoroughly. Let's make another batch and we'll taste it together, then you tell me which one you prefer."

I started mixing the ingredients all over again, first the dry ones—flour and sugar—then a little milk and the egg yolk. In the meantime, I put the rest of the milk on the stove with the vanilla and the orange peel, ready to pour into the mixture as soon as it neared boiling point.

"Why did you become a chef, Leo?"

"Who knows. I guess because the things I cooked had the right look about them." Then I tried to clarify. "I mean, when I cook things, they come out exactly as I imagined them before I even started making them."

"I thought it was something simpler, like because you make a good living."

"And what about you?"

"It was just a coincidence. In jail there were some courses you could take, and you got good-time credits. Then the cooperative gave me a chance to get out on work release and stick my nose out the door."

"And now?"

"Now I'm happy with the way things are. I've only got a few years left of my sentence. Maybe when I'm out I can start up a little place of my own, but not in Italy. I've got some contacts in Tunisia. There, with twenty thousand euros, you can live like a king."

I saw the flashing yellow light and decided to go through it.

"Listen, you must've done something pretty big if you've been inside for so many years."

He handed me the whisk without a word. The light had turned red.

"We're not going to use the whisk," I said. "We just stir the cream so it doesn't stick to the pan. Can you pass me the spatula, please?"

"Go on," he said.

"Well, there isn't much more to do now, just work in a circular motion and scrape the bottom of the pan..."

"I'm not talking about the cream. You were starting to say something."

I wanted to hit the brakes, but when you're in the middle of an intersection that's the worst thing you can do. When in doubt, accelerate, I remember someone saying.

"I don't want to butt into your business, I want that to be clear. I know nothing about the lives of the people who end up here at the restaurant, and that's the way it should be."

"Don't worry, Leo. I don't tell everyone my story, but I do tell some."

"I'm not worried."

"Murder. I killed a loan shark. I don't know how many chances you get in your life to stay outta trouble, and even if I did have a chance that day, I didn't pick up on it. I'm telling it to you straight, that guy was an asshole and he deserved what he got."

That's when I should have either slammed on the brakes or hit the pedal to the metal; instead all I could do was let inertia carry me along and hope I wouldn't smash into anything. He continued his story.

"I was working in my father's company. I was about twenty and I wanted to set up my own business. Banks don't lend money to kids, so I borrowed some from a guy who used to come over to our house. Everyone knew he was a loan shark, and my dad wasn't the least bit happy when that guy lent me fifty million lire, but I didn't care. I started up my business, worked my fingers to the bone, and every month I'd pay him the vig. Then, just when I'd nearly paid off my debt, I skipped a couple of payments. When I took him the final amount, the guy said the debt wasn't settled yet because I'd been late, the interest had increased, and I still owed him another five million lire. I said maybe he was mistaken, that I'd given him all the money I owed him. Then he started to bust my balls; he'd wait for me when I'd meet up with my friends and then go on and on about it. One time, in front of everyone, I even said to him, 'Leave me alone or I'll shoot you.' I wasn't scared of him, he knew everyone in my family, just like we knew everyone in his, but I refused to be bullied. I was busting my ass, working Saturdays and Sundays, and I liked to spoil myself. I was living the high life, you know, new cars, going to a target-shooting range. I had a few guns and a firearms license. I was allowed to carry my weapon—disassembled—only from my house to the shooting range and back. I hardly ever disassembled my pistol, very few people ever do, and that night I had it in my car.

"Just as I was unlatching the gate to go home, I felt a sudden pain in my thigh. That motherfucker had hung around and waited to stab me in cold blood. He was blind drunk and his wife was with him. He was screaming that I had to learn respect and I was still wet behind the ears, and in the meantime he kept coming at me with the knife. It was a split-second decision. I circled him and opened the car door, got my pistol out from under the seat, and shot him in the arm. He must have been so damn drunk or stoned that it didn't stop him, so I shot him two more times in the stomach, but he kept coming at me. He grabbed me around the neck, and I managed to shove the gun under his chin and blow his face off. His wife testified in court—she told them the truth about the knife, the stabbing, his hands around my neck, exactly as it happened. They didn't arrest me right away. The case dragged on and on, and I thought I'd get away with self-defense. I even left Italy and went to Tunisia. I opened a business there and met a fantastic girl called Dalila. She'd never been out of her country, didn't know anything about what had happened, and never wanted me to use a condom. When they came to arrest me in Tunis, we had just found out she was expecting a baby. They sent me packing back to Italy like I was some kind of fugitive from justice. Someone had testified that I'd threatened the asshole before I shot him: murder and attempted escape, thirty years without parole. Those shots cost me a life behind bars. My son was born while I was in the slammer, my woman moved to Italy, and I'm lucky she hasn't turned her back on me. The warden of the penitentiary married us and our honeymoon was two days' leave at my parents' place. But I would do it all again in a heartbeat. Like I said, that asshole deserved to die."

So there you have it. So much for remorse, I thought to myself. Marco gave me a serious look that said, *Keep it to yourself.* Then he smiled and asked if we could taste the frigging pastry cream stirred with a spatula. The intersection was behind us and the traffic was flowing smoothly again.

"Look, forget what I said about the pastry cream. Yours is fantastic, perfect, silky soft, and mouth-wateringly delicious.

Disregard whatever I told you before, keep making it just like that," I joked, putting on a wild-eyed face and groveling.

"So what are we going to do with my glue?" he asked, laughing too.

"We'll wait until it cools down, then we'll jazz it up with some whipped cream and rum, and tonight's dessert will be fantastic almond cookies with sabayon and mixed berries. Do we still have some frozen berries somewhere?"

"Yeah, I think we do. I'll go and check." And off he went, leaving me on my own.

And there you have it. People still ask me why I continue to work as a chef. The truth is that I could have tried any number of improbable careers without finding one I love as much as this. What other job would allow me to peep through so many cracks in the wall of life?

That defeat was the first of seven more for Floyd Patterson. His career at the top of the world was over, although he didn't know it yet. When he did realize it was over, he hung up his gloves and became a coach and gave bittersweet interviews. He died of cancer at seventy-one. Sonny Liston never lost a bout, except when he sold out to the gambling mafia. He was thirty-eight years of age when they found him lying facedown on the floor of his home with needle tracks in his arm and a massive amount of morphine in his bloodstream. Everyone knew he was terrified of injections.

Being a bittersweet coach has its advantages. My name is Leonardo Lucarelli, and it's embroidered in dark red on the black uniform that defines me. I have a natural talent for giving people better answers than the ones I give myself. Every so often I think I should have stayed in the one-star restaurant with its Pasta all'Amatriciana at €40 a pop, and eventually opened my own restaurant, which is what every chef is expected to want, but life goes on, and there you go.

Marco returned to the kitchen holding a bag of frozen berries.

"Hey, man, you get to ask me why I'm in jail and you haven't even told me your son's name."

"My little boy? Matteo. His name's Matteo."

You continue working in a kitchen because you've been following politics for years but you never go to vote. Because one day you might have a casual conversation that will take you somewhere else. Because when they say it's too late, to you it always seems too soon. Because nothing defines you as perfectly as this job does. Because you never know how it's going to end, but you know you have to whisk egg yolks in a copper bowl. You continue to work in a kitchen because you can't find what you've learned in the lyrics of a song or on TV, and some nights, when you feel like God's right-hand man, you know you're not exaggerating.

You continue working in a kitchen because you want to live to tell the tale of all the great things that keep happening to you, and because if you truly know what it feels like to be in a good place, then maybe now you say, convincingly, Yep, I'm in a good place.

You continue to work in a kitchen because knowing how to cook immerses you in reality and history, because the kitchen is a theodemocracy and fools always lose.

You continue to work in a kitchen because chefs are the fifth quarter of Roman cuisine, an oxymoron, the offal that most people regard as waste, but the only part of the animal that distinguishes a real chef from a wannabe, that differentiates someone who knows how to live from someone who doesn't. Living life as a fillet steak or a rump steak is easy. Only an artist knows how to survive as tripe, brains, intestine, spleen, or testicles. You continue working in a kitchen because the world of restaurants and food service is a contradiction in terms and it can give you a good laugh. You continue to work in a kitchen to transform scraps into flavors. Because cooking's right on trend but you got there a nanosecond ahead of the curve. Because outside the kitchen you are a consummate good-for-nothing, and cooking is all that stops you from smoking more than you breathe, drinking more than you eat, standing still more than you sleep, and spending more than you earn. You continue to work in a kitchen because you need boundaries, and because knowing how to handle knives is a useful skill to have when the days seem to meld into each other and form a single dangerous whole.

You continue to work in a kitchen because by now it's become pretty obvious that you'll always choose sneering mockery over subtle irony.

Without the friendship, support, advice, steadfastness, and help of Matteo, I'd never have written this book.

LEONARDO LUCARELLI was born in India and has since resided in regions all across Italy, including Lazio, Emilia-Romagna, Veneto, Trentino, and Tuscany. He entered the culinary world as a college student, and after completing a degree in anthropology, he continued his career in the kitchen. He has worked in fifteen restaurants—some Michelin-starred, and seven of which employed him as chef. Lucarelli currently lives in L'Aquila, where he consults for several restaurants in Rome.

⚎ OTHER PRESS

You might also enjoy these titles from our list:

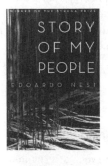

STORY OF MY PEOPLE by Edoardo Nesi

Winner of the 2011 Strega Prize, this blend of essay, social criticism, and memoir is a striking portrait of the effects of globalization on Italy's declining economy.

"A searing indictment of globalization's failures, and the inability of politicians and pundits to consider its impact on real lives...much of the book is sad, honest, and biting; overall it is an important work."
—*Publishers Weekly*

SECRECY by Rupert Thomson

In this highly charged novel, Thomson brings Florence to life in all its vibrant sensuality, while remaining entirely contemporary in his exploration of the tensions between love and solitude, beauty and decay.

"Thomson paints a suspenseful picture of the moody, factional world of Florentine politics and draws parallels with the inner life of an artist whose work imitates darkness and decay." —*The New Yorker*

LIVE BAIT by Fabio Genovesi

This is the story of a small Italian town where fishing, biking, and rock 'n' roll make the news, until tragedy turns everything upside down. Told with the tenderness of a Fellini film, this contemporary novel continues the great tradition of Italian literature and cinema.

"If John Irving had an Italian son, he would be named Fabio Genovesi." —*Schnüss, Das Bonner Stadtmagazin*

Also recommended:

BALZAC'S OMELETTE by Anka Muhlstein

"Tell me where you eat, what you eat, and at what time you eat, and I will tell you who you are." This is the motto of Anka Muhlstein's erudite and witty book about the ways food and the art of the table feature in Honoré de Balzac's *The Human Comedy*.

"This effervescent volume celebrates Balzac's use of gastronomy as a literary device and social critique."
—*The New Yorker*

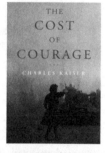

THE COST OF COURAGE by Charles Kaiser

The heroic true story of the three youngest children of a bourgeois Catholic family who worked together in the French Resistance

"*The Cost of Courage* documents, through the life of an extraordinary family, one of the twentieth century's most fascinating events — the German occupation of the City of Light." —*Wall Street Journal*

THE SUITORS by Cecile David-Weill

In this amusing insider's look at the codes, manners, and morals of French high society, two sisters devise a scheme for attracting a wealthy suitor who can purchase their family's estate.

"This novel is a delicious romp...I loved reading it!"
—Ina Garten, Barefoot Contessa cookbooks and TV

▉ OTHER PRESS

www.otherpress.com